Unwin Education Books: 11

FIFTY YEARS OF FREEDOM

A Study of the Development of the Ideas
of A. S. Neill

Unwin Education Books

Series Editor: Ivor Morrish, BD, BA, DIP. ED. (London), BA (Bristol)

Unwin Education Books: 11
Series Editor: Ivor Morrish

Fifty Years of Freedom

A Study of the Development of the Ideas of A. S. Neill

RAY HEMMINGS
M.A. (Cantab.)
Lecturer in Education, University of Leicester

London
GEORGE ALLEN AND UNWIN LTD
RUSKIN HOUSE   MUSEUM STREET

ISBN 0 04 371020 4 hardback
    0 04 371021 2 paper

Printed in Great Britain
in 10 point Times Roman
by Cox & Wyman Ltd.,
London, Fakenham and Reading

Contents

Plates

Acknowledgements

In researching into the early years of Neill's career I was fortunate in having the generous co-operation of the Directors of Education at Forfar and Dumfries, Mr A. Crawford and Mr J. Lamont Brown. Both gave me considerable help, as did Mr D. Miller, the Headmaster of Kingsmuir School where Neill spent his childhood, and Mr W. Kerr, the Headmaster at the Gretna School where in 1915 Neill started to explore the roads to freedom. Both introduced me to many people who knew Neill in those early days. I am grateful to the Authorities at Forfar, Dumfries and Fife for allowing me to examine the log-books of the various schools through which Neill progressed from pupil to pupil-teacher to assistant teacher to headmaster.

I am indebted also to the managements of the *Daily Mirror* and the *Daily Mail* for giving me access to their library files. I would also like to acknowledge a small grant from the University of Leicester that helped towards the cost of research.

Many individuals have helped by sharing with me their personal knowledge of the events with which this book is concerned. I would particularly like to thank Mr John Layard, Mr J. W. Brown, Miss D. E. M. Gardner and Mr Leslie Morton. And of course A. S. Neill, whom I first met in 1948 in an ABC restaurant near Liverpool Street Station where he 'interviewed' me for the post of teacher of mathematics and physics at Summerhill. Ever since then I have had the benefit of his practical and inspirational help, and also of his friendship. Though he has been aware of my working on this book – and we talked about it in the early stages – it is only in the direct quotations from his own writing that the book necessarily expresses Neill's own opinions. I am grateful for his permission to make these quotations, but I do not wish to claim his authority for anything else that is included in this book.

R.E.H.

The author and publishers are also grateful to the following for supplying the photographs numbered below, and for permitting their use:

Plate 2: Reproduced from *The Student* by permission of Edinburgh University. Copy supplied by the British Museum.

Plate 3: Education Sub-Committee, Dumfries.

Plate 4: Copy supplied by the Cambridge University Library.

Plates 5 and 7: © Copyright 1963 by Herb Snitzer from *Living at Summerhill* (Collier Books).

Plate 6: Photographs by John Walmsley.

Plate 8: Photograph by Phil Méheux.

Introduction

Shortly after the publication in the United States of the compendium that Harold Hart made of A. S. Neill's writings, *Summerhill: a radical approach to child-rearing*, as the book was called in America, a huge tide of enthusiasm for the 'Summerhill idea' swelled apparently out of nothing. One outcome of this sudden vogue was the formation of an American Summerhill Society which intended to open an American Summerhill School. This provoked *Id*, the magazine which the original English Summerhill Society published, to print an 'Important Notice' denying any connection between the two societies. As to the proposed school, *Id* was emphatically outraged. 'Both Neill and the British Summerhill Society oppose absolutely this use of the name "Summerhill" ... No one has the right to institute another Summerhill. Everyone has the right to draw inspiration from Neill's work and run their own schools under their own names.'

The motive behind this notice seems to have been a jealous protection not just of the name, but rather of the reputation of Summerhill. In a later issue of *Id* an exchange of open letters between Paul Goodman and Neill was reprinted from the American publication *The Voice*, from which it appeared that there had been good reason to fear this unsought association. Neill told that he was receiving letters from the States which reported unsavoury rumours surrounding schools which, while not actually using the name, were being associated with Summerhill. One correspondent had told him that 'the name of Summerhill was becoming mud in the U.S.A. for it was being used as a sanction for anything calling itself freedom for children'. Others wrote of 'adults who, they allege, encourage promiscuous sex, dope, homosexuality; one says that girls were jeered at because they were virgins'. These rumours may all have been quite false, and yet, Neill pointed out, the mud was likely to stick. 'Anything new, anything anti-Establishment can be killed by talk and bigotry and hate in general. I can defend my own school. Let the others stand up and protect their schools.'

These sentiments were not likely to find favour with Paul Goodman who follows in the line of Kropotkin, author of *Mutual Aid*. He responded aggressively, arguing that it was 'neither happy nor necessary' to have such 'a proprietary attitude towards one's contribution and influence' as

Neill seemed to exhibit. He quoted Neill as saying that he was 'proud to have any school acknowledge the inspiration of his work', but added that 'he is squeamish about directions (and "excesses") that that inspiration might take . . . Certainly nobody likes to be misunderstood, but I would rather risk that than suffer the illusion that "my" ideas are my property.'

However strong one's sympathy for Neill may be in this little squabble, it may still be admitted that Goodman had a valid point. Summerhill has been Neill's creation, but it has also been a creation of his time. It is not a question of his indebtedness (which he has often acknowledged, and sometimes even exaggerated) to people like Homer Lane, Freud, Wilhelm Reich and others. It is a matter of history, and Summerhill is a part of the long history of the struggle for, and against, man's freedom. Neill's school is a part of a social process which has included the Russian revolution and Black Power, *Ulysses* and *Mein Kampf*, Freud and space travel, Moral Rearmament and the hippies.

While thus claiming Summerhill as 'ours' we do not mean to minimize the unique qualities that enabled Neill to persevere in its creation and to preserve its existence long enough to make it more than a mere 'experiment'. Its fifty years have been time enough to develop as a result of internal experience and also to interact with changing moods and events around it. What this book attempts to do is to trace this development and these interactions so as to help to clarify the present context of the ideas that Summerhill has embodied. Neill has more than once expressed his dislike of the notion of anyone writing his biography, asserting that it is not what a man is, but what he does, that is important. This study is not a biography; biographical material is introduced only to give roots to what Neill has done. These are the personal roots but they are not simply personal, for the experience out of which a man moulds his actions is a particular sample from a common fund.

Likewise, the selection of the events and movements which this book deals with is my choice, based on my conception of relevance, from the vast matrix of human activity in this century. It has been a century preoccupied with freedom, denying and asserting, extending and restricting, freedom in all spheres of human activity. Previous ages have also had this preoccupation, but perhaps the peculiar contribution of the twentieth century has been its exploration of the psychological aspects of freedom in the context of the extensions of intellectual, economic and political freedoms that we have inherited. Neill has, I think, made an important contribution to this exploration, which of course continues.

The indications seem to be that the gravest present threat to freedom is from a social collusion in a non-terroristic totalitarianism which is producing extremes of conformity and non-conformity. We have to find means of liberation from society, without actually destroying society in the process. I am suggesting that in this situation Neill's form of education is peculiarly relevant, and I have presumed in my final chapter to feel out for a conceptualization which may help to realize this. In doing so I do not wish to pretend that Neill himself would concur. About that I do not know.

1 Origins

The ideas that are embodied in the practice of modern educators who are commonly referred to as 'progressive' have a long history. One might suppose that this would be a kind of recommendation to their conservative critics, but curiously it is often suggested that the discovery that these ideas are not simply a modern invention in some way detracts from their value. The fact is that freedom has been a continuing preoccupation over many centuries and there have long been men concerned to defend and extend its frontiers. But to pretend that all that has been said and done in this sphere, or even that all of any importance, is to be found, for instance, in the writing of Rousseau is ridiculously to oversimplify an elaborate and unfinished struggle.

Rousseau was the first great philosopher of the modern era to question why man should allow himself to be chained when his potentialities require a free development. In education, this question has long troubled the more sensitive minds, and after Rousseau there have always been individuals who have tried to break the fetters of childhood. Pestalozzi and Froebel were the most renowned of these pioneers but, as R. J. W. Selleck describes the more recent situation (in an appropriately horticultural metaphor): 'The seeds of [their] thought lay dormant through the long winter of the payment-by-results period, or, if they grew, produced misshapen plants with meagre blooms. In the spring of the New Education they sprouted in profusion, grew rapidly and often strongly. Some outgrew themselves and others could not survive the return of winter. But for a while a walk in the garden was very exciting.'[1]

A. S. Neill's own education did not take him into this garden. He spent his school-days under his father-dominie in the village school of Kingsmuir, a few miles outside Forfar. George Neill had been appointed there in 1876 just two years after it had opened in a new single-roomed building with twenty-five pupils on roll. He accepted the missionary task of schooling the sons and daughters of this farming community in the formal learning dictated by the payment-by-results system, and of bending them to the moral discipline of a stern Calvinistic tradition. Numbers at the school grew rapidly, though it was not until they had reached their peak at 139, ten years after George Neill had come to the school, that a second room was added. Even with this amelioration, the dominie, with his one assistant and a pupil-teacher, was obviously working in difficult conditions. But he managed, apparently with success – at least as success was then measured. Her Majesty's Inspector reported that the school was being 'conducted with very great care . . . The teacher deserves the greatest praise for such excellent work among a class of children by no means very intelligent looking.'

No doubt in such conditions George Neill felt the need to keep a firm control on these children and no doubt he did this sometimes with the help of the ubiquitous Scottish tawse. But I have talked with some of his surviving pupils, now in their seventies or eighties, and most remembered the old dominie with an affectionate respect and certainly they refuted any suggestion that he made any cruel use of the strap. 'If a boy got it, he was deserving it,' was the common opinion. These memories must be overlaid with adult values, of course, and with the solidarity of a village community whose standards George Neill himself had done much to form. In some cases, too, they must have been coloured with a gratitude for his earnest, perhaps relentless, teaching which had ensured that those 'with brains' passed their examinations to the Academy at Forfar, and thence worked their way into one of the professions. As one who was enjoying retirement from years of successful work begun in that old schoolroom put it to me: 'He couldna do with backsliding. He'd give them one or two then, to keep them going. Ah weel, he used his old tawse quite a bit. But stories that he burnt the thongs at the ends to make them harder – these are just old stories.'

Yet there were such stories, mainly current among the later generations of his pupils who were perhaps not so inclined to accept the old dominie's discipline as a part of the inevitable pattern of childhood. The idea, however, that Neill's appetite for freedom has been nothing but a reaction against an over-repressive upbringing is not one that can stand unqualified, especially when one reads the dedication of his first book, *A Dominie's Log*, to his father: 'As a boy I attended a village school where the bairns chattered and were happy. I trace my love of freedom to my free life there.' In fact as far as schooling was concerned, Neill's early revulsion for the traditional kind stemmed mainly from his experience as an assistant teacher at Kingskettle where he spent three wretched years under a headmaster whom he later described as 'a sadistic tyrant' who 'tawsed the pupils most savagely and expected me to do likewise'.[2]

On the other hand there is no doubt that Neill suffered acutely from the very austere moral training which his parents gave their family. He recalls, for instance, the painful memory of being locked in a dark room after he had been discovered in some exploratory sex play with his sister.

1a. Class group at Kingsmuir School (c. 1900)
A. S. Neill is at the extreme right of the back row, and his father is at the extreme left. Three of his sisters are also in the group: Hilda is in the front row, sixth from left, and in the row behind is Mary, fifth from left, and Adie, seventh from left.

1b. Kingsmuir School buildings. This photograph was taken in 1968, but the buildings have changed little since Neill's day.

2. A. S. Neill in his student days.
This portrait appeared in *The Student* in 1912 at the end of Neill's year of editorship.

Neill has largely avoided references to his mother: others who remember her describe her as 'jolly and kindly'. But if she was more gentle than her husband, she probably did not treat the moral welfare of her children lightly. For Scotland was then gripped by Calvin's harsh puritanism enforced by threats of demonic torments, and it was not only from his father that Neill learned fears of retribution. 'We were told that almost everything we did was a sin to be punished by hell-fire. I used a forbidden word when I was nine and my granny made me read from a book ... The sentence she selected was something like this: "If you want to know what hell is like, hold your finger in the flame of a candle." It was a grim religion which inspired nothing but fear.'[3]

Another difficulty that Neill had in his relationship with his father arose out of his lack of interest in study. 'He must have roared at me a thousand times, "You've no ambeetion! You'll end in the gutter." '[4] His elder brothers had had no difficulty in satisfying their father's aspirations for them: the first had become a minister and the second a doctor. But, to quote from a close childhood friend of Neill's: 'Allie had more devilment in him than the others. He was not too bright at his lessons. He was more mischief than anything. He was the kind of fellow who'd paint his bicycle blue when everyone else's was black.' There was little in his father's classroom that excited his imagination, except perhaps the subject called Intelligence 'where we made a semi-circle, and my father asked us the meanings of words and phrases from our Readers'.[5] The sums on acres and pecks and poles, the vulgar fractions, the copy books, the strings of rivers and names of towns and their products to be learnt, the parsing and dictating, drove him to a boredom that he tried to relieve with surreptitious games with his white mice, daydreams, and playful pranks. Outside in the fields and farms he could find fun enough. It is engagingly described in *Carroty Broon*, a book which Neill based on incidents of his boyhood. The villagers of Kingsmuir have been able to identify themselves among the characters of this book and clearly Peter (Carroty) Brown is Neill himself. However, the insensitive dominie of the book is no portrait of his father, but is based on the Kingskettle schoolmaster under whom Neill worked later. Peter had the kind of father that perhaps Neill would have liked – a simple cattleman, 'a good-natured sort of man who ... did not ask much from life: a dram on Saturday night, kirk on Sunday morning, and *The People's Journal* on Sunday afternoon ... He had no ambitions for himself, but he had ambitions for his family.' He tries to persuade Peter to become a chemist (the career through which Neill's elder brother rose to become a doctor). But Peter says he is going to be a ploughman, 'or maybe a minister'! He is twelve years old, and more occupied with his first sweetheart, and his pigeons, and games of 'bools', and fights and dares, and smoking a clay cutty, than with adult ambitions. His mind was too full of fun and sadnesses, of the adventures and conflicts of life, the real entangled with the imaginary, to apply himself seriously to the routines of lessons – except briefly when he sets out to win the Angus Club prize, an enticing gilt-edged volume, awarded to the best arithmetic scholar each year. And he would have got it, but that the dominie could not bear to see this harum-scarum take first place above his favourite. So Peter took the second prize, lost interest in that game and turned his skills to arranging a fiendish death for the cat who was attacking his rabbits.

Neill himself was early cast in the role of the family ne'er-do-well and at fourteen he was sent off to Edinburgh, seventy miles away, to be a clerk in a gas-meter factory. Miserably homesick, he soon persuaded his parents to let him return to Kingsmuir, at first to study for the Civil Service, and then, when he was unable to support this fantasy, to become a draper's assistant in Forfar. This entailed a two-mile walk to and from work each day and twelve hours standing in the shop. He has recurrently suffered from a weakness in his legs, and he was unable to endure this regime. So finally and almost in despair, his parents decided that the only thing he was fit for was to become a teacher!

In 1899 he began a four-year apprenticeship as a pupil-teacher under his father, returning to the scene of his earlier maladjustments. At first he evidently did not find it any easier: at the end of the report on the school for 1901 there appears the first (and not last) disparaging judgement on Neill from one of His Majesty's Inspectors: 'A grant under Article 19E is paid in respect of A. S. Neill. This candidate is warned that his work all round is weak.' However, he redeemed this poor impression sufficiently to complete his apprenticeship, though he failed to gain a place in the Normal School in Glasgow from which he might have emerged a fully qualified teacher, and he had to work as a mere 'ex-pupil-teacher' at neighbouring Kingskettle. It was here that he suffered under the 'sadistic tyrant' mentioned above, but it was here also that he met the Rev. Aeneas Gunn Gordon – 'a man whose kindness helped me greatly during an unhappy period of my life'.[6] Perhaps in a mood of desperation, Neill thought of joining the Church and it was with this object that he went to Aeneas Gordon for tuition in Greek. He soon abandoned the idea of a career in the kirk, but with the minister's help he found at last sustained enjoyment in academic study. He moved to Newport, a suburb of Dundee, to a school which had a more humane headmaster and, besides the Elementary Department in which Neill worked, a Higher Grade Department staffed by graduates. It was both the stimulation of this company and the comparison of their prospects with his own poor status* that gave him the deter-

---

* 'I saw myself living for ever on £100 p.a.' (*Id*, 2, p. 3).

mination to get into a university. His resolve was all the stronger because he had acquired from the Minister at Kingskettle a taste for learning. 'I wanted to be educated,' he has explained simply.[7] This experience may well have influenced his later conviction that it is a child's own feelings towards learning, rather than any external compulsions, that determine success. For now Neill was able to reverse his twenty years of baffling failure. He studied for the entrance exams and to his delighted surprise the University of Edinburgh offered him admission.

He spent his first year in studies that would have led to a BSc in Agriculture but then, realizing that he had no real taste for science, he moved into the honours English School under Professor Saintsbury. At least a part of the motivation for this change was the ambition he was now beginning to formulate to become a writer, an ambition quite largely inspired by the example of J. M. Barrie whose home-town, Kirriemuir, lay only seven miles from Neill's. Nowadays, Barrie seems to be the main industry of Kirriemuir and at the top of the hill overlooking the town stands his birthplace, a low white-washed cottage with the inscription 'A Window in Thrums' beside its door. From Thrums, as Barrie had dubbed the town in his writing, he had worked his way to Edinburgh University; there he, too, had read Honours English, and he had gone on to write the books and plays that had given him fame. It was a log-cabin – or at least a stone-cottage – story of the classical mould which inspired Neill, as it did many of his compatriots, and he was strongly affected by Barrie's strange imagination. *A Window in Thrums* he found particularly moving: one may suppose that he linked it with his own struggle to free himself from his oedipal knots. *Sentimental Tommy* was another of Barrie's novels which Neill read with strong feeling, though his own *Carroty Broon* may well have been an attempt to re-write a Scottish boyhood without Barrie's fantasizing sentimentality. But the story whose influence lingered longest was that of Peter Pan: reviewing *Peter and Wendy* in the undergraduate magazine *The Student*, Neill described it as the 'sweetest story ever written . . . a song of childhood . . . of innocent joys and delicious make-believe'. It was in terms of the Peter Pan metaphor that he worked out the psychology of his first 'problem child' (see Chapter 5), and in his earlier books he frequently returns to its imagery. Later he came to realize the weakness of this fantasy, though he did retain at least a part of its message: 'To be a Peter Pan is to remain an infantile neurotic, fearing life; to be a Peter Pan in play is a sign of healthy sanity. When a man has lost the ability to play he should die physically, for he is already dead psychically, and a danger to any child who comes into contact with him.'[8]

But if he responded emotionally to Barrie, there were stronger intellectual influences which opened during his student years. These did not come from the English School: he found there only a remote and uncomprehending authority and the reality of academic study soon began to depress him in its contrast with the heady intellectual emancipation which he found in his reading of such men as Ibsen, Shaw, Wells and Nietzsche. These were the thinkers who made a more permanent impact on him than the sentimentality of Barrie or the academicism of Saintsbury; but he had to learn to keep their influence well segregated from the discipline of honours English. Once, when he wrote a critical essay on Hamlet in the style, and from the standpoint of Ibsen, he received from his professor a reprimand for immoral impudence. 'After that, I just quoted Hazlitt,' Neill comments. On many occasions since, he has spoken with derision of academics, and he has acquired the reputation of being anti-intellectual. But really it is the unimaginative intellectualism that he despises. Twelve years after leaving Edinburgh, for instance, he wrote: 'For four years I studied for exams in English, Old, Middle and Modern. Chaucer, Spenser, Shakespeare; dullest of all, Dryden. Professor Saintsbury had an unfortunate liking for Dryden, and we all had to pretend to an interest in Dryden. Today I could not read any of these writers; today I could not contribute anything at all to a discussion on post-Popian poetry or pre-Paterian prose . . . A man should be awarded a university degree for creative work. Instead of spending four years reading up what Hazlitt or Coleridge said about Shakespeare (I had no time in those days to read Shakespeare's plays), I should have been writing a play. To write a bad limerick is better than to learn *Paradise Lost* by heart.'[9]

The last remark in the foregoing paragraph is of a kind that is a hallmark of Neill's writing (as it may be of his actions, too) – the extrapolation to a shocking extreme of an otherwise just acceptable idea. It was a device that he began to exploit when he was appointed editor of *The Student* in his final year at Edinburgh. Until he took over, this had been an undergraduate magazine of inoffensive conventionality: he set out to make it one that would provoke, and in this he succeeded too well for some. He was accused of yellow-press methods and in defending himself he wrote frankly: 'An editor wants to increase circulation,' and he suggested 'give him enough rope, and he will either hang himself (The Immorality of Prof. Spooks) or use it as a lasso or a skipping-rope.' Neill took the rope and did not hang himself – though perhaps he tripped himself up by spending so much time on the job that, in spite of leaving the last issue of the year for his successor to edit so that he could 'cram a year's work into three weeks', he had to be content with a mere second-class degree. An appreciation of his work that was printed at the end of the year declared: 'One is bound to admit that it marks a new tendency in university journalism. The editorial has become the leading article of the magazine, and has always had an interesting, if somewhat sensational, title.' This notice also gives some indication of his *persona* at this time: 'The most notable thing about Neill is his versatility. As a volunteer he was a good shot; he writes, sketches, makes (and creates) his own golf clubs, sings, recites . . . In private life he is quiet, and somewhat inclined to be shy on first acquaintance, but when one gets to know him better, he opens out considerably. He is an accomplished *raconteur*. We hear he is probably going to adopt journalism as a profession. In this he should certainly make his mark.'

Neill's editorials still make lively reading even though they are concerned with issues that are dead. He attacked the apathy and snobbishness of students, 'the damnable frigidity that meets you everywhere'. He appealed for tolerance and *camaraderie*. 'There are the Class Bloods and the Old Quad men; but few Old Quad men have the manners of dustmen, and few Bloods are brainless. What if a man be inane? What if he wears patches in his trousers? What if he uses his fish-knife for the meat? Leave Suburbia to trouble about these little things.' And then he confessed: 'We hate what is fashionable. Yet human nature is frail. Personally we are revolutionary, anarchic, yet our one ambition is to have a pair of spats.' He was impatient of the shallowness of student debate and he derided the Union for wasting its time on Home Rule and Tariff Reform . . . 'There is infinitely more food for thought in questions like Eugenics, The Superman, The Marriage Laws . . .' His social comment had an obvious Shavian flavour. 'Religion and social convention are at one in decreeing that humility is a virtue . . . they are responsible for the cowardly hypocrisy we call self-depreciation.' 'As we are Early Victorian in our morals, we wish to condemn the modern attitude to liars and to point out the moral rectitude of the deliberate liar . . . Heroic mendacity is reprehensible because it is so stupid. Cowardly mendacity is the province of the clever person only. He is the salt of the earth.'

In one of his first issues to sell out completely he posed the question, 'Are teachers socially impossible?' Society classes the school teacher with the mercantile clerk, or sometimes with the dustman, he observed; and this was quite largely the teacher's own fault. 'There are teachers in our schools who don't know that to expectorate in the street is a disgusting proceeding. There are men in our schools who talk as broadly and as badly in dialect as a coalheaver does.' The article brought letters of protest at its 'vulgarity', to which Neill nonchalantly responded that 'the truth when it is unpleasant is always considered vulgar'. More seriously he attacked 'the Cursed Examination System' for its basic dishonesty in forcing students to cram and to reproduce their professors' opinions. 'That we are all apathetic and disinterested [*sic*] is not our fault, nor our professors', but the fault of the exams.' However, the following week he withdrew his exoneration of the professorial ranks. He had been looking into the matter more fully and had 'reluctantly decided that our Profs are far from being ideal teachers. Indeed many of them are not teachers at all, but merely lecturers.' Why should students be forced to suffer arm-cramp by taking notes from lectures, he asked, when the information could as easily be conveyed in book-form? Tutorials were as bad, for there 'a lecturer asks a student a question and uses the answer as a text on which to preach a pseudo-professorial sermon. That's not education. Education is etymologically a leading or drawing out: university education is really a ramming in.' Neill went on to contrast this with the practice in an elementary school where a good teacher will 'handle a class for an hour and tell them nothing; that is education in its true sense.' He then castigated his professors for their aloofness: 'They stand upon their dignity and their whole attitude says, "I don't want any of your familiarity. I am a Professor . . ." If he fails to be a man of charity, of kindliness, of love, the honorary degrees count for nothing; he is unfit to be a professor, for, in teaching, the man is greater than his subject.'

This was Neill's first public comment on the existing form of education as he had experienced it. His three-week cram enabled him to fulfil its formal requirements; but he had not absorbed the culture, and looking back on it later he could only regard his own education as 'useless', and as a teacher himself he was at first paralysed with a sense of futility. Jules Henry has pointed out how 'an intellectually creative child may fail . . . simply because he cannot understand the stupidities he is taught to believe as "facts". He may even end up agreeing with his teachers – in Neill's case, his father – that he is stupid. The child who finds it impossible to learn to think the absurd the truth, who finds it difficult to accept absurdity as a way of life, the intellectually creative child whose mind flounders like a poor fish in the net of absurdities flung around him in school, usually comes to think of himself as stupid.'[10]

Neill had been thus caught, but his unhappiness at Kingskettle had impelled him to use the net itself to climb out. As a Master of Arts he was now almost free, and he decided to move in the direction of what he plainly regarded as his more creative university activity – the editing of *The Student*. He joined Jacks, the Edinburgh publishers, to help edit an encyclopedia and then for the same firm compiled a 'Popular Educator', to which he himself contributed articles on English Literature, Mathematics and Sketching. This he knew was only bread-and-butter stuff; but the doors to the literary world began to open for him when he was appointed Art Editor to a new London magazine – *The Piccadilly*. From a Fleet Street office the outlook now was bright. Only a recurrence of his phlebitis (for which he had an operation at this time though not one that was permanently effective) dulled the glamour of working with such men as Alec Waugh, H. A. Vachell, H. G. Wells even, all of whom offered material for *The Piccadilly*.

But the excitement was short-lived, for this was 1914 and *The Piccadilly* was among the first casualties of the war. Its first issue, though set up for print, never appeared – and Neill was without a job.

REFERENCES

1 R. J. W. Selleck, *The New Education*, p. 217.
2 *Id*, 2, p. 3.
3 *Queen*, 27 September 1961. (Interview with Neill by Maurice Richardson.)
4 *The Free Child*, p. 156.
5 *Is Scotland Educated?*, p. 110.
6 Ibid. p. 68.
7 *Id*, 2, p. 3.
8 *The Problem Family*, p. 157.
9 *The Problem Child*, p. 178.
10 Jules Henry, *Culture Against Man*, p. 287. In the passage quoted, Henry is writing particularly about 'social studies', but he makes it clear that he sees education generally as having a basis of absurdity.

2 Dominie

When Neill's hopes for a literary life collapsed he saw no alternative but to return to the obscure schoolrooms of Scotland; he became the temporary head teacher of the village school at Gretna to stand in for one Thomas Blackburn who had been granted leave of absence from the task of civilizing young Scottish barbarians to quell the German vandals.

The blacksmith legend was not the mainstay of Gretna's economy in those pre-tourist days. Then the villagers quietly planted and dug their potatoes and cut peat from the wide bog that stretches over the border, with no thought of exploiting the peculiarities of the Scottish marriage laws in the manner of today's vacuous commerce. The Public School (the term is used in its American sense) stood, and still stands, between the villages of Gretna Green and Springfield. Except that it is built in red stone rather than grey, the school is almost identical with that in Kingsmuir where Neill was brought up. In its two rooms, 130 scholars (when all were present), aged from five to fourteen years, worked under three teachers. The Infants and Standard One children were in the smaller room – thirty feet by twenty-one – where long desks and benches rose in tiers. The other room, ten feet longer, was partitioned so that the children in Standards Two, Three and Four could be taught in one group, and those of Standards Five, Six and Seven (which were to be Neill's special concern) in another.

Obviously when the children were not kept at home by snow-storms or by measles epidemics, or when they were not in the fields helping with the potato harvest, the rooms would have been even more overcrowded than in schools of today. Conditions were made more uncomfortable by the mean furnishing of the building; and it was poorly heated and indifferently maintained. In fact, Neill seems to have used the school log-book mainly to record the incidence of burst pipes, the lack of coal and kindling-wood, the absence of the caretaker, and his unproductive struggle with the doctor and with the School Board to effect some improvement. 'I object,' he wrote, 'to dust in a badly ventilated room, and I am taking the school in late and closing early.' And a fortnight later, when he found the school had remained uncleaned for five days, he recorded that 'I asked the Chairman of the Board for permission to close the school . . . He replied verbally by messenger that he had nothing to do with the cleaning of the school. I at once acted. I told the scholars that there would be no school tomorrow.'

These were not the physical conditions ideally suited to an educational experiment; but of course the school had been designed for no such purpose. It was merely one of hundreds of almost identical schools that were built to apply the established educational formula to the children of villages all over Scotland. Nor, for that matter did Neill come to Gretna with any revolutionary intentions. He had no preconceived plans, no theory of education to translate into practice. He had simply memories of his father's school and of the repressive regime he had worked under in Kingskettle, a dissatisfaction with the academics of Edinburgh and a mind (or a heart) churned up with the free-thinking notions that had excited him at university and that had filled the air during his brief excursion into the literary circles in London.

Coming straight from this heady atmosphere, he must have found the conventional conception of a dominie's role almost humiliatingly irksome, and it is not difficult to imagine his feelings when he read the routinely correct entries with which his predecessors had filled the school log-book which it was now his duty to continue. He was certainly riled at finding in the heavy black instructions pasted inside its front cover the injunction that 'no reflections or opinions of a general character are to be entered in the log-book.' His reflections and opinions were not to be so easily suppressed and he resolved to keep a private log in which 'I shall write down my thoughts on education.' This was the origin of his first book, *A Dominie's Log*. It was not a work of fiction, as Professor Stewart suggests,[1] but a reasonably accurate account of the day-to-day events of Neill's first year at Gretna. Despite the pseudonyms that he used, many who were in his class and who are still living in and around Gretna have found no difficulty in identifying themselves and their friends both from the character portraits and from incidents that Neill related in the book.

The official log-book received scant attention from Neill. Entries are irregular and terse, and there is little to suggest that there was anything unusual happening. Only two entries give any such hint. The first of these was on 14 May 1915: 'Open-air school dropped for the time being owing to cold weather.' This was a euphemism for Neill's rambles with the children, kite-flying expeditions and the free use of the playground which are described only in his 'private log'; and later, after the *Log* was published, there was the construction of a fish-pond in the school yard and of a pigeon-house. The second hint as to how things were developing is contained in the Inspector's report which Neill copied (as he was required to do) in full into the log-book. It is dated 9 July 1915 and opens promisingly enough: 'Under the present Headmaster the work of the school is being carried on with much earnestness,' though the Inspector, Mr MacPhee, added rather ambiguously: 'Results are on the whole pretty satisfactory in the circumstances.' He found the children in Neill's class to be 'intelligent and bright under oral examination' and making 'an exceedingly good appearance' in class subjects. 'More attention, however, should be paid to neatness of method and penmanship in copies and jotters.' In his other log Neill observed that 'some men are born tidy and some have tidiness thrust upon them,' and that being in the latter class himself (the thrusting being done by his landlady and by the school charwoman), he was incapable of teaching neatness. But when Mr MacPhee went on to comment that 'discipline, which is kindly, might be firmer, especially in the Senior Division, so as to prevent a tendency to talk on the part of the pupils whenever the opportunity occurs', Neill was in more serious disagreement. Why, he wondered, if the Inspector found the children intelligent and bright, did he want them to be silent? 'You must learn not to talk in school,' Mr MacPhee had said to the class as he left them. 'I am a peaceful man,' wrote Neill, 'and I hate a scene. I said nothing, but I shall do nothing. If he returns he will find no difference in the school.'[2]

On the cover of *A Dominie's Log* is a quaint picture of the schoolmaster, pipe in one hand and a dangling tawse in the other, looking uncertainly as a boy kisses the cheek of a pretty young girl with dark tresses falling over her shoulder and a school slate in her hand. The conflict implied by all these symbols Neill tries to argue out in the book. Very quickly he felt a futility in his task. What does it all mean? he asked himself when he was left in the empty classroom at the end of the day. To teach the three R's when he knew they would read no more than the 'drivelling weeklies', and write only pathetic, semi-literate notes to their children's dominie? Education had done no more for their parents than to encourage them to sing Tipperary and to hang in their homes the 'vile prints' that were given away with a pound of tea. But this sense of purposelessness was almost as quickly dismissed by that kind of hope that has enabled him over many years to sustain his brand of seemingly eccentric faith against so much ridicule and material pressure. 'I am hopeful because I have found a solution. I shall henceforth try to make my bairns realise. Yes, realise is the word. Realise what? To tell the truth, I have some difficulty in saying. I think I want to make them realise what life means.'

He had found an aim but the means by which to achieve it was still obscure. He knew of only one ready-made recipe – the Scotch Code – and he had no time for that. 'There has been no real authority on education, and I do not know of any book from which I can crib.' In fact, there were people working at that time from whom he might have gleaned ideas – Dewey and Montessori, for instance, or in a smaller way, in England,

Norman MacMunn and Edward O'Neill – but he was unaware of them. There is no educational influence in his writing or practice of this time that can be identified; perhaps the most dominant theme which coloured his thinking was a kind of compassionate and utopian socialism.

Yet in politics too he could find no acceptable authority. 'Capitalism is un-Christlike, and we must destroy it,' he declared; but also, 'Heaven help us from the bureaucratic socialism of the Webbs!' His resolution to make the children 'realise' involved him quite often in breaking the teacher's traditional vow of silence on politics and this occasionally brought protests from parents. From one he received a note: 'I send my son Andrew to get education at the school, not Radical politics.' Neill told Andrew to assure his father that 'I hate Radicalism possibly more than he does.' This brought an apology from the father: 'Aw thocht ye was one o' they wheezin' Radicals. And what micht yer politics be?' Neill's answer, 'I am a Utopian' led the confused man to talk about the weather, but it was not made just to fob off a simple villager: it was as near the truth as he could get. For all his hatred of capitalist values he had only a wavering faith in the ability of the masses to take charge of their own concerns. More than once he quoted Ibsen's thunder: 'The Majority *never* has right on its side. *Never*, I say.' And the reason for this Nietzsche seemed to give: 'If we have a degenerate and mean environment, the fittest will be the man who is best adapted to degeneracy and meanness: he will survive.'

The adaptation to such an environment that was forced on Neill's bairns distressed him. Being country children they would not have to endure the industrial squalor that Neill glimpsed from railway carriages. It was rather the ignorance and prejudices of their homes and the hours of consuming toil that lay ahead which would inevitably brutify them, however imaginative an education he might provide for them. That was the real futility. When Robert Campbell reached the age-limit and left school to start work the next morning as a ploughman, Neill, depressed, reflected, 'Truly it is like death: I stand by a new-made grave, and I have no hope of resurrection. Robert is dead.' He would be 'gathered to his fathers', taking up the attitudes of his neighbours, going to church, voting 'Radical or Tory', marrying and living in a hovel. And there was Margaret Steel, a bright girl who, Neill thought, should be given a free university education but who 'will go out into the fields, and in three years she will be an ignorant country bumpkin'. In fact she went to a factory and as she left school Neill wrote: 'Today Margaret is a bright-eyed, rosy-cheeked lassie; in three years she will be hollow-eyed and pale-faced. Never again will she know what it is to wake naturally after her sleep: the factory siren will haunt her dreams always. She will rise at half past four in summer and winter; she will tramp the two-mile road to the factory, and when six comes at night she will wearily tramp home again. Possibly she will marry a factory worker and continue working in the factory, for his wage will not keep up a home.'

He contrasted this forlorn prospect with the pampered lives enjoyed by the daughters of Bruce, the factory owner, and he fulminated against the way in which this profiteer used women as instruments to exploit the men. He saw Bruce advertising for labour: '"No encumbrances" says the ad. . . . He breeds cattle for showing, he breeds pheasants for slaughtering, he breeds children to heir his estate. Then he sits down and pens an advertisement for a slave without "encumbrances".'

But to have right on its side did not mean that the Majority was not wrong. It was, as always. The workers played their parts in the capitalist game, going to church, voting Radical or Tory, . . . When there is a strike of coal beneath the fields of the local farm* the children are excited: they'll build a town here bigger than London. Neill tried to de-glamorize the prospect for them. In three years, he told them, this bonny village would be a smoky blot on God's earth like Newcastle. But lacking the quixotic fervour of a Blake to build a New Jerusalem, he supposes that in time he will have alone to 'trek inland to seek some rural spot where I can be of some service to the community'. It seems that the only service he felt he could give was to the still innocent – the non-industrialized village, or to children whose imagination was still unconfined by the servitudes of adulthood. Perhaps he was a Peter Pan who would take the Darling children off to some Never-never land; or a Piper who would lead infants away from their greedy and plagued parents into some utopian mountain.

In fact this image was taken up by Neill in a short play he wrote for the children at King Alfred School at Hampstead four years after leaving Gretna.[3] It was set in the Country of the Free to which the Pied Piper had led the children of Hamelin. The second generation is growing up, schooled by the Piper himself. Now for the first time the harmony of this utopia is interrupted by one child who shouts in protest: 'I am tired of sweet music. I want the music of the hurricane, of the rainstorm, of the thunder.' The Piper's music, he suggests, is the music of a man who wears a mask. What has happened to the anger that the Piper felt when the Mayor of Hamelin refused him his fee? the child asks. Perhaps it is slumbering within you!

This allegory, performed on the occasion of the retirement of a 'well-loved headmaster' of King Alfred's – John Russell – was probably intended as a comment on what Neill disparagingly called the 'higher life' pre-occupations of the staff of that school, but perhaps he was also expressing his own realization that his own romanticizing of childhood was an idyll

* The incident was presumably based on the building of a munitions factory at Gretna.

that could not survive when his bairns were forced to face the reality of adult life.

In other words Neill's problem, as for all teachers, was as much to do with his own role and attitudes as it was concerned with the proper content and mode of the education of his children. When he first went to Gretna he assumed much of the stance of a conventional dominie, even to the extent of sometimes using the tawse – he leathered Tom Wilkie for hitting the diminutive Dave Tosh on the nose, and he even whacked Lizzie Smith for talking while he was reading the war news to the class. It was only as he got to know the children better that he unconsciously shed the attitudes that these actions implied. When spring came in 1915 he became aware, for instance, of the rivalry between Tom Dixon and Georgie Steel for the love of pretty Katie Farmer, and he recalled the 'noties' that he used to write to his own Violets and Katies. Then in a few weeks the boys were playing football and 'bools', and the girls were ignored. There's no chivalry, he observed – thankfully; none of the chivalry which makes us open doors for nice ladies and banish the prostitutes of Piccadilly from our minds. He wanted no such hypocrisy from the children: he refused to teach them manners which were, he thought, nothing but a sham. Correspondingly, his own relations with the children became more direct. When he came across a boy surreptitiously smoking a cigarette, Neill simply told the lad that he too, as a boy, had smoked an occasional Woodbine, but that it isn't really good for you. The boy grinned and, explaining that he did it only for fun, tossed the cigarette over a wall. Earlier, Neill would automatically have given the boy a welting but now a physical assault on a child had become unthinkable: it was no studied forbearance on his part, but rather the result of his coming to see things more and more from the children's point of view.

Schoolwork of the conventional kind became increasingly difficult to stomach as the child-view took over. He found that children had a genuine love for poetry, but like them he hated the poems that crowded the standard school anthologies – Little Jim, Lucy Gray, The Wreck of the Hesperus, and the rest of them. The teaching of history was all wrong, he thought, with its snobbish preoccupation with kings and queens. It should tell the story of the people; and geography likewise should tell what living is like in different parts of the world rather than be concerned with lists of exports and rivers. He hated (and abandoned) such tortuous compulsions as parsing and sentence-analysis, just as much as the children hated them. This progressive rejection of the traditional curriculum led to its substitution by a sometimes very hedonistic version of activity methods. 'I try hard to share the bairns' joys,' he wrote. 'At present I am out with them every day flying kites.' One of these kites became entangled in a tree, and a branch was broken in the retrieving of it. The tree-owner came to Neill in a fury: 'That's what comes o' yer nae discipline ideas. Dawm it, Aw'll no stand that! Ye'll just go doon to the school and gie the boy the biggest leathering that he's ever had in his life.' Neill explained that he was the schoolmaster, not the policeman, and the broken branch was no concern of his. 'Had it been my garden,' he added, 'I should have sworn possibly harder than you have done. On the other hand, had it been twenty years ago and my kite, well, I should have done exactly what the boy did.' And to himself he reflected: 'I find that I am on the side of the bairns. I am against law and discipline; I am all for freedom of action.'

This realization led to a thorough revision of his classroom methods so that very soon he was able to say 'I force no bairn to learn in my school.' The result he exhibited to Mr Simpson, a neighbouring headmaster, who came to see the school 'at work'. He was shocked at the noise Neill tolerated during registration, and then confused as the children rushed about to their several occupations: Jim Burnett to take the *Glasgow Herald* from Neill's desk, Lizzie Smith to borrow *The Invisible Man*, Tom Mac-Intosh to get the key to the manual room to finish a boat he was making. As Neill was getting ready to give an arithmetic lesson to those who had not gone outside with a novel, Mary Wilson held out a bag of sweets to him; 'and then she said: "Please sir, would the gentleman like one too?" Simpson took one with the air of a man on holiday who doesn't care what sins he commits.'

At the end of the first year Neill wrote in the official log-book: 'The school closed today for the summer holidays. I have received Form 9b from the clerk.' In his other log he wrote: 'When Jim Jackson came to school he had a bad look: if a girl happened to push him, he turned on her with a murderous scowl. Now that I think of it I realise that Jim is always a bright cheery boy now. When I first knew him I could see that he looked on me as a natural enemy, and if I had thrashed him I might have made him fear me, but the bad look would never have left his face. I close my log with the solemn declaration of my belief that I have done my work well.'

With that it seems that Neill had found his commitment to education. On the previous day, Jim Jackson had marched up the road towards Neill with his gang behind him and his wooden gun in his hand. At twenty yards he had fired, and cried out: 'Please sir, you're dead now. But we'll take you prisoner instead!' He had no desire to escape – nor evidently has he ever had since. He stayed at Gretna for another year and a half until he joined the army in March 1917.

Even before he left he had published his second book *A Dominie Dismissed*. This is a work of fiction which opens with his departure from

Gretna being forced by pressure from dissenting parents. Though he never suffered such a dismissal in fact, there was plenty of opposition to his libertarian methods, though in the main he seems to have been regarded as just an oddity and not taken too seriously. A few parents, however, objected strongly to Neill's refusal to force children to work at subjects they had no taste for, especially when this threatened their success at the examinations for entrance to the Academy. A few removed their children when the Ministry of Munitions opened another school for the children of the workers at the new factory in Gretna. On the other hand Neill is remembered now with affection and some admiration by several of the people still living in the neighbourhood who as children were in his class or who had friends or brothers or sisters there. It is generally an amused pleasure that lights the faces of these people when they are reminded of this distant dominie, and however unfavourably some of the older people may have regarded him there is no doubt that those who were his pupils thought him 'the cat's whisker' (as one of them put it). If, for most, their year or two with Neill is just a pleasant and curious memory, some were affected more deeply by his example. I was told, for instance, that Margaret Steel (as she was called in the *Log*) had two children whom she brought up in what was called 'complete freedom'. The phrase suggests that she may have let them stray over the line that divides freedom from licence (as Neill later found many parents were apt to do). Mr Brown, who took over the headship at Gretna after the war (and who stayed there for nearly forty years), remembered these two children as wild, difficult pupils with much undisciplined talent. There is a story too of a teacher who had worked with Neill and who had extrapolated the libertarian doctrine to the extent of bathing in the nude with her pupils – a piece of unteacherly behaviour which led to her having to remove herself to another part of Scotland!

Neill himself has always sailed close to the wind of scandal but has never been capsized by it, and though he has shocked many people, and shocked them so deliberately and continuously that they have professed finally to have become bored by it, he has always had access to a humour that has deflected angry actions. In fact humour was such a strong element in *A Dominie's Log* that the book was not always taken as a basically serious piece of educational writing. Even his publishers seem to have been in some doubt: in an advertisement for the Dominie books they wrote: 'His chief trouble is that the public persists in accepting him as a humourist – but this is typical: Charlie Chaplin's chief ambition is to play Hamlet.' Actually the situation may have been the reverse, for it seems that Neill, still harbouring literary ambitions, saw his future more as a humorous writer than as an educationist. He wrote two books – *The Booming of Bunkie*

(1919) and *Carroty Broon* (1920) – which were clearly aimed in that direction, though neither met with much success. The latter was by far the more accomplished of the two, and it was so because Neill was using the humour as a medium for expressing what was to him a serious – that is to say, important – subject, the struggle between an adolescent boy's fantasies and his realities. So his second book also, *A Dominie Dismissed*, exploited the humorous in conveying a serious argument – in this case a statement of the rationale for the actions that he had described in the *Log*.

These actions had been performed as a more or less instinctive response to the Gretna schoolroom to which he had come with no ready-made theories. It was not that there were no theories then available which might have supported his intuitions. On the contrary, the subject of freedom in education was being discussed fairly widely at this time and there were at least a few who were putting the idea into practice. The movement in this direction had started at the turn of the century with the founding of such schools as Abbotsholme (1889), Bedales (1893) and King Alfred's (1898), and with their alliance in the New Schools Movement. Their immediate inspiration had been largely a reaction against the narrowness of the classical education and the Arnold ethos which were almost universal in the Public Schools and which were translated with little essential change into the grammar schools; but the New Schools were started by men and women whose minds were open to new ideas and they soon widened their reforms to constitute a serious challenge to many of the hitherto secure values of orthodox education. This challenge was most impressively articulated by Edmond Holmes in his book *What Is and What Might Be* which appeared in 1911.

Holmes, at one time Chief Inspector of Elementary Schools, was a man of vision. At odds with most of the ideas that lay behind the policies of the Board of Education, he must often have felt out of place as one of its officials, and his book reads like the venting of an enormous expostulation after years of professional constraint. Certainly he was no revolutionary in the political sense and he was far from being the free-thinking libertarian that many of this camp were taken to be. He had been deeply influenced by his reading of oriental philosophies, and though he was strongly critical both of the practice of religious instruction and of much of the Christian doctrine, his criticisms were not motivated by anti-religious attitudes. On the contrary what he deplored was the absence of true religious feeling in most of the Scripture lessons that he had seen over the years; he linked this with an evident lack of faith, stemming he thought from the Christian dogma of original sin, in the valuable outcomes of the unimpeded process of human growth. It was this dogma, he asserted, that led to teachers feeling that they had to coerce their pupils into the ways of right thinking

„ 29ᵗʰ	Mr MacPhee. H. M. I. S. called to day & examined all classes.	
July 9ᵗʰ	The Report of H. M. I. S. has arrived. It is as follows :—

"Under the present Headmaster the work of the School is being carried on with much earnestness, and the results on the whole are pretty satisfactory in the circumstances.

The pupils in the Senior Division are intelligent and bright under oral examination, and make an exceedingly

good appearance in the class subjects. More attention, however, should be paid to neatness of method and penmanship in copies & jotters.

In the Junior Division Spelling is a weak subject. The Infant division is in capable hands, and the pupils generally do well in all their subjects.

Discipline, which is kindly, might be firmer, especially in the Senior Division, so as to prevent a tendency to talk on the part of the pupils whenever opportunity occurs."

July 15ᵗʰ	School closed to day for Summer Vacation
Aug 16ᵗʰ	School opened today.
Sept 17	School closed for autumn holidays

3. From the Gretna School log-book. Neill refers to the Inspector's Report, which he has here copied out, in his book *A Dominie's Log* (pp. 132–3).

A NEW TYPE OF SCHOOLMASTER.

Comic Papers and Musical Comedy Tunes as a Part of Education.

One of the wisest, one of the most human, and one of the most refreshing books that have been written for many a year is "A Dominie's Log," from the pen of A. S. Neill, which Herbert Jenkins publishes at half-a-crown. Mr. Neill is a Scottish schoolmaster who has the tremendous courage to run his school on the no-discipline lines and (among other things) the sympathy to encourage love-making between his bairns. We introduce him to our readers with the following excerpts from his "log":—

I FORCE no bairn to learn in my school. The few who dislike books and lessons sit up when I talk to the class. The slackers are not always the most ignorant.

* * *

The inspectors refuse to allow teachers to use slates nowadays on the ground that they are insanitary. To-day I reintroduced slates to all classes. My one reason was that my bairns were missing one of the most delightful pastimes of youth—the joy of making a spittle run down the slate and back again.

* * *

I have not used the strap for many weeks now. I hope I shall never use it again.

* * *

At last I have attained my ambition. As a boy my great ambition was to possess a cavalry trumpet and bugle. I have just bought both. I call the bairns to school with "Stables" or the "Fall In," and I gleefully look to playtime so that I may have another tootle. The bairns love to hear the calls, but I think I enjoy them most.

THE COMIC PAPERS.

I wonder why so many parents and teachers cuff boys' heads when they find them reading comic papers and "Lloods." I see no harm in either. I wish that people would get out of the absurd habit of taking it for granted that whatever a boy does is wrong. I hold that a boy is nearly always right.

THE STORY OF THE SQUIRE.

Howlers bore me; so do most school yarns. The only one worth remembering is the one about the inspector who was ratty.

"Here, boy," he fired at a sleepy youth, "who wrote 'Hamlet'?"

The boy started violently.

"P-please, sir, it wasna me," he stammered.

That evening the inspector was dining with the local squire.

"Very funny thing happened to-day," he said, as they lit their cigars.

"I was a little bit irritated, and I shouted at a boy, 'Who wrote "Hamlet"?' The little chap was flustered. 'P-please, sir, it wasna me,' he stuttered."

The squire guffawed loudly.

"And I suppose the little devil had done it after all!" he roared.

STYLE.

When a man writes too musically and ornately I always suspect him of having a paucity of ideas. If you have anything important to say you use plain language. The man who writes to the local paper complaining of "those itinerant denizens of the underworld, yclept hawkers, who make the day hideous with raucous cries," is a pompous ass. Yet he is no worse than the average stylist in writing.

* * *

There must be something in style after all. I had this note from a mother this morning:

"Dear Sir,—Please change Jane's seat, for she orings home more than belongs to her."

I refuse to comment on this work of art.

WHY NOT "HITCHY COO"?

If I could play the piano I should spend each Friday afternoon playing to my bairns. I should give them "Alexander's Ragtime Band" and "Hitchy Coo"; then I should play them a Liszt rhapsody and a Chopin waltz.

CO-EDUCATION.

The more I see of it the more I admire the co-education system. To me it is delightful to see boys and girls playing together. Segregate boys and you destroy their perspective. I used to find at the university that it was generally the English public school boy who set up one standard of morals for his sisters and another for shop-girls.

* * *

Seldom is there ever any over-familiarity. The girls have a natural protective aloofness that awes the boys; the boys generally have strenuous interests that lead them to ignore the girls for long periods. At present the sexes are very friendly, for lovemaking (always a holy thing with bairns) has come with spring; but in a few weeks the boys will be playing football or "bools" and they will not be seen in the girls' playground.

THE QUESTION OF SEX.

How can I bring my bairns to take a rational elemental view of sex instead of a conventional hypocritical one? How can I convey to them the realisation that our virtue is mostly cowardice, that our sex morality is founded on more respectability? (It is the easiest thing in the world to be virtuous in Padanaram (a place in Forfarshire); it is not so easy to be a saint in Oxford-street. Not because Oxford-street has more temptation, but because nobody knows you there.)

* * *

If a philanthropist would come along and offer me a private school to run as I pleased then I should introduce sex into my scheme of education. Bairns would be encouraged to believe in the stork theory of birth until they reached the age of nine. At that age they would get the naked truth.

* * *

The present evasion and deceit lead to the dirtiness which constitutes the sex education of boys and girls.

ODD SAYINGS.

I object to age and experience; I am all for youth and empiricism. After all, what is the use of experience in teaching? I could bet my boots that ninety-nine out of a hundred teachers use the methods they learned as pupil-teachers.

* * *

No man, no woman, has the right to make the skies cloudy for a bairn; it is the sin against the Holy Ghost.

* * *

Few bairns have a sense of humour; Theirs is a sense of fun. Make a noise like a duck and they will scream, but tell them your best joke and they will be bored to tears.

* * *

I know that I am teaching badly if the class is loafing, and I am honest enough in my saner moments not to blame the bairns.

* * *

I want to teach my bairns how to live; the Popular Educator wants to teach them how to make a living. There is a distinction between the two ideals.

4. The popular Press discovers Neill: *Weekly Dispatch*, 14 November 1915.

and right behaviour. On this basis he castigated the practice in schools – 'the path of mechanical obedience' – that he had watched as an Inspector. In all its parts – Scripture lessons, arithmetic lessons, payments-by-results, rewards and punishments, examinations – the whole of 'What Is' in education was based on the thesis that the only way to salvation for a sin-ridden humanity was through a strict adherence to rules and an insistent suppression of 'instinctive' or 'natural' behaviour – a suppression of 'growth', in fact. 'The aim of his teachers is to leave nothing to his nature, nothing to his spontaneous life, nothing to his free activity: to repress all his natural impulses: to drill his energies into complete quiescence; to keep his whole being in a state of sustained and painful tension; . . . to turn the child into an animated puppet who, having lost his capacity for vital activity, will be ready to dance, or rather to go through, a series of jerky movements, in response to the string which his teacher pulls.'[4]

In contrast, Holmes set out What Might Be – 'the path to self-realization' – by describing a school in a village that he misleadingly called Utopia (it was an actual school which Holmes knew well) run by an enlightened headteacher whom he called Egeria. In Roman times the nymph Egeria was worshipped as the goddess of childbirth, and Holmes commented that this lady 'has certainly been my Egeria'. It is impossible to know how far he idealized the actuality: certainly his descriptions of 'the radiantly bright faces of the children . . . the brightness of energy and intelligence and the brightness of goodness and joy . . . the ceaseless activity of the children . . . the air is electrical with energy . . . there is no need for punishment or any other form of repression . . . it is equally true that there is no need for rewards . . .' – these eulogies understandably provoked some scepticism at the time. Today Egeria's school might be any one of a large number of advanced primary schools, but in 1911 the description had a much less familiar ring. It also provoked scorn and criticism, as did the rationale by which Holmes explained his ideal.

Some measure of this opposition can be gauged from the fact that within three years Holmes published a second book *In Defence of What Might Be* which was almost entirely devoted to answering attacks on his first volume. His defence was strengthened by the addition of the theories and practice of Montessori to the intuitive approach embodied in Egeria's work, and this appearance of a scientific methodology added confidence to the quite widespread social idealism which had rallied to Holmes' enthusiasm, and the movement became much more buoyant. Holmes declared in his second book: 'I write as one who is championing a revolutionary movement . . . which, in its attempt to get to bedrock, threatens to undermine the very foundations of our western scheme of life.'[5]

Holmes became one of the key figures in a small group which discussed

c

these ideas at first informally, and which later initiated a series of conferences out of which eventually grew the New Education Fellowship. The first of these conferences was held in 1914 under the title 'New Ideals in Education' and its debates centred upon the work of Montessori. Present at this conference was a man who gave reinforcing strength of a different kind. This was Homer Lane who had come to England in 1912 and had started his famous Little Commonwealth the following year. The extreme daring, and extraordinary success, of his dealing with delinquents must have given heart to the movement which was rather lacking in practical demonstrations of the efficacy of its faith. Lane gave such demonstrations in dramatic measure. 'None is more wonderful and inspiring than the Little Commonwealth for young delinquents . . . Surely every logical and progressive teacher should be tempted by such victories of the principles of liberty.' So wrote Norman MacMunn in the Preface to his *A Path to Freedom in the School*, another significant contribution to this freedom movement. This little book appeared in that same year, 1914, and sounded the same revolutionary note as Holmes: 'The leaders of our movement have all the proofs, all the plans, all the necessary faith,' MacMunn wrote. 'For what, then, do we wait? To put it bluntly, for men and money.'

If this optimism was somewhat premature, at least it is clear that Neill was not so much alone in his ideas as he thought when he published the *Log*. The issue of freedom in schools was a live one, a part of the widening debate about education, popular interest in which expanded as the hope grew for a new life to follow the horrifying destructiveness of war. One indication of this growing concern was the decision of the editorial board of *The Times* to publish a monthly supplement – which very soon became a weekly one – devoted entirely to educational matters. This was not to be a revolutionary tract, of course, yet the yearly issues of the *Supplement* were sprinkled with items which suggest that the question of freedom was not one which was discussed only by an esoteric fringe. 'The most important of all educational questions hinges on that of freedom,' wrote Professor Culverwell in a lengthy letter that was printed in the *Supplement* of March 1916. So it is not surprising to find that this paper gave a long and largely commendatory review of *The Dominie's Log*.[6] The reviewer properly linked the book with the Holmes thesis – 'it belongs to the category of What-Might-Be's' – and describes it as 'the revelation of the soul of a teacher struggling to emancipate itself from the shackles of formalism and tradition'. Neill was complimented on his honesty and humour, rapped over the knuckles for some unspecified lapses in 'good taste', and reminded with avuncular indulgence of 'two important truths he has forgotten: first, that pupils cannot evolve the material of thought from inner consciousness, they must be instructed; second, that liberty and authority are mutually related and one without the other is, if not at all events, ruinous'. The next fifty years were to show that these 'truths' were not so simple as that: the reviewer's hope that 'we have not heard the last of this author' was not to be disappointed.

The book received other mostly favourable notices in papers and journals that were not specifically educational in their appeal. The sensation-mongers were quick to smell the possibilities: the *Weekly Dispatch*,[7] for instance, under a banner headline 'A New Type of Schoolmaster', proclaimed the *Log* as 'one of the wisest, one of the most human, and one of the most refreshing books that have been written for many a year'. Mr Neill 'has the tremendous courage to run his school on no-discipline lines, and (among other things) the sympathy to encourage love-making between his bairns'(!). The yellow press was thus prompt in identifying the titillating element in Neill's work, and has not since neglected it on that score. The *Dispatch* on this occasion followed its introductory commendation with two columns of quotations. Neill could not have found unmixed pleasure in these attentions especially from a paper which smeared its pages with lurid atrocity stories, savage attacks on 'the cowards who skulk under the guise of conscientious objections', and with bloodthirsty yelps of jingoistic fervour. This contrasted strikingly with the humane values that he had been trying to convey to his bairns at Gretna, and which the *Dispatch* affected to applaud.

There were others who presented a more credible understanding of Neill's intentions. The review in *The Bookman*[8] again illustrates that Neill was writing to a public far more ready to accept his ideas than he had thought. 'There is nothing new in Mr A. S. Neill's little volume, but . . . there is much that is fresh.' The review went on to suggest that his ideas, though happily presented were 'the usual commonplaces of modern educational theory mingled with the social opinions of the up-to-date young man who reads "The New Age" and the "New Statesman"'. *The New Age* (then under the inspiring editorship of its creator, A. R. Orage) was the most notable radical weekly of its time – as necessary a part of a young advanced thinker's reading as the *Statesman* became under Kingsley Martin in the thirties and forties. Neill was certainly a regular reader of this journal; in fact, he was a contributor – a light, satirical piece of his, 'The Lunatic', appeared in its columns early in 1915.

But *The New Age* was not so approving of his book as other journals had been: five months were allowed to pass after its publication, and then[9] a full column was given to laying out the folly of his ill-informed revolt. 'His heart is in the right place, but where, oh where is his head?' His unaware-ness of other progressive educationists was treated with schoolmasterly scorn, he was given a reading list to study – Rousseau, Pestalozzi, Froebel,

Montessori, Dewey – and he was advised to visit Mr Caldwell Cook at the Perse School, Cambridge. The criticisms were valid, but they were expressed with what seems an unnecessary, and certainly an uncharitable, severity, and one is led to wonder why a new writer should have been attacked with such vehemence.

It seems probable that this delayed review only appeared at all because the book was having such a success and that it was an attempt to discredit the author whose threat was as apparent to the progressives as it was to the die-hards. Neill has always embarrassed the more intellectually, as well as the more spiritually, inclined of the radicals, and it may be that when the reviewer wrote: 'He is not quite alone in the world,' he was expressing a hope rather than a statement of fact – a hope that he would come into the fold and observe their rules of intellectual and moral decorum: 'There is no good reason why he should appear before the world in deliberate *déshabillé* of style and thought.' This appeal to Neill to behave was made more explicit: 'There is no real reason why his new-found sympathy with children should be made offensive to adults; and Mr Neill must be told not to prejudice his case' – our case? – 'by an apparent preference for anarchy. We all know what he means when he objects to discipline; but why should he go to the other extreme and say: "Dignity is a thing I abominate"?' Apparently not everyone did know what he meant, or would allow him to mean it. After warning Neill against an excessive admiration for 'advanced' writers like Ibsen, Shaw, Wells, and Galsworthy, who were 'mere revolters', the reviewer tells him now to concentrate on essentials. 'The questions are: "What does Mr Neill want to teach?" and "How is he going to teach it?"'

These are hardly the essentials that Neill was suggesting, though his reply that was printed in the next issue of *The New Age* does not offer any positive alternatives. 'My chief aim,' he wrote, 'is to counteract the influence of the home. I hold that revolt is urgently needed. Every advance in ideas is a revolt against something.' He had yet to find a coherent philosophy to support that revolt.

REFERENCES

1 W. A. C. Stewart, *The Educational Innovators*, vol. 2, p. 284.
2 *A Dominie's Log*, p. 127.
3 Printed in *Education For the New Era*, vol. 1, No. 3.
4 E. Holmes, *What Is and What Might Be*, p. 48.
5 E. Holmes, *In Defence of What Might Be*, p. 315.
6 *Times Educational Supplement*, 7 December 1915.
7 *The Weekly Dispatch*, 14 November 1915.
8 *The Bookman*, December 1915.
9 *The New Age*, 13 April 1916.

3 Homer Lane

Neill's second book, a fantasy based on his supposed dismissal from the school and his return to the village as a cattleman on a local farm, he used as a vehicle to argue out a kind of rationale for the actions he had described in the *Log*. The argument is dramatized in his attempts to rescue some of his former pupils from the effects of his successor's reimposition of a conventional education. Particularly, he fights for Jim Jackson, the boy who had taken him prisoner at the end of the *Log* and whose imagination Neill had previously delighted in. Now it is being beaten out of the lad by Macdonald, the new dominie. 'I'll do all in my power to help the lad preserve his own personality . . . Professional etiquette be damned. I'm not in the profession now anyhow, and all the professional etiquette in the world is as nothing to the saving of a soul.'

In this proselytizing spirit he sets about his anti-education of Jim and some other of the more hopeful young souls, in the fields and in his bothy. But it is a losing battle. The children are drawn helplessly into an acceptance of the lot which Macdonald and the irresistible norms of village living assume for them. 'I am losing Jim Jackson. The battle for his soul is unequal. Macdonald has him all day, while I see him only at intervals . . . His father and mother are people after Macdonald's own heart. They are typical village folk, stupid and aggressive. Oh I loathe the village; it is full of envy and malice and smallness.' But this bitterness subsides as he drifts into a love affair with his boss's daughter Margaret. They become engaged and he again takes up his work as teacher with Margaret as his pupil. He instructs her (and us) about his thoughts on all manner of subjects: on education, of course, and on pacifism and politics, on morals and manners, on literature and religion. Using their romance as a kind of centre of interest, he is also able to gather together a small band of his more devoted ex-pupils, three girls and Jim Jackson, for whom his hope revives. The book ends with his marriage, of which Jim writes a fanciful description: 'Mr Macdonald was there, but he did not sing . . . After it was finished the happy cupel went over to the bothy to there honeymoon and Martha Findlay said it made marriage common and that anybody could have a bothy for a honeymoon, so I just said to her . . .'

Like the essays that earned Jim a strapping from Macdonald more than once, the book is 'all lies', and though it is dedicated to 'the original of Margaret' it was many years before Neill was to get married, and then not to this Margaret. Perhaps this wedding and the immediate return to the bothy speak of a decision to marry himself to, and work with, a toiling humanity. Yet despite this more joyful ending the book is not written from the same light-hearted optimism as the *Log*. *The Times* reviewer, in a less indulgent notice than the previous book had been given, suggests that 'there is a bitter undercurrent in the book: a sense of failure, failure that must follow when the doctrine of freedom in education becomes a doctrine of licence.'[1]

The sense of failure was certainly there but of course Neill would not have agreed with the reviewer as to its cause. He was aghast at the enormous social forces that resisted the changes which he wished to initiate. On the other hand he was convinced that education, besides being the prime culprit, was the only instrument by which change could come. 'Obviously present-day civilization is all wrong. "But," a dominie might cry, "can you definitely blame elementary education for that?" I answer, "Yes, yes, yes."'[2] Alone, he had been unable to counteract the influences outside his classroom: this was his failure as he saw it. And on a national scale he felt no more optimistic. All the eloquent speeches from eminent men about post-war education seemed only to be concerned with the commercial interests of the country, and the schools' main aim would be, as before, to turn out efficient wage-slaves. Who is there to save education? he asked. Not the teachers, who would go on talking about Compulsory Greek and then perhaps Compulsory Russian. The teachers would humbly adapt themselves, he thought, to whatever schemes the 'commercially-minded gentlemen of Westminster' drew up.

However, to offset this pervasive pessimism, Neill had found one supporting hope. This was Homer Lane, to whom he yearned with a passionate idealism and who became a dominating influence in his work. He confessed that he thought always in black and white: Lane was a dazzling white. 'There are two ways in education: Macdonald's, with Authority in the shape of School Boards and magistrates and prisons to support him, and mine with the Christlike experiment of Homer Lane to encourage me.'[3] The epithet is significant. Perhaps at this stage he was not attributing the messianic qualities with which others later invested Lane; rather he was admiring the message and practice of Christlike love that he saw Lane bringing to education – a message which, he added, Lane combined with the message of freedom from Shelley. Unlike most others in the progressive movement who were nervously unsure of the proper limits of freedom, Lane would have no compromise and chided those who did. '"Give the child freedom" is the insistent cry of the New Education, but then its exponents usually devise a "system" which, although based on the soundest of principles, limits that freedom and contradicts the principle.' Such a system was implied by the much-quoted casuistry of Rousseau's: 'No doubt Emile ought to do only what he wants to do, but he ought to do nothing but what you want him to do. He should never take a step you have not foreseen, nor utter a word you could not foretell.' And for all his attempts to dissociate himself from 'anarchical theories of education such as we are apt to associate with the name of Rousseau', Edmond Holmes was one who followed the master in this respect, declaring that the child should be allowed to choose only from things that were worth doing.[4] In much the same way MacMunn paraphrased Rousseau's dictum: 'The boy has the right to choose, but his choice is far more likely to fit in with our wishes than it would be if a training in freedom had not taught him to correlate his natural activities with the idea of useful development.'[5] Lane would have none of such contrivances. 'The point is,' he declared, '*Freedom cannot be given*. It is taken by the child . . . Freedom involves discovery and invention, neither of which, by their nature, can be embodied in any system. Freedom demands the privilege of conscious wrong-doing.'[6]

Lane had come from America in 1913 already with experience in the education of delinquents, for six years having had charge of a reformatory for boys called the Ford Republic. Like Neill, he had been feeling his way towards his own methods, working by instinct rather than by theory. Theory overlaid his work, developing out of his experience in three main stages – the first he formulated after he had been working with adult prisoners for some years, the second after he left the Ford Republic, and the third when his English school, the Little Commonwealth, was on the point of collapsing (or more accurately, exploding).

When he began to work with adult prison convicts, he took it for granted that human nature was bad and regarded crime as 'a reversion to nature'. Then when his work brought him into contact with young first offenders he recognized 'a tendency in them to do right which had been twisted by environment into what had the appearance of wrong . . . I found no less altruism and spirituality among my juvenile delinquents than among normal children.' Then, watching still younger children at play, he found 'the child in the playground was not the same child as the one who came to school' where he showed none of the heroic, fearless, resourceful, and powerful qualities that were apparent in his spontaneous play. His search took him to observations of infants as a result of which he claimed to have found 'the clue to the mystery of crime and failure. Even the infant was denied freedom to his self. Crime is no greater denial of nature's intention than is failure. One is the expression of a human soul still fighting against domination, and the other is a soul defeated.'

He thus arrived at the thesis that the perversion of young children was the result of their loss of freedom, of the training given to them from infancy onwards, and that the perversion might take the form either of a loss of power or of delinquency. The original power of their natures he claimed was evident in the play activities of normal children as in the criminal activities of the delinquents; and in both he discerned the remnants of their 'original goodness'. This view determined the way in which he organized his programme for young offenders in the Ford Republic. His methods and ambitions he described in a series of newspaper articles published in 1909. He explained that the boys had initially to be helped to regain their self-respect, and then to be helped to develop a self-reliance by which that self-respect could be maintained. But 'he has not been developed into a permanent social value until his self-reliance is modified by self-restraint and public spirit ... It is in the solution of this problem of how to teach self-restraint that the farm-school has developed a unique method. Self-government, the personal responsibility of the individual for the social worth of the community. That is the key.'[7]

Lane was forced to resign his position at the Ford Republic as a result of an unfortunate scandal in a teacup, and he then had a short while (working as a navvy) which Wills describes as a regenerative period of withdrawal, 'a spiritual, or at any rate mental, stocktaking'.[8] In thus reflecting on the work which he had been doing he arrived at a new and important formulation. 'He knew he had been doing something unique,' writes Wills. 'Now he knew what it was. He had been using the reforming and regenerating influence of love, where most people use the stunting and corrupting influence of hatred, condemnation and punishment. Henceforward this was to be at the core of his work and the centre of his teaching. The self-determination which he had hitherto preached was now seen to be merely a corollary of this startling fact; that those who would help the delinquent and anti-social and unhappy must "be on their side" – must love them.'

Such a position would not be acceptable to present-day psychologists and sociologists as a sufficient basis for an educational programme; however much they might respect it, they would demand a more objective analysis and a scientifically verifiable methodology. Lane was conscious of such a demand at the time when there was great excitement at the possibility of an education based 'scientifically' on the New Psychology and he was persuaded by this excitement to develop explanations in these terms. Neill was likewise seduced by the psycho-analytic theories – though probably to a lesser extent: for him this notion of the regenerating influence of love was always the central and most significant element in Lane's 'Christlike experiment'. But through all Lane's scientific ambitions, and certainly through Neill's, there seems to run a stronger conviction that the real issues have to be argued out in terms of children and parents and teachers and their relationships rather than in 'scientific explanations'. H. J. Home[9] has put the point like this: 'That the symptom has meaning, if it is neurotic, is Freud's basic discovery, the basic insight which opened up the way to an understanding of functional illness and the principles of psycho-analytic treatment. It is not surprising that, in the excitement of so great a discovery . . . Freud should have overlooked the logical implications for theory of the step he had taken . . . In discovering that the symptom had meaning and basing his treatment on this hypothesis, Freud took the psycho-analytic study out of the world of science into the world of humanities, because a meaning is not the product of causes but the creation of a subject. This is a major difference; for the logic and method of the humanities is radically different from that of science, though no less respectable and rational and of course much longer established.'

Lane's first attempts to assimilate the 'science' of psycho-analysis into his recipe of love are set out in a paper he prepared for the Little Common-wealth committee at the time of the inquiry into the allegations of sexual misconduct preferred against him by two girls who were in his charge at the school. This statement is reproduced in full in Wills's biography;[10] it needs to be read bearing in mind that it is addressed to the managers of the school who were sympathetic to Lane, but probably quite ignorant of any psycho-analytic theory, and also that Lane himself had read his first book on the subject less than two years before writing this document. Both these factors contribute to the obvious naïveté of the exposition.

He introduced his audience to the concepts of the Conscious and Un-conscious mind: 'Seven-eighths of our thinking is undirected by our wills.' The content of the Unconscious, the libido, consists in unmoral craving or desire – though not merely lustful. 'Its impelling, never-ceasing voice is continually urging the Conscious to remove all moral barriers to the gratification of its desires . . . It is plausible, compelling, never-tiring . . . It disguises a sense of inferiority behind swagger and boasting and vain display. It produces hypochondria as a cover for indolence . . . In a thousand ways it impedes the conscious will in its striving for social and vocational success.' (Lane is quite clearly ascribing meanings to symptoms, in Home's terms.) Then, rather like the seller of patent medicines, having convinced his audience of the malignancy of their symptoms, Lane reveals the remedy: 'Thanks to the brilliant and profound research of Professor Freud . . .' we now had a technique to redirect the 'tremendous energies' of the unconscious towards the services of our life-purposes. He describes the two functions of psycho-analysis: diagnosis on the one hand, the analy-sis of the unconscious mind; and sublimation on the other, the re-directing of the libido. This, he says, 'is education pure and simple.' While the nonanalytic teacher produces a 'titanic unconscious conflict' in his pupils, applied psycho-analysis will solve all problems. 'Does your boy hate arithmetic? He can be made to love it by analytic pedagogy. Is he rude and ungracious? It is a conflict easily removable ... Does he bite his nails? Fidget in his chair? Has he an obsession for drumming his fingers? Sucking the end of his pen? Teasing his brother or sister? Whistling? Throwing stones? ... All these things and thousands of others ... can be dealt with certainly and scientifically by analysis.'

This brash salesmanship is however counterbalanced by a more thoughtful self-criticism, and in particular his explanation of his failure (as he called it) at the Little Commonwealth is interesting. He first describes the conflicts of adolescence as a struggle between the libido and the developing moral and social consciousness. In cases in which the latter is 'weak and artificial – not based upon experienced truths', then he expects some forms of perverted libidinal expression to ensue – sexual perversion, purposeful lying, obsessional thieving, hatred of parents and teachers, cruelty. 'The conflict is not intense – the libido speaks with a direct but slightly disguised, voice.' If the balance of power is in the other direction, the relatively weak libido disguises its effect in the conscious mind, with resulting hypocrisy, parental fixation or obsessional love with hysterical symptoms, penuriousness, snobbery, over-fastidiousness, competitiveness, or in extreme cases, masochistic self-destruction and sadistic murderous tendencies. Lane then suggests:

> The conscious moral principles instilled deeply into the minds of the citizens of the Commonwealth by our form of self-government is so intense and so surely based upon logic and reason and experience that the libido which is definitely directed towards erotic or love objects by the co-educational features of our school, must assume the deepest disguise in its power in order to evade the censor and affect the consciousness of the individual. Hence the prevalence of masochism or self-accusation in the Commonwealth.

This appears to be a quite damning criticism of the principles underlying the Commonwealth; but Lane continues his analysis to demonstrate that it was not the principles, but his application of them, that was at fault. His explanation is in terms of the phenomenon of transference, which he represents as a directing of libidinal energy, of love or hate, towards 'anyone who comes within the range of our senses'. The psycho-analyst harnesses this energy so that the patient's libido may, at the will of the analyst, be sublimated into 'channels of happiness and success'. But he saw this as happening not only between an analyst and his patient, but also between every boy or girl and their teacher; and he suggested that a large part of a teacher's success depended upon the degree to which he felt able to accept and use this transference. If it were rejected it might take on the negative form of hate.

Lane then goes on to confess that in his own case he knew that such transference was inevitable, but that he 'shrank from the responsibilities entailed by [his pupils'] consciousness of it'. And to avoid these responsibilities he devised the system of self-government, thinking that he could in this way secure their transference on to the community. If, moreover, he made himself a member of that community on equal terms with the pupils, he hoped that whatever transference was made to him would result in an increased love for the community. He adds, incidentally, that in this way he hoped to set a pattern which other schools could adopt even though the head was not a psychologist. However, it did not work out as he had anticipated. 'I see now clearly that the adolescent must still have a parent substitute to accept his libido temporarily for purposes of dissolving complexes and conflicts before that libido can be transferred to the community in which he lives.' He thus implies that his refusal to accept the transference phenomenon personally resulted in particular in the two girls' virtually successful attempt to destroy him, and more generally in the painful abreaction to the self-government of the Commonwealth. But his conclusion is not to condemn that system: it remained an essential element in his scheme.

The official inquiry into the affairs at the Little Commonwealth led to the Home Secretary's refusal to renew the certificate of the school if it remained under the superintendence of Homer Lane, and the committee of managers preferred to close the school rather than appoint another headmaster. In 1918 Lane moved to London where he free-lanced for several years as a lecturer and 'consultant in psycho-analysis'.

Soon after he had joined the army, Neill was posted to the Royal Artillery School at Trowbridge in Wiltshire. This brought him close to Lane's Little Commonwealth in neighbouring Dorset and he seized the opportunity to spend a week-end there. The experience enthralled him, and before leaving he had agreed with Lane that he would join the staff as soon as he was free to do so. As it turned out, however, by that time the Little Commonwealth had been closed; but Neill did not abandon his intention to learn from Lane. He secured a job at King Alfred School (which kept him in London) and engaged himself as one of Lane's 'pupils'. The term was adopted because Lane had no professional qualifications as a psychotherapist, but in fact his 'private lessons' were no less than a course of psycho-analysis though of a kind peculiar to Lane. As Isherwood has described it: 'Lane's practice seemed to have been as sensational as his preaching. He detested the conventional pomposities of the psychologist: the solemn consulting-rooms and shaded lights. If his patients needed it, he took them to night-clubs, or tearing about the countryside in his car.'[11] This may have been a part of Lane's attempt to correct his self-confessed error in not accepting the transference from his pupils at the Little Commonwealth. If so, it seems at times to have been an over-correction which later brought him trouble. But in Neill's case the friendship which developed was a genuine and intimate one. Neill spent a lot of time with Lane outside consulting hours, as well as with the Lane family – two of the children were at King Alfred School and one, Allen, in Neill's class there.

Neill was not only imbibing Lane's educational philosophy which articulated for him many of the conclusions he had groped towards at Gretna but he was also rapidly acquiring an understanding of psycho-analytic theory which was becoming an essential part of that philosophy. This 'New Psychology' was a subject which fascinated intellectuals generally and was treated regularly in articles in the advanced journals. Neill absorbed the study so readily that a piece he wrote entitled 'Psycho-analysis in Industry' was accepted for publication by *The New Age* in December 1919. It seems now a curious choice of subject for him, but it appears to mark his transition from a preoccupation with socio-political affairs to his later and more permanent interest in individual psychology.

He was concerned to argue for the primacy of crowd psychology over economic considerations in social planning. In his view it was the inferiority feelings of the industrial crowd which were the main roots of its behaviour – its 'slave morality' (in Nietzsche's phrase), and this in turn was produced by the authoritarian education to which future wage-slaves were insistently subjected. The factories replicate the authoritarian structure of the school, ruling by fear as the teacher does. He argued from this that the advocates of national guilds – the panacea that *The New Age* was constantly pressing for – should be making a psychological appeal rather than an economic one, and he looked forward to 'guildsmen' working out some form of self-government that would be practicable in factories. Here he was borrowing one of the more important of Lane's educational ideas, as he acknowledged in the article: 'In a small room in Regent's Park, Mr Homer Lane talks nightly to a small group of enthusiasts. His subject is always authority. He contends that every child is born good: if he becomes bad the blame lies at the door of Authority. And those of us who knew the Little Commonwealth know that his work there proved his contention. If authority is wrong in the home and the school, it is wrong in the factory.' But he claimed more positive virtues for self-government than merely that it removes authority from the scene: 'Self-government breeds altruism. What proof have I? Only the proof that every schoolmaster who tries self-government discovers in the process.'

These remarks showed a greater confidence in self-government than

Neill's experience at King Alfred School at this time might have supported. One of the founding members of the New Schools Movement, this day-school in Hampstead was patronized by parents mainly of the intellectual middle-classes. Neill had spent half a day there in the summer of 1916 and had found the atmosphere 'delightful' and the children self-motivated, free of rewards and punishments, marks and competition. He had been inclined to envy the teachers working with children whose parents had chosen freedom, though on reflection he had decided then that it was more worth while to be working at Gretna where the children 'need freedom more'.[12] However, when he came to work in the school he found the staff less committed to freedom than he had supposed. In particular they resisted his attempts to persuade them to adopt a form of self-government until the headmaster, John Russell, suggested that Neill should try it in his own class so that they could see how it worked there. The demonstration was not successful. In a letter dated 25 February 1919 Homer Lane's wife wrote: 'Our poor Mr Neill is having an awful time here in King Alfred School where he has just started self-government. Allen is the Chairman of his class and he is in hot water most of the time.'[13] It is not clear whether it was Allen or Neill who was in the hot water, but from other accounts it becomes obvious that Neill was getting into trouble. The staff were out of sympathy with the idea and what passed in his class was not supported by what happened in the rest of the school. The difficulty is illustrated by an incident which Neill related[14] in which the class brought him to a meeting to tell him that one of their number, Mary, had called him, in his absence, 'a silly ass'. When he merely agreed with this assessment of him and gave them licence to call him whatever they liked the class was indignant; but there was an even greater outcry when Mary was thus encouraged to blurt out an accusation of favouritism against their French teacher, Miss Brown. Mary must withdraw her charge. She refused. Neill is told that, as a member of staff, he must squash Mary. He refused. And then the bell rang for lessons and the meeting dispersed.

Naturally, other members of the staff agreed with the children: professional etiquette demanded that Neill should not have listened to, let alone tolerated, such comments on a colleague. Neill maintained that his action was correct (though admitting a secret pleasure in the discomfiture of Miss Brown!). But for the bell, he thought, the meeting would have realized that Miss Brown was the proper person to hear the accusation, and she would have been sent for just as Neill himself had been called when Mary had said that he was a silly ass. Then the substance of the charge could have been helpfully dealt with.

This would still have depended on Miss Brown's willingness to play the same game. Neill commented that 'unless the staff can lay aside all dignity and become members of the gang, education is not free.' It seems that King Alfred's was not free in this sense, and the tensions that were created by Neill's experiment led to his having to resign his position. 'I had to leave the freest school in London because it wasn't free enough to tolerate me,' he wrote later.[15]

REFERENCES

1 *Times Educational Supplement*, 7 December 1916.
2 *A Dominie Dismissed*, p. 65.
3 Ibid. p. 53.
4 E. Holmes, *In Defence of What Might Be*, p. 134.
5 N. MacMunn, *A Path to Freedom in the School*, p. 152.
6 H. Lane, *Talks to Parents and Teachers*, p. 112.
7 Quoted in D. Willis, *Homer Lane: a Biography*, p. 90.
8 Ibid. p. 123.
9 Quoted by P. Lomas in *Psychoanalysis Observed*, p. 120.
10 D. Willis, op. cit. pp. 253–67.
11 C. Isherwood, *Lions and Shadows*, p. 301.
12 *A Dominie Dismissed*, p. 75.
13 Quoted in D. Willis, op. cit. p. 197.
14 *A Dominie in Doubt*, p. 169.
15 *A Dominie Abroad*, p. 64.

4 The New Era

His resignation from King Alfred School left Neill free to accept an invitation from Mrs Beatrice Ensor (a founder member of Holmes' Ideals in Education group) to join her as co-editor of the quarterly *Education for the New Era*. The first issue of this journal had appeared in January 1920 with avowed interests in internationalism and experiment in education and, as its title implied, with a confident hope that the ideals which had inspired the New Schools Movement, strengthened by twenty years of experience and theoretical development, would now be given wider application.

Its opening editorial (under the evangelical title 'The Outlook Tower') had proclaimed that 'Freedom, Tolerance and Understanding have burst the doors so carefully locked upon them in the secret chambers in the souls of men ... in all realms of thought and action they move: not least in education.' The new era was quickly to become an empty illusion but immediately after the trauma of war it was almost necessary to believe in a life fit for heroes; and the considerable social and intellectual liberation which the war had facilitated bolstered hopes that the era could really be a new one. 'Educational ideas that seemed startling in 1914 are hardly likely to perturb the world of 1920,' wrote Norman MacMunn.[1] 'Not only have men supped full with horrors, but through those horrors their vision has penetrated to primitive realities.' Now, he thought, they were ready to accept 'the failure of courses hitherto considered good and wise and safe ... and to examine more closely, and with less confidence, the foundations of their own judgements'.

In other fields than education men were rejecting previous assumptions though not always did they embrace new hopes with the fervour that Mrs Ensor's editorials displayed. In describing the temper of Cambridge undergraduates at this time, for instance, Kingsley Martin writes: 'Most of us were pacifists of one sort or another, angry with "the wicked old men" who had stumbled into war and worse still carried through a peace that mocked the ideals for which so many of our schoolfriends had died.'[2]

The seeds of disillusion evident there were not as yet sprouting among the utopian educationists. MacMunn concludes that he was left 'finally convinced that the world can be saved from still worse catastrophes only by its children, and this by nothing less than a new and fundamental conception of education'.[3] He was certainly not alone in this conviction: 'Pioneers everywhere,' the Outlook Tower claimed, 'are endeavouring to apply the New Ideals.' Montessori is quoted: 'We are the sowers. Our children will be those who reap. To labour that future generations may be better and nobler than we are – that is the task,' and Benjamin Kidd is cited even more optimistically: 'Give us the young. Give us the young and we will create a new mind and a new earth in a single generation.'

But apart from such crusading trumpet-blasts as these sounding from the editorial Tower, it is not really a revolutionary spirit that one catches from the pages of the first couple of issues of *Education for the New Era*. The world was to be reformed . . . by the teachers' greater respect for their children's feelings and opinions; through the medium of self-government; through the abolition of all competitive elements, marks, form-orders, and the like; through the abolition of punishment ('there is correction but no punishments'); through some reform of curricula (history in particular was to lose its parochialism and jingoism, more emphasis was to be given to arts and crafts); through an emphasis on humanistic values though by no means at the expense of religious values; and above all, through giving children an environment infused with Beauty. Into this serene pool of platitudes Neill hurled his first depth-charge from the Tower which Mrs Ensor had temporarily vacated to catch up on her work as Secretary to the Children's Famine Area Committee. She explained in a short note that 'as his interest is in the psychological side of education the portion of this issue is devoted to the new psychology'. Actually, there is only a two-and-a-half-page article on psycho-analysis. Mrs Ensor might well have been more apprehensive about Neill's editorial – he had evolved a style for such an assignment when he was revitalizing *The Student* at Edinburgh, and one can feel his exhilaration as, like Toad in the washerwoman's clothes, he finds himself in a driving-seat once again.

He first bears down on what he calls the 'crank schools'. Having praised the crank for standing apart from the crowd and being ready to think, he pointedly remarks that soon the crank 'becomes arrogant and imposes his crankiness on the poor children. He worships "good taste" – his own good taste, and he expects children to accept his standards. Hence at our crank schools we find too many ideals. Children whose natural liking is for Charlie Chaplin are surrounded with art pictures, portraits of Walt Whitman and Blake: they hear the music of Schumann and Beethoven – while they prefer listening to a fox-trot on a gramophone, and they listen to moral lectures about good taste.' Educators, he says, should aim at providing release for *all* of a child's emotions – good-taste teaching merely drives 'the more earthy part of a child's psyche underground'. His next point of attack was the way in which self-government was being used – 'it never goes farther than a miniature Bow Street proceeding. The children become spies and policemen ... It will never succeed unless the teacher believes that all authority is dangerous for the child.' He goes on to tell how psycho-analysis has demonstrated the need for the child to be released from the constraining influence of authority so that his egoism can find a full expression. Selfishness in a child is not a vice; it is natural, and only by expressing it can the child grow towards altruism.

So he would expel authority: 'Obedience is tolerable only when it is a mutual contract.' Punishment certainly must go; 'it deals with results, not causes.' Respect too, is not an attribute for the teacher to cultivate, because it contains fear. 'The only way to teach is to love ... Read Froebel, Montessori, Freud, Jung; but read and re-read the life of Jesus Christ.' But no moralizing. '"Shall I teach my children the difference between right and wrong?" asks a young teacher. "No," I reply, "for you do not know the difference between right and wrong." "I do!" she protests indignantly. And I answer: "Suppose you know what is right and wrong for you; do you know what is right and wrong for a child?"'

No protests against this were actually published – strangely, the journal gave no place to readers' letters – but it is clear from the next editorial that Neill had provoked much indignation and outrage. Mrs Ensor tried to calm the storm firstly by a plea for tolerance for the opinions of others. It is ironic that she should have found this necessary only ten months after she had inaugurated the first issue of her magazine with the words, 'Freedom, Tolerance and Understanding have burst the doors ...' and it seems to give point to Neill's assertion that the New Ideals were but a thin veneer covering more earthy realities. Mrs Ensor's veneer attempted to cover the cracks by suggesting that really it was all a question of terminology: but Neill himself was adamant. Is Charlie Chaplin of greater educational value than Shelley? asks one lady. 'Life is so difficult to understand,' Neill replied, 'that I personally cannot claim to settle the relative educational value of anyone.' And that is his point: that children must determine their own values, in culture as in morality. 'Another lady writes angrily of my advocating the abolition of respect and dignity ... I hold that the dignified teacher is a danger to children. For the child in the presence of dignity represses much of his nature ... and even the upholders of dignity agree that self-expression is the greatest aim in education.'

The uneasy partnership between the two co-editors continued in fact for a couple of years. They were using much the same vocabulary, but more and more they came to be talking different languages as Neill moved into an increasingly extreme position. Throughout this period he was trying out ideas both in his editorials and in his books. Norman MacMunn, reviewing *A Dominie in Doubt* (which appeared in 1920), praised Neill for his courage in daring to search his soul in public, to describe his thoughts in process. Homer Lane had provided him with his basic premises; he was now searching out the implications. He made some progress towards this through his reporting for *The New Era* (as the journal came to be called) on many of the schools where experimental work was in progress. He went to MacMunn's school, for instance, and wrote about it enthusiastically, admiring the play-way methods and the absence of compulsion and regretting only that it was not co-educational. When he visited Wychwood School, in Oxford, he found the headmistress having some difficulty in persuading her upper-middle-class girls to govern themselves. Neill gave her a helping hand as she described: 'The council behaved like a good-natured dog who will fetch a stick to please you if you insisted on throwing it, but feels in his heart that the afternoon is too warm . . . Things were at a deadlock when Mr A. S. Neill came down for a week-end. We were in quarantine for mumps and bored to extinction; in half an hour he had started a blaze of enthusiasm "for the real thing this time", which is bidding fair to burn a steady fire at last. We found on consideration that we disagreed with him on most things, but that merely added fuel to the blaze.'

Neill was extending his influence in other ways. Advertised about this time was a course of lectures 'by A. S. Neill, M.A., author of *A Dominie's Log* and *A Dominie in Doubt*, these lectures to take place on Tuesday evenings in the Eustace Miles' Restaurant; half a crown a lecture, or half a guinea for the full course of six lectures.' And it was not only in London that he spoke. In January 1921 the *Forfar Dispatch* announced that he was to give a talk in his home-town. 'Mr Neill has been lecturing recently in Edinburgh and Dundee, and his views have provoked a good deal of discussion and comment . . .' The report on this lecture gives some idea of the ideas that Neill was propagating. 'He gave a clear and reasoned outline of the scope of this new science [psycho-analysis] and its bearing on education and life. One specially interesting part of his lecture dealt with the expression of the ego and the personality . . . Many of the supposed vices and original sins of children like lying, laziness, obstinacy, unresponsiveness, even stealing, were often due to thwarted or suppressed personality through children being obsessed with fear, or misunderstood, or distrusted.'[4] This reporter was obviously appreciative without actually committing himself to a judgement; at least he considered that it caused 'many of us "furiously to think" as our French friends say'.

Neill may have been received more sympathetically on this occasion, being on his calfground, as he called it. It is probable that his father was in the audience, and it would be fascinating to know how furiously the old dominie was caused to think. I was told by Neill's brother-in-law that when

Neill came home for his holidays, father and son would have long talks together in the evenings, and that George Neill 'changed to Allie's ideas completely'. This is hard to believe, but both parents were apparently properly proud of their once problematic child, as he was devoted to them. He had dedicated his first book to his father, and *A Dominie's Five* is inscribed 'To my mother who, in her seventieth year, began to travel in foreign parts' – the book told the adventure story of five children's journeying through Africa, the children being five of Neill's pupils to whom the tale had been originally told. With her husband, Neill's mother had, in fact, travelled to Dresden to visit her son when he was running his International School there.

But whatever converts he made in the provinces, Neill was fighting a losing battle in London for the control of *The New Era* with those whom he sarcastically called 'the Higher Life enthusiasts'. In 1921 the first of a long series of international conferences was held in Calais with the theme 'The creative self-expression of the child'. Neill spoke on what he saw as a vital corollary – 'The abolition of authority'. He argued that the use of authority for instilling an adult morality had the particularly damaging effect of stifling the natural morality of the child. Authority in schools should be abandoned and with it all forms of moral teaching. His lecture was not at all in tune with the well-meaning cosiness of this advanced, though thoroughly respectable, gathering. Neill's doctrine seemed dangerous – 'libertarian, anarchic', some people called it.[5] The conference resulted in the formation of the New Education Fellowship of which *The New Era*, with French and German editions as well, was to be the official organ. On the back cover of the October issue of that year appeared the principles and aims of the Fellowship. The first of these read: 'To train the child to desire the supremacy of spirit over matter.'

Neill could have had little sympathy with such sentiments. He had declared: 'Moralists have wronged humanity by insisting on ideals, and personally I had rather see a child educated by a drill-sergeant than by a higher-life person.'[6] In fact, that first principle seems to contradict the thesis that Holmes, who had been mainly responsible for forming the group from which the Fellowship grew, had put forward that it was just such a dualism as that between mind and matter that had been the root error of western philosophy and which the New Educationists were to correct. Neill was at one with Holmes in this, arguing that the problem for mankind was to find the means to reconcile the God and the Devil within himself, to accommodate simultaneously his own Christ and his own Crippen. He might have quoted Blake, whose portrait, he complained, always stared at children from the higher-life walls: 'Without Contraries is no progression. Attraction and Repulsion, Reason and Energy, Love and Hate, are necessary to Human existence. From these contraries spring what the religious call Good and Evil. Good is the passive that obeys Reason. Evil is the active springing from Energy.'

After the Calais conference Neill stayed on the continent to report for *The New Era* on the new schools in Germany. He does not seem to have taken this assignment very seriously, but Mrs Ensor did receive one lengthy report from him when he got to Dresden. The school there was housed in the buildings that had been provided for Dalcroze in 1912 by a wealthy family. Dalcroze himself had been there only for two years before his work was interrupted by the war, and then in 1919 the school had been re-opened by Frau Baer, the American wife of a Dresden architect, who had herself been trained in eurhythmics by Dalcroze. She had combined the dance institute with a school for German children; both wings Neill described enthusiastically in his report and declared that he would not return to London until he had taken a full course at the Dalcroze School. In fact he stayed even longer, for it was in partnership with Frau Baer that he started the International School of which his wing grew eventually into Summerhill.

Thus his work for *The New Era* virtually ended though he remained nominally one of its co-editors for a few months more. There were two issues however on which his disagreement with Mrs Ensor became inescapable. These were the work of Montessori and that of Coué, both in their different ways of some significance.

Neill concluded his report on the Dresden school with this comment: 'One thing that pleases me among the Dalcrozians, there does not seem to be that unfortunate Montessorian habit of waiting for guidance from the Fountain-head. I see Montessorianism becoming a dead, apparatus-ridden system, but I see Rhythm extending its influence in all branches of education.' This was more than a mere rejection of another authority, although it was certainly that, for Montessori was one of the most respected prophets of the New Educationists. Her ascendancy in England dates from 1912 when Edmond Holmes wrote an enthusiastic report on her work for the Board of Education. Homer Lane had perhaps been the only one of the 'New Ideals' group who had not become a convert, and his remark that all devised 'systems' of education are incompatible with a child's freedom was probably directed particularly against Montessori, for hers was a most highly developed system. In fact, this was the main reason for her widespread appeal that she appeared to be marrying the idealism of the New Educationists with the scientific method* so much respected in an age

---

* R. W. Selleck has pointed out that since the 1880s there had been a series of painstaking observational studies amassing an extensive, scientifically-based knowledge of child-development, and that the 'naturalist' school of thought (which sought to follow the 'natural' development of the child) both required such knowledge and

dazzled with its own technical innovations. The motor-car, the aeroplane, the wireless were new enough, but common enough, to excite visions of the new era, but they had been exploited so far largely as instruments of destruction. It was necessary to find a less menacing aura for them if the power of scientific promise was to be made acceptable. Montessori seemed to be using the scientific method as a means to the ennoblement of humanity.

The New Era was in no doubt about this from its beginning, and promised articles on Montessori in every issue. The first of these was written by C. A. Claremont. He expressed the hopes invested in Montessori unequivocally: her work 'suggests that in the study of these little children under their conditions of freedom, with their physical, material and spiritual needs provided for, it is not impossible that we may discover general laws of human life; that here indeed is initiated a true "Science of Humanity" . . . The idealist, the dreamer of dreams, undoubtedly points the goal of our endeavours. It is possible that Montessori is destined to show us the way to its attainment.'[7]

The principle of freedom was central in Montessori's discussion of her method, but hers was no such simple conception as Neill's. In this she would have the approval of most philosophers of education. 'It is not only necessary to give freedom,' she said, 'but also the conditions of life.' Enlarging on this dictum, Claremont wrote: 'The Freedom of Man must imply the possibility of his growth, of his fullest and most perfect development, not only physical, but mental and spiritual. And this implies the means of growth or nourishment, which must be studied, discovered and supplied on all three planes. Hence freedom is a question of positive and complex construction; and this is not only in the world of the school but in that of adult society.' Claremont supports the interpretation of freedom as a positive and complex construction by an examination of adult society in which he claimed that the older idea, of Adam Smith and John Stuart Mill, that freedom is the sole and necessary condition for economic welfare had been discredited: enlightened self-interest had not in practice been found to be trustworthy and government had been required to step in with various Factory Acts, Education Acts and the like. The validity of the analogy between a complex industrial society and a community of a hundred or so children is not discussed. The difference between the purposes of these two organizations is dissolved in the phrase 'the fullest and most perfect development'. The two situations are in fact so far apart that

---

derived support from it. (See Selleck, *The New Education*, vol. 1, pp. 273–95.) Montessori continued in this tradition but had the added appeal of an elaborate pedagogic methodology and didactic apparatus at least partly based on this accumulated knowledge.

the argument from one to the other seems to require rather more than the mere observation that the same words are used in both contexts.

What freedom meant in a Montessori classroom is spelled out in the subsequent succession of articles that appeared in *The New Era*, particularly in one by Margaret Drummond.[8] The first sense in which the 'Montessori child' is free is that none is compelled to take a lesson or to use the apparatus, and every pupil is free to cease work when he likes. Implied in this freedom is the freedom of movement which 'is necessary for the formation of the self.' There are however two important codicils. The first is the statement that 'what makes this arrangement possible (the child's freedom to start and stop lessons at will) is that the lessons correspond to felt needs within the child.' Secondly, 'liberty of movement does not mean that the child is to be left to the mercy of his impulses. That is not freedom.' The well-worn example of the child at a fire leads on to the conclusion that 'it is only through knowledge that the child becomes free.' But knowledge alone is not enough: 'If in the beginning he is not guided to form good habits, then in the end even knowledge will not make him free. He will be bound by chains which in his ignorance he has forged himself. Dr Montessori is no apostle of licence. *At every step the little child is patiently and lovingly directed*' (my italics) 'until through knowledge he can direct himself.' The essentially authoritarian nature of the system becomes apparent in this passage; it is the paternalistic variety – or rather, maternalistic, perhaps even more insidious in its effects. The scientific authoritarianism is made quite explicit in a later passage of the same article: Dr Montessori forbids the use of the didactic apparatus except for the purposes for which it is designed. The child may work with it; he may not play with it . . . The didactic apparatus is a scientific apparatus designed to give little children clear, fundamental ideas of the nature of our world: it may be compared to the microscope or the telescope.' And of course no one would want one of these pieces of scientific equipment to be turned into, say, an Eiffel Tower: this would 'degrade it. Dr Montessori, by the respect she inculcates for it, gives a lesson much needed by the young people of today.'

This reverence for the scientific method and scientific paraphernalia was one essential of the Montessori doctrine that Neill could not stomach. 'I feel that she is always a scientist but never an artist. Her system is highly intellectual, but sadly lacking in emotionalism.' He deplored her disapproval (as he thought) of 'phantasy', which he saw as an indispensable part of a child's mental life. It is his 'means of overcoming reality . . . It might be objected that phantasying is the first stage of insanity. Yes, but it is the last stage of poetry . . . I rather fear that one day a grown-up Montessori child will prove conclusively that the feet of Maud did not, when they touched the meadows, leave the daisies rosy. No, the Montessori world is too scientific for me; it is too orderly, too didactic. The name "didactic apparatus" frightens me.'[9]

Another of Montessori's short-comings, according to Neill, was her failure to accommodate the child's unconscious mind. The boy who is interfering with the work of another child is merely segregated and treated 'as a sick person'. But Neill wants to ask, 'What is behind Jimmy's aggressiveness? Jimmy does not know, nor does the Montessori teacher, because she has been trained in the psychology of the consious only.' Her apparatus likewise he saw as having been conceived with only the child's conscious mind in view. The distance between the two standpoints led to analyses which were radically different while offering superficial similarities. For instance, Montessori observed: 'When we leave the child to himself, we leave him to his intelligence, not, as is commonly supposed, to his instincts, meaning by the word "instincts" those commonly designated as animal instincts. We are so accustomed to treat children like dogs. And so accustomed are we to regard as manifestations of evil instincts the rebellions of a child treated like a beast . . . that by way of elevating him we first compare him to plants and flowers, and then actually try to keep him as far as possible in the state of physical immobility of vegetables, subjecting him to the same sensations, reducing him to slavery . . . His human substance mortifies and dies.'[10] Neill uses the same animal metaphor: 'The chained dog soon becomes savage, and the chained libido reverts to savagery also.' But for him freedom is not just a freedom for the child's intelligence: 'The ultimate cure (for war) is the releasing of the beast in the heart of mankind . . . not the releasing after chaining him up, but the releasing of the beast from the beginning. Personally I do not believe that he is a wild beast until we make him one by chaining him; he is primitive and animal and amoral, but I believe that by kind treatment we can make him our ally in living a goodly life. The Devil is merely a chained God.'[11]

Montessori's refusal of a place for the child's unconscious in her scheme, her insistence on the importance of intellectual development, her rejection of the fantasy-life of children, and to a large extent of their creative expressions ('Intellectual education allows no freedom for the creative impulse.'[12]) were all reasons enough for Neill's antipathy to her doctrine. Underlying all this, perhaps, was her morality which for Neill was the last straw: 'Her religious attitude repels me. She is a church woman; she had a definite idea of right and wrong. Thus, although she allows children freedom to choose their own occupations, she allows them no freedom to challenge adult morality. But for a child to accept a ready-made code of morals is dangerous; education in morality is a thousand times more important than intellectual education with a didactic apparatus.'[13] The morality appears to be the underlying influence since it puts boundaries which delimit the kind of behaviour that is tolerable, and within the boundaries it assigns values to the different modes of behaviour. In these respects, Neill regarded Montessori as being as much a 'character moulder' as any, and this was for him an ultimate condemnation. He liked to quote Shaw's remark: 'The vilest abortionist is the person who tries to mould a child's character.'

Most of the New Educationists would have rejected the idea that they were 'character moulders', yet most saw it as their task to improve children despite their talk about laws of natural growth and the like. Montessori seemed to be working out the proper means to do this. Hopes were likewise pinned on Coué's 'suggestion theory', though this was a more short-lived vogue. Coué described suggestion as 'an active process which goes on in the interior of an individual and whose starting-point is an idea'. In an issue of *The New Era* devoted to this new doctrine (October 1922) Mrs Ensor explained that 'it is for the teacher to supply that idea, to surround the pupil with influences that make for beauty, strength and growth. It is for the teacher to see that the suggestions that reach the child are the right suggestions.' This was done very deliberately; in one school the teacher would write 'the resolution of the week' on the blackboard and the children would copy the formula and collectively take the good resolution. At Tiptree Hall, Norman MacMunn would have his pupils at morning assembly put themselves into 'a quiescent state' and he would then repeat the Coué formula and enumerate the qualities to be awakened.

The practice was accompanied by a fairly elaborate theory expounded in a jargon which is not easy to penetrate. It seems that there were two ways in which a person might assimilate external influences – by suggestion and by auto-suggestion. It was the latter which was aimed at, where the Imagination (which resides in the subconscious) and the Will ('at the mid-point of conscious awareness') act in concert. Then the subject can attend to the right stimuli – and it is the teacher's responsibility to see that these are present. Otherwise there will be an unselective adoption of external influences. 'There is no complete freedom at this stage of evolution for we are all subject to suggestion,' Mrs Ensor declared. She went on pointedly to expose the error of 'the extremist in education' who supposes that if the child is left 'perfectly free' he will be guided from within and will express *himself*.

In reality there are a myriad of influences which may become stimuli for imitation in action: the child can never be simply 'left alone'. Of course this is an argument which the 'extremist' has to face, but Mrs Ensor took it to a point which came near to denying the existence of the person as an autonomous entity, and her previously vaunted ideals of self-expression in education seemed quite to lose their place. In fact, she seemed to be setting up conformity and convergence as the valued attributes by pointing out that the results of intelligence tests show that 'high suggestibility indicates the normal or supernormal intelligence, while unresponsiveness is a sign of subnormal mental capacity.'

There is little doubt that the 'extremist' whom Mrs Ensor had in mind was Neill, and she was quite right in anticipating his opposition to Couéism. To him it was as much an anathema as the more sinister methods of brainwashing appear to us today. In the issue that followed the special number on the subject, Neill wrote that he was 'frankly annoyed' that *The New Era* should champion this doctrine which he described as 'a crime against childhood'. It was criminal because it imposed on the child moral standards which set up intolerable strains of guilt resulting in all the neurotic symptoms and consequent unhappinesses and inefficiencies. Likewise the imposition of standards of taste prevented the child from developing, and perhaps living through, his own interests. 'It is not one whit better than the suggestion of the old Puritans who told the child he was born in sin. I assert that every suggestionist believes in original sin; he tries to make the child better . . . as if God didn't know his job.'

Mrs Ensor wrote blandly that 'Mr Neill has very definite views on education and psychology, and it is probable that I print many opinions with which he would not agree. This has occurred in connection with my October editorial on Suggestion and Auto-Suggestion, and therefore, in fairness to "The Dominie", I think his name must be dropped from the magazine as co-editor.'

REFERENCES

1 N. MacMunn, *The Child's Path to Freedom*, p. 1.
2 K. Martin, *Father Figures*, p. 103.
3 N. MacMunn, op. cit. p. 2.
4 *Forfar Dispatch*, 27 January 1921.
5 W. Boyd and W. Rawson, *The Story of the New Education*, p. 69.
6 *The New Era*, vol. 2, No. 7, July 1921.
7 *The New Era*, vol. 1, No. 1, January 1920.
8 *The New Era*, vol. 2, No. 7, July 1921.
9 *A Dominie in Doubt*, p. 146.
10 Quoted by M. Drummond in *The New Era*, vol. 2, No. 7, July 1921.
11 *A Dominie in Doubt*, p. 247.
12 Ibid. p. 246.
13 Ibid. p. 148.

5 The International School

Neill's dismissal from the co-editorship of *The New Era* probably did not upset him overmuch. He did not want to remain simply a commentator on other people's work. His urgent need was to demonstrate his developing ideas, but there seemed no place for him. Already the 'freest school in London' – King Alfred's – had proved not free enough for him; his encounters with the progressives in England had proved frustrating and offered no likely alliances. Only to Homer Lane did he feel any real affinity, but that relationship, fruitful as it had been for Neill, now promised no possibility of partnership. Lane was engrossed with, and rather jealous of, his own work as therapist; and in any case both he and Neill were so enmeshed in the complexities of a psychological transference which neither knew how to resolve that any normal reciprocation was impossible. Neill later asserted that he was unable to do any original work until after Lane's death in 1925, and it may be that his flight abroad was in part an effort to escape this entanglement. Yet what he really had in mind is made clear from a note that he inserted in *The New Era* (April 1921): 'I give grateful thanks to "A Lover of Freedom" for sending me a handsome subscription towards setting up a Self-Government School. The school will materialize when the present housing trouble is over.'

As it turned out he did not have to wait for that. In Dresden he found an old friend, Frau Doktor Neustatter. She had been on a visit to England when war was declared so that she and her young son had been separated from her husband – a Bavarian eye-specialist – until 1919. She had sent the boy to King Alfred School and it was thus that Neill had first made her acquaintance, for her son had been in his class. She became a convert to his educational ideas, so much so that they had thought of working together. 'I had already planned one day to have a free school, and she shared my enthusiasm, but we had no money.'[1]

At Hellerau, a Dresden suburb, she was living with her husband at the Dalcroze Institute. Here Frau Baer conducted her eurhythmics school and in another part of the buildings there was a German school under the management of a committee of parents. The idea had already been mooted to establish a third wing in the form of an international school when Neill arrived. Coming as a visitor from the recently established New Education

Fellowship, and moreover bringing with him £400 in savings, the more substantial because of a very favourable exchange rate, he was regarded with some respect, and a particularly strong mutual regard quickly developed between himself and Frau Baer: he admired the skill and manner of her teaching, while she was excited by the promise of his ideas.

They began to plan and dream 'of a school where creation will be the chief object, where the child will do rather than learn, where he will make his own books rather than reading lesson-books, where he will spend a month making a ship if he wants to.'[2] They would provide three channels – Art, Crafts and Eurhythmics – along one of which each child would chose to go from the age of about fourteen. A fourth channel – Science – they had to reject because it would have been too expensive to cater for properly. They would focus their limited resources where it mattered most. 'And because the world has had too much intellectual education and too much education of the conscious mind, we concentrate on creative education, that is the release of the unconscious.'[3]

Neill also wanted the school to become a centre for the people of Hellerau to which they would come in the evenings to use the workshops, hear about psychology, see films and use the library. Already Frau Baer's eurhythmic classes were well attended by local people, and Hellerau was a promising place for this kind of community centre. It was 'a village planned for craftsmen and artists, the original model for places like Letchworth with pleasant houses set irregularly on the slopes of a sandy hill among pinewoods and hedged everywhere with sweet briar.'[4] Neill has often been accused of isolationism, and it is interesting to find him at the outset sketching a blue-print for a village college of the kind that Henry Morris established in Cambridgeshire in the thirties and that are now being copied in various parts of the country. Isolation was not of his first choosing.

There were local difficulties in the way of these plans, however. It soon transpired that the already existing school – the Neue Schule – did not agree with Neill's ideas as he had at first supposed. It was 'run by idealists, most of them belonging to the Jugend movement of Germany. They disapproved of tobacco, alcohol, foxtrots, cinemas: they wore Wandervögel clothes. We on the other hand had other ideals . . . Our intention was to live our own lives while allowing the children to live their own lives. We intended that children would form their own ideals.'[5] But some kind of merger was necessary: not only did Neill want the use of the buildings but the Neue Schule held an all-important concession from the State without which Neill would have been able to take only foreign children, of whom it would have been difficult to attract a viable number. On the other side, the German school was in financial difficulties and Neill, for the first and last time in his life, was the powerful capitalist.

So with one pupil of his own whom he had brought over from England, Neill moved into the hostel. Frau Neustatter was to be the school matron. The position of her husband was somewhat ambiguous. 'As a government official who needs three valets and Emma (the maid) to find his hat every morning, and the whole household to find his valise, he is no fit person for a *schulheim*.'[6] Yet he *was* the Frau's husband, and 'with the manner and appearance of a duke' he had a certain usefulness. He was made chairman of the Neue Schule Limited Liability Company, and it seems he was content with the arrangement so long as 'his bowl of thick sour milk, Topfen, was waiting for him in the evening when he came home from the office.'[7]

Not all the ambiguities were so easily resolved. The dismissed staff of the Neue Schule continued to live on the premises for some months and not all their former pupils transferred their loyalties to Neill. There was difficulty in finding new staff in whom Neill could feel confidence partly because of the scarcity of qualified people committed to his way of thinking and partly because of his own insecurity in introducing men who might rival and eclipse him. One whom he greatly admired and could accept with gratitude and without fear was the Swiss artist-craftsman, Professor Zutt. His aim in teaching handwork was to help children experience the joy of creation, of which all were capable, he thought, given the freedom to make what they wanted, learning techniques as they created, unrestrained by practice exercises. 'What Zutt calls *Freude* [joy] I call interest,' Neill wrote, 'and although our terms are different we are completely at one in our attitude to education.'[8] Another close ally that he acquired was Willa Muir whom he had known (as Willa Anderson) in his university days. He had met her again the previous year in London when she had been in charge of the Day Continuation School at Selfridges which she had organized on sufficiently advanced lines as to merit both a report in *The New Era* and subsequently her dismissal as a subversive influence among the young employees. She had married the poet Edwin Muir and they were wandering about Europe when Neill met them at a bus-stop in Dresden. She recounts in her auto-biography that as soon as he set eyes on her there he decided that she was the very person he needed to help him, and she and Edwin straightaway joined the growing community.

Neill's third and most important ally was of course the Frau Doktor Neustatter who was later to become his wife – and a vital personality in the development of Summerhill. At Hellerau she became the 'confidante and mother-figure', as Willa Muir puts it, 'to all the Eurhythmic students as well as to Neill's younger pupils' – and, it seems probable, to Neill himself. She read the manuscript of the book he was writing, and her comments (on which he reports in the book, *A Dominie Abroad*) are as much comments

– invariably of a supportive nature – on Neill himself. Yet his references to her are scant and surprisingly casual.

As with the difficulty of staffing the school, many of the conflicts in which Neill found himself involved were both external and internal to him. He was in a very self-analytic phase at this time and in *A Dominie Abroad* he was prepared, even eager, to display this analysis publicly. There was, for instance, the question of internationalism which aroused deep suspicions in many of the Germans connected with the school, and for his part Neill confessed that in Germany he never felt more like wearing a kilt – surrounded by foreigners his nationalistic sentiments welled to the surface. However, intellectually at least he was committed to this principle – not that he wanted to change English children into Germans, or Germans into Swedes, but rather he hoped that his pupils would learn to appreciate the characteristics of other nationals (and at one time there were pupils from every European country except Spain) while firmly retaining their own. He confessed himself to be often irritated, and sometimes quite angered, by what he took to be the German character, though for the most part he was tolerant of it, and often amused.

Particularly hard to tolerate was the intervention of the bureaucracy (which he considered peculiarly Germanic). An official from the Ministry of Education informed him that he was not permitted to teach the English language and that he must appoint a German teacher for this purpose. This seemingly perverse ruling, and others, led eventually to a reversion to the original arrangements at Hellerau – the re-establishment of the German school under a German headmaster with the International school officially a part of it – though in practice it was an independent wing. In *The New Era* Neill described the tripartite structure: 'Rhythmus, Plastic and Music School (late Dalcroze School) – Directors Prf. Freind and Frau Baer-Frissell; School for German Children (about 100 pupils) – Director Herr Harless from the Odenwald School; International division, begun Sept. 1922 with 2 boys and 8 girls, Director A. S. Neill. Harless specializes in the Group system. I specialize in no system . . .'[9]

The argument about these regulations came at a time, however, when Neill was himself debating his own interest in teaching a language – and his ability to do so. He oscillated irregularly between enthusiasm and boredom, and his eventual polarization towards the latter may be one of the origins of the subsequent neglect of traditional learning that was to be a critical feature of Summerhill. With no previous experience of language teaching he started with the direct method – his own lack of fluency in German may have forced this on him. This became a kind of audio-visual approach in the approved modern style – though without any of the modern hardware, of course, and with typical Neillian idiosyncrasies –

pictures of horses with wheels in place of feet, cows with ducks' feet, motor-cars with paws; all provoked great interest. Then he had a revulsion against such devices. 'I have decided to ostracize brilliant teaching for ever. It is all wrong, fundamentally wrong.' Good teaching was not necessarily good education. 'The interest should come from within the child.' At the obvious level this may seem nonsensical: it is surely inconceivable that a child should want to learn a foreign language without an external stimulus of some kind, and anyway would not the response to such a stimulus be coming 'from within the child'? But it was not at this trivial level that Neill was thinking. He was objecting to the assault on the child's own powers of decision-making that 'brilliant teaching' (like clever advertising) involves. The brilliant teacher diminishes the child's autonomy by the continuous exercise of powers of persuasion.

Any teacher who allows himself to be committed, as Neill was in this instance, to teaching a group of children a particular knowledge is faced with this dilemma. The fact is that in this situation the crucial decision has already been made and the teacher has simply to persuade the children to accept that decision. Neill did not formulate it in this way and he tried to resolve the anomaly by setting the children to teach one another. They made up stories in English to tell each other: one boy brought a copy of *Tiger Tim's Weekly* and that became their textbook for a while. Then Neill veered in another direction: he tried activity methods, having the children cutting out advertisements and writing descriptions and cutting up books to make new sentences from the words. He put up notices about the school buildings: 'Please walk on the grass' appeared in the dressing-rooms, and suchlike. 'Perhaps it is my mission in the educational world,' he reflected, 'to apply humour to teaching, but to apply it in a serious, scientific way.' Probably he was also using it to make a dull job more tolerable, his conclusion now seems almost predictable: 'It has come to me with something of a sudden shock that I am no longer interested in teaching. Teaching English bores me stiff. All my interest is in psychology.'[10]

He reflected that school subjects had no particular value and should really be totally abolished. 'Life is no subject, and education is life.' He wanted his school to be 'a school for libido not for intellect' but he was not confident that that was what they were achieving except perhaps in Zutt's workshops and in Frau Baer's Eurhythmics. There was still the need to prepare children for a career, or rather to prepare them for the acquisition of qualifications that acted as passports to careers but which were largely irrelevant to the work at which the children might be aiming.

Another set of unwelcome realities that Neill had to face were embodied in the German school. He had felt quite hopeful when Herr Harless came to take charge of it, regarding him then as 'one of the really modern teachers of Germany'. But the initial harmony did not last. Neill 'suffered a good deal from conferences he had to attend with the headmaster and staff from the German school who, being inclined to be authoritarian, were suspicious of self-government and psycho-analysis. One of Neill's most successful turns of an evening was an imitation of Herr Doktor Harless making a speech, which always began with: "Die Psÿcho-analÿse, zwar, . . ."'[11]

On the other side, it seems that the German earnestness towards work and culture was difficult for Neill to endure. Work that was creative or was a voyage of discovery he fully approved of, but the German staff and parents wanted to use work as a means of character-building and this was anathema to Neill. Their insistence on high culture he found equally unacceptable. He countered with jokes and jazz. 'Of an evening we would all be dancing to a gramophone upstairs, while downstairs the German was reading Goethe or Nietzsche to his flock. One by one they crept upstairs to dance and naturally he was indignant.' In part Neill's attitude was the bravado of an outsider. 'It was here that I realised how ignorant I was. My university degree seemed a small thing; I had to listen to talking on art and music and philosophy, sitting dumb.'[12] Willa Muir recalls his defiant low-brow preferences, but adds that 'he was rather inclined to sport chips on his shoulder and no one paid much attention, except that Edwin told me privately he thought Neill was being silly about Bach. I said it didn't really matter, because whatever theories Neill might air his practice with children was almost infallible.'[13]

It is reassuring to have this remark from someone who worked with him daily (yet who was clearly no sycophant) because Neill's is the only detailed account that we have of this work. There were two groups on whom he practised his untried techniques of therapy – the few pupils in his own International wing, and the older girls in the School of Dance. He gave talks to these girls about psychology and he found that quite a number of them were 'badly in need of help'. He was bold enough, or rash enough, to offer them some form of therapeutic sessions, in spite of the difficulties presented by his also meeting them socially every day – having lunch with them and dancing with them in the evenings. Willa Muir recalls that he and 'a handsome young Bavarian assistant in the German school, the only two bachelors among so many girls, became emotional centres for the "hopeless passions" which young girls seem to need for practice.' These were unavoidable difficulties which Neill could only try to minimize. Certainly he did not adopt Lane's cavalier attitude to his role as a therapist. The fact that he did not charge fees added, he felt, yet another difficulty – 'I become not only the substitute for father and mother, but I become a sort of Christ who helps people without thought of reward.'[14] How he managed is illustrated with the case of nineteen-year-old Hedwig who was 'almost pathological – psychically a baby', with sudden temper tantrums and weeping when her dancing lessons proved too difficult for her. The transference on to him proved very strong and, in his efforts to discredit her deification of him, he tried giving her work to do for him, kept insisting that his interest in her was a scientific one, not altruistic, and interpreted all the love she poured on to him as infantile love for her parents. He seems to have steered a safe course and reports her improvement with restored self-confidence, claiming that in six months she had made twenty years' growth.

Dora, a twenty-six-year-old Slav, danced suicide dances. He avoided treating her at all for 'if her fantasies were disturbed heaven only knows what would happen'. But Lotte who came to talk about Marie, and Marie who wanted to talk about Lotte, were more straightforward. And so too was Rita, a girl with 'a very strong Personal Unconscious (Conscience)'. Neill had adopted a partly Jungian model of the Unconscious having the two components – the Impersonal or Collective Unconscious which is a racial inheritance, inborn, and the Personal Unconscious which is a subsequent acquisition from the individual's environment. 'The Impersonal comes from God; it is the original life-force that urges us to self-preservation (Ego Instinct) and race-perpetuation (Sex Instinct) . . . The Personal Unconscious is first formed by mother and father, and later teacher and parson add their quota to it.'[15] He believed that 'every neurosis and every unhappiness' comes from a conflict between these two areas of the Unconscious, and in such a conflict there is no doubt which side Neill is on: 'The Impersonal Unconscious comes from God, while the Personal Unconscious comes from people who think that God didn't know His job when He created man.' So he saw the girl Rita as being caught in this struggle: after he had expounded this theory in his psychology class, she had 'fought him with fury' but with gradually weakening resistance until one day she announced to him that she had got rid of her conscience. The previous night she had gone into Dresden and had had 'a fine old time at a Maskenball with wines and cigarettes galore'.[16] Neill however refused to accept the function of her conscience which she seemed to be unloading on him by telling him of her adventures. They proceeded to examine her reactions to the evening, and Neill concluded that her choice of a masked ball indicated that the conflict was still unresolved and that she was able to exercise her Impersonal Unconscious only by hiding behind the mask. However, 'she is making a brave attempt to square her conscience with her life-force. Rita will come through all right.'

Whether she did so or not Neill does not tell: as with most of these cases, as well as in his later writing, he only sketches the kind of problems he met and his handling of isolated incidents. This is tantalizing. It also has the effect of making it appear that Neill claimed instant cures. Only in the case of his first pupil, whose tale is scattered through the pages of *A Dominie Abroad* (which was written as the events were happening), can we gain an impression of the gradual development of his relationship with a 'problem child'. For this reason it is a story which is worth piecing together.

When it had been finally decided to start the International School, Neill went back to Scotland for a short holiday and while there he collected David. The parents explained that they had started bringing David up 'the wrong way', correcting him and trying to make him good. Then deciding that this was mistaken, they switched to 'complete freedom'. (Neill's ideas on child-rearing have always been subject to this misunderstanding – the confusion of freedom with licence.) This abrupt change from control to *laissez-faire* had no doubt aggravated David's difficult behaviour. Neill's first meeting with him was not a success. David straightaway demanded a cigarette which Neill supplied thinking that a few puffs would be enough to convince him that smoking was not really very much fun. Neill was a little put out when David's five-year-old brother (David was eight) also asked for one; and even more so when both boys smoked their cigarettes to the end and then each demanded another. Neill would have supplied them but for the look of alarm on the mother's face.

There followed a trying journey across Europe during which Neill was exposed to a series of embarrassments as David ran through the whole repertoire of any spoilt boy aggravated first by the excitement, and then the tedium, of a long journey. After this, Neill was not sorry to lose his protégé as he explored the novelty of Hellerau from breakfast-time to bed-time for the next few days. But peace was not long-lasting: in a short time David had blunted Dr Otto Neustatter's surgical scissors by cutting wire with them, and had borrowed and lost Neill's slide-rule, knife, scissors and razor-hone. The Doctor forbade him to touch any of his things in the future; Neill invited him to use anything of his that he wanted. Neither policy affected David's actions at all, and Neill concluded that a respect for property would be learnt only in David's contact with his peers – any complaint from adults would 'touch his authority complex'.

The first penetration into David's underlying feelings came when Neill discovered the boy's attachment to his Bible with which, he explained, he guarded himself against ghosts that he saw in his room at night. Hell was full of ghosts which are the bad parts of people, and there were bad parts of him, he thought, which made him do naughty things like meddling with other people's possessions and losing his temper. He was interested when Neill suggested that the ghosts were just the parts of himself which he thought were bad, and when Neill added that *he* did not think they were bad at all. The ghosts did not reappear that night, but subsequently David went to sleep in the Herr Doktor's room, 'because he is big and fat and he could fight anything.' His Bible was neglected (Neill surmised that Otto was now God) until the Doctor went off to Berlin for a few days, and then it reappeared.

Shortly after this David received some money from home and went off to town and bought himself an air-gun. It was a lethal weapon and the adults were considerably disconcerted to see it in David's hands. But it did at least provoke a further set of associations which gave Neill more insight into the ghosts. David told Frau Neustatter that the gun was to protect her against bad men, like the Kaiser, and against ghosts. He went on to talk about Oliver Cromwell who had usurped the King's place, and whose body the King later ordered to be taken from its grave. Neill concluded that he was himself Cromwell, the man who had taken the King's (father's) place, and he said to David: 'I shouldn't wonder if you didn't buy that gun to shoot me.' David laughed heartily, and Neill reports that he subsequently lost interest in the gun (partly no doubt because Frau Neustatter had prevented him from buying ammunition for it). But he found another weapon – his tongue – to use in this Oedipal conflict, as Neill now formulated it. ('His ghosts are symbols for father, but subjectively they are symbols for the unconscious hate of father.') This new weapon was one for which he was never short of ammunition, and he set up a kind of verbal blockade of Frau Neustatter allowing no one, and particularly not Neill, to have any conversation with her. The occasion arose when David had interrupted an important conversation four times and Neill said to him, 'All right, Peter Pan.'

'He was interested. "Why do you call me Peter Pan?" he asked. "Because Peter never grew up," I said. "But haven't I grown up, then?" he asked. "Yes and no," said I. "Long ago, when you were a wee boy, you were very, very angry when anyone took your mummy's interest away from you. You wanted her all to yourself, and that wee baby has never grown up. He is Peter Pan, and it is this wee Peter Pan that always wants Frau Doctor all to himself."'

This explanation apparently ended the interruptions, though it was by no means the end of David's other difficult behaviour. Neill had invented a significant piece of vocabulary which he seemed to use now rather too ruthlessly. Whenever David behaved in 'an unconscious, objectionable way' Neill would say: 'Good, Peter, my lad!' and this would madden David until he got Neill to promise not to call him Peter so often. It seems, however, that they continued to irritate each other until one day, after 'quarrelling all the morning' they signed a Peace Treaty. This was a playful though serious document which bound 'Herr von Neill' not to mention

Peter von Pan more than once a day in return for David's restraint in inter-fering with Neill's peace and property.

Though the Treaty was not adhered to very strictly (in fact it had to be revised in a few days), it did provide a language in which Neill could talk about the points of everyday conflict without becoming too involved personally. He continued also to use the language of associations. David, resisting the Treaty's clause which required him to sell his air-gun to Neill, told Frau Doktor that he wanted it to protect her. 'People might want to kill you,' he said. Neill asked him if he had ever heard of anyone who had been killed, and David quoted a poem (which Neill identified as about Eugene Aram) in which, David said, 'a man killed someone and hid the body in a wood. He was a teacher...' Frau Otto asked him who was the first teacher who came to mind and David responded pleasantly, 'Mr Neill, of course.'

Shortly after this, David became involved in a fight with some neigh-bouring children over a ball which he wanted to purloin. Their aggressive defence of their property produced such a furious violence from David that Neill had to intervene. David was difficult for the rest of the day and the next morning he woke still in a temper. Neill thereupon set up a couple of cushions which he represented as the next-door children and invited David to 'biff 'em'. This David did with sadistic energy but after half an hour he announced the trick had not worked. He still had his temper. So Neill changed the casting. 'This big cushion is David, and this little one is Peter Pan. Now *Los!*' David looked at them thoughtfully. Neill tried to explain that it was not the next-door children that he was in a temper with, but himself for being in a temper.

'He thought this out. "It isn't me I'm angry with," he said, "it is Peter Pan." And he kicked Peter roof high, and incidentally burst one of Frau Doctor's best cushions. After that he began to laugh uproariously, and all signs of temper disappeared.'

Neill adds that he discovered a further clue to David's violent tempers, though he does not say how he made the discovery. This was to do with David's younger brother, Jack, who would always put the blame on David for his misdeeds. David would never deny Jack's story, but shortly afterwards he would break into a violent temper. Neill inferred that his tantrums were at least in part a regression to this situation. 'Every thwart-ing, every criticism seems to send him back to his earlier stage; uncon-sciously he is always the innocent person suffering for the sins of his little brother.'

David persisted in such provoking behaviour as throwing stones and old boots into neighbours' gardens (choosing particularly the more anglophobic ones), until after three months, when negotiations about the school had been completed, David was absorbed into the crowd. His dependence on Frau Doctor disappeared, or at any rate, was transferred on to his class-teacher whose favours Neill was surprised to see him share amicably with six other children. On reflection, Neill supposed that this supported the theory that it was only the father whom David felt to be a rival.

This comparative peace was short-lived and a new phase was triggered by an incident at an entertainment held in the hostel. An improvised dancing display by some of the children, and in particular by David's special friend Heinz, drew some warm applause of which David badly wanted a share. He seized two pieces of wood and banged them together, but his exhibition provoked protest rather than appreciation and he reacted by yelling and screaming. At this the Herr Doctor forcibly removed the sticks from him and his tantrum was drowned in the noisy jollity of the dance. He appeared to subside, joining in the merriment. It had been a familiar act of the 'spoiled-child' syndrome, irritating to adults, especially to those who, like Otto, are burdened with their own egocentricity. Otto had stopped that unseemly display abruptly, and David's feelings, whether they were a relief or a fury at having his Peter Pan summarily suppressed, remained unexpressed at least until after the party when he sought out Neill in his room. Then he screamed out his hatred of Otto: 'He is a beast. He is so big I can't fight him. He had no right to take my sticks away.' Neill agreed with this and David went off to bed more quietly, but the following day the housekeeper came in some alarm to tell Neill that David had dressed himself up in his waterproof with rucksack and waterbottle and was asking for his dinner because he was going away, exploring. Neill sent for David who told him in a far-away voice, that he wanted to go away alone, 'to Africa, I think'. He talked dreamily about needing his gun in case he met snakes and lions. Neill probed for associations. A lion was an animal with a big head. 'Heinz has a big head, and so have you but the biggest head is Dr Otto's. A snake is a worm, and a worm is a snake, and a snake has a forked tongue and stripes like a tiger, and a tiger is like a lion.'

When David wistfully admitted that he could not really go to Africa, Neill suggested that he might go to Dr Otto's garden instead. 'You may get a pot at something there; Dr Otto, for example.' David grinned and grinned at this idea but did not follow it up. Instead he went for a walk with Rose, one of the Dalcroze girls, and came back apparently satisfied. However, somewhat to Neill's dismay, it appears that David had taken his Bible with him on this walk. Neill was disappointed to find that David was still ready to regress to the protection of the Bible and puzzled as to why 'he takes God's Word with him when he wants to do God in. It looks like a case of fighting the enemy with his own weapons.'

Although David had abandoned his expedition he had not forgotten Africa and a little while later he began a fantasy exploration of the dark continent with Neill. He took to coming to Neill's room at eleven each day, sitting on the couch and dictating the story of two boys shipwrecked off the coast of Africa. Neill typed. And while he made the story, David also destroyed, tearing up Neill's table-cover with a nail and then breaking up a pencil. At the end of one session he seemed particularly unsettled and Neill suggested that they might make Africa in plasticine. David was delighted at the notion, though he poured scorn on the idea of doing it in plasticine. He wanted 'a great, big Africa, an inch to the mile . . . lots of black men made of wood, but only one white man, me of course, and the Sahara, and . . .' That afternoon he came into Neill's study with a pick and shovel, and dragged Neill off to a sandy patch behind the hostel, and there they began to make Africa.

How far they got with it is unclear. Another day, Neill asked him if they were to go on with Africa. A far-away look came into David's eyes. 'Africa or Frau Doctor,' he said, 'it's all the same.' Neill thought of this remark as confirming Jung's speculation that the mother symbolizes the unconscious, but David himself seems to have cleared up the symbolism in a way which at least satisfied him so completely that he thereafter lost interest in Africa.

'We were talking about birthplaces, and I asked him where his mother was born. He told me she was born in Africa. "I do believe," he said, after a thoughtful pause, "that's why I want to go to Africa so much. It's really my mummy that I want."' The last we read of David, he is writing a letter to his mother.

Neill was feeling his way in this work with David and he had some uncertainties both about the place of such therapeutic attempts and about some of the technical details. Of the latter he seems most concerned with the use of the child's symbolism – the use, that is, by the child. He seems more definite that he himself should use the symbolism simply as a means to understanding. He considered that it would have been quite wrong for him to have said, 'Yes, David, the lion means Dr Otto.' He thought that he had to be careful to hide from David the fact that he was thinking and talking in symbols, and that a teacher also should hide his technique as much as possible. It seems that to some extent Neill failed in this – when David finally made the interpretation himself Neill was somewhat disconcerted: 'I am annoyed at his self-analysis, for I had thought that my study of him had been so carefully disguised that he saw no connection between his symbols and their meaning.' What Neill wanted was that his own understanding of the symbols would have enabled him to help David to work out his conflicts in the medium of those symbols. So when the story-telling seemed not to satisfy, Neill suggested 'making Africa' in order to 'offer a new channel for his libido'.

Neill was at pains to emphasize that he was not psycho-analysing David; by which he presumably meant that he had no ambitions to bring David to a consciousness of the origin of his conflicts. His aim as an educator was to make the unconscious conscious, but by this he did not mean to bring his pupils to make psycho-analytic formulations about the working of their unconscious mind – rather that they should come to *feel* its effects. He hoped this would happen mainly in two ways: through their self-expressions in various artistic activities and in their play, and through their interactions with other children in the social life that they all shared. Thus when he is credited with having effected a striking change in David ('everyone says that in four months he has become a more social, more lovable lad') he discounts this: 'I am willing to give much credit to the influence of his free environment. Indeed I have much more faith in that than in psychological treatment, and if he were not such a difficult problem I should certainly allow the environment to do all the work.'[17]

There is a postscript to David's story in *The Problem Child*: he stayed with Neill when the school returned to England and when he was twelve Neill seems to have found him well-adjusted, 'learning everything'. 'When he had chicken-pox I found him sitting up in bed working simple equation problems for amusement.'[18] Yet there was a hint also of some of the old David surviving: 'When he volunteers to help me with the weeding I know that he is going to renew his request for a pocket-knife of mine that he covets.'[19]

REFERENCES

1 *Hearts Not Heads in the School*, p. 157.
2 *A Dominie Abroad*, p. 65.
3 Ibid. p. 67.
4 Willa Muir, *Belonging*, p. 73.
5 *A Dominie Abroad*, p. 119.
6 Ibid. p. 121.
7 Willa Muir, op. cit. p. 77.
8 *A Dominie Abroad*, p. 159.
9 *The New Era*, vol. 4, No. 13.
10 *A Dominie Abroad*, p. 196.
11 Willa Muir, op. cit. p. 76.
12 *Id*, No. 3, p. 4.
13 Willa Muir, op. cit. p. 76.
14 *A Dominie Abroad*, p. 207.
15 Ibid. p. 44.
16 Ibid. p. 77.
17 Ibid. p. 207.
18 *The Problem Child*, p. 110.
19 Ibid. p. 112.

6 Summerhill

The economic and political disturbances in Europe resulted in the disintegration of the Hellerau school in 1923. The French occupation of the Ruhr effectively stifled the hope of healing the bitterness of defeated Germany, and Neill found that the political passions that surrounded him, and had always made his position as an alien internationalist suspect, were becoming increasingly uncomfortable. On one occasion he was mobbed in the street by a group of angry Germans who had mistaken him for a Frenchman, though he claimed that when he convinced them that he was actually a Scot the mobbing changed to cheering as he was recognized as a member of another oppressed nation! More inescapable was the galloping inflation that reduced every pound which he had, on poor advice, converted into marks, to the value of about a halfpenny. The Muirs, receiving a dollar-made income, found themselves in the reverse situation of embarrassing affluence amid a plague of poverty. The most expensive meal in Dresden would cost them no more than ninepence; cigarettes came at seventeen for a penny, and fourpence bought them a bottle of the best hock. 'Suffocated by a sense of guilt', as Willa Muir puts it, they left Germany altogether. For some time a communist uprising was feared and parents had been taking their children away from the school so that the German section had already been forced to close, and when the street fighting began Neill deemed it then prudent to take the remaining half-dozen children of his International wing out of the battle-zone. They went to Vienna. Dr Neustatter remained in Dresden to protect his property and played Vicar of Bray to the changing political regimes; but his wife elected to go with Neill. To Willa Muir she explained that although she and her husband were still on good terms they had drifted apart during their wartime separation and now her interest was irretrievably with Neill's school.

In Vienna a Youth Organization offered Neill the use of part of a hostel in Lower Austria; the Education Authorities raised no objections to his establishing his school there, and so Neill led his small party up the 3,500-foot mountain, Sonntagberg, at the summit of which an enormous church loomed over the long yellow-stuccoed building that had once been a monastery and was now to house this strange refugee school. Neill described it tersely in a notice that was printed in *The New Era*: 'An hour and a quarter's climb up: six minutes down on skis or toboggan. House with 200 beds, electric light, and a farm with sixteen pigs, oxen, mules. A paradise for children.'[1] He added that he wanted to take in as many 'hungry German children' as possible, and he appealed for subscriptions to help him: 'Twelve shillings a week will feed one child.' But it turned out not to be so paradisical: apart from the purely physical difficulties – the dragging of supplies up the long mountain slopes, the terrifying storms that sometimes made it impossible to stand upright out of doors – the feeling of isolation was intense and the children particularly missed the fun of the larger social life that they had left in Hellerau. 'Children require to live in a grown-up community,' Neill commented.[2]

However, when the weather improved in the spring, visitors began to appear. Their Hellerau carpenter, a man with musical talent, came to join them. Then a Welsh girl, with a rucksack on her back, climbed the Sonntagberg to see the school she had read about in *The New Era*. She did not come with the subscriptions Neill had asked for, but better she brought herself, Bronnie Jones; and she stayed on to teach mathematics. In fact she stayed with Neill until the war and became one of the most valuable points of stability of his staff. When she died in 1967 he wrote a loving appreciation of her work:[3] it was, he said, as if she 'were born to be in Summerhill . . . Everyone liked Jonesie. Her bright brain never seemed to be in evidence; we thought of her not as a clever scholar and teacher, but a warm, dear friend who was superhumanly human.'

Professor Zutt did not come to Austria, but supported by Frau Neustatter and now by Jonesie, Neill was at least adequately staffed for his small group even though some of them were very difficult children – one, an incendiarist, he had to shadow constantly for six months. He was joined, too, by the Muirs in the summer. They had gone to Italy from Hellerau, and thence to Austria, but when their source of income suddenly disappeared Willa's thoughts 'turned to Neill's school on the Sunday mountain . . . Edwin instead of simply not minding was eager to go.' At Hellerau, Edwin had seemed not wholly in tune with the spirit of Neill's community but this was probably because he felt more a resident visitor than a part of the school and he seems somewhat to have resented his wife's keen absorption in the work. However, Neill was pleased to have them back again – 'dear Edwin, a fine poet and a fine man,' he wrote later.[4]

But though this little community was happy enough within itself, relations with the local villagers were difficult from the first and became more and more strained as time progressed. Theirs was a closed society, suspicious of foreigners and especially of such bizarre ones as these. 'A less suitable place for a "free" school could not have been chosen,' Willa Muir commented. Sonntagberg was a holy mountain and Neill and his startling company were seen as heathen desecrators. This was a view not without some justification: at their first arrival, one boy – the incendiarist – pelted the wayside shrines with snowballs, and there were other such incidents to provoke the villagers' hostility. They disliked the children's bathing and threw broken glass into the pond; they objected to the appearance in the roadway of a girl clad only in a swimsuit (she was, it is true, only nine years old, but then the village girls wore long black stockings even on the hottest of summer days); there were allegations of illicit relations between staff and pupils based apparently on a glimpse of some innocent romping that had been misinterpreted.

Understandably, Neill found all this quite distasteful: years later even, he wrote that 'the Roman Catholic peasants were the most hateful people I had met. To them we were pagans and unwelcome foreigners. They were priestridden.'[5] It does not seem unlikely that the villagers, or perhaps their priest, were responsible for the intervention of officialdom. The local policeman arrived one day at the mountain-top with his bayonet fixed and a document from the Education Office which posed a number of pointed questions about the internal arrangements of the school. According to Willa Muir, Neill refused to provide any answers, or even to accept the questionnaire. Probably he had already decided that the villagers' antagonism, added to the physical difficulties and isolation of a mountain-top existence, made a prolonged stay there inadvisable. He returned to England which, he declared, was 'still the freest country in the world'.[6]

He pronounced this conclusion after two years' work in the little seaside town of Lyme Regis; it replaced the memory of those Austrian antagonisms with an experience quite free of complaints from the local inhabitants. The English people he found more tolerant of children than the Germans; he found that his boys and girls were now free to go where they liked and to do what they liked, and in return he found that the children never behaved 'as the proverbial problem children behave'. They stole no telegraph poles, chased no cats with bricks, trespassed on no orchards. 'It is the law that makes the crime. Freedom does not make children good, it simply allows them to be good.'[7] These were children whom he described as 'incendiaries, thieves, liars, bed-wetters, bad-tempers, children who live their lives in fantasies'.

The suggestion has been made that Neill did not in the first instance seek these difficult children but that they were passed to him like so many bad coins. A notice in *The New Era* controverts this idea:

The Dominie Returns to England with his School. A. S. Neill, the dominie, has brought his International School home, and has set up at Summerhill, Lyme Regis. He is specializing in problem children and says that he wants boys and girls that other schools find troublesome, lazy, dull, anti-social.

He steadfastly refuses to compromise . . . 'Here is my school,' he says to parents, 'absolute freedom to work or play. Take it or leave it.'[8]

Unkindly one might suggest that he was desperate for pupils, but however true that may have been, it was not his main motivation. That is rather to be found in the Introduction to his next book, *The Problem Child*, where he wrote: 'Since I left education and took up child psychology . . .'; and like the psycho-analysts he saw that he must first study the pathological.

However, it was also the case that during the first few years at Lyme Regis finances were difficult, for the five children he had brought back from the Continent (some of whom were on reduced fees) were obviously insufficient to make the school economically viable, and even two years after the move there were still not more than ten children (according to Ethel Mannin who sent her daughter there in 1926).

Fortunately, Neill had Frau Neustatter still with him. She now fully shared his aspirations – they were married in 1927 – and she had the organizing ability which, according to his own confession, Neill completely lacked. She was also indomitably optimistic, patient, loving and understanding. Mrs Lins, as she came to be known (a corruption of her family name, Lindesay), turned the school into a boarding-house during the vacations of their first few years at Lyme, and by way of a more long-term investment Neill wrote the first of his 'problem' books. He had by now produced five 'Dominie' books which had been searching, wondering, doubting; the change in the form of the titles marked a move out of these years of speculative debate to a greater certainty. *The Problem Child* was received very sympathetically and it established him, if not as an authority – that was to come later – at least as a man of note. The book was widely read, running to five editions in ten years, and it was probably largely responsible for the rapid expansion of his school that followed after the first couple of years in Lyme Regis. By 1927 Neill was secure enough to take a mortgage on a larger property – this time near the east coast, at Leiston in Suffolk, where Summerhill has remained ever since. At the time of the move he had thirty-one pupils; four years later this number had grown to forty-two, and by 1934 he had about seventy children and a staff of fourteen.[9]

One who was attracted by the book was Ethel Mannin, a self-consciously emancipated woman who became a fervent convert to the Summerhill idea and herself wrote several books on the upbringing of children. Generally her excited idolatry of Neill makes her a rather unacceptable witness, but in her *Confessions and Impressions* she gives a description[10] of her first view of Summerhill which seems to me authentic because I find it easy to root in it the Summerhill I knew twenty years later. Coming to

Lyme Regis on a hot June day to keep an appointment as a prospective parent with the headmaster, she was 'encouraged' to see the gates painted in black and orange, but then a little disconcerted to find in the white-washed hallway (decorated with 'wildly futuristic paintings') no one to answer her ringing of the bell and to usher her in to see Mr Neill. There were only noises off – yells and whoops and shrieks of laughter. However, after a while a 'black-haired, stockingless, sandalled young woman' smilingly appeared and led her into another somewhat shabby room with basket chairs, rugs on bare boards, rickety shelves overflowing with books, 'English and German, novels, poets, works on psychology and psycho-analysis,' and a grand piano. The cedar tree outside stretched towards a tennis lawn, and beyond that was the sea.

After a while people began to appear. A boy and a girl rode up outside on ponies (Ethel Mannin later learned that the girl was Homer Lane's daughter). And then Neill came in, 'a tall, thin, slightly stooping figure with a lean, clever, sensitive face . . . He wore grubby white flannels, an old and sagging tweed coat and a gay, careless sort of tie – and sandals . . . He gave the impression of shyness, and one felt that he hoped he wasn't going to be asked a lot of tiresome questions.'

Other members of staff drifted in, and though there were no introduc-tions there was a feeling of casual acceptance 'because you were there'. This is recognizably the manner in the Summerhill staff-room today, a casualness that can be felt as an off-hand lack of interest when you are unused to it, but which is actually a routine absence of formality and an assumption of privacy within the community. 'You can turn up at any hour of the night or morning and people will just say "Hello", even though you may not have been near the place for months. Nobody questions your comings and goings. Nobody minds any queerness in anyone else. The atmosphere is really "free". You can read at table if you want to and get up and leave it as soon as you have finished eating. Nobody minds.'

What is less recognizable is the rumbustious joyfulness of the place. That it has become so much more quiet as Neill has aged suggests how much its character reflected Neill himself. Ethel Mannin describes the gusto of a Summerhill sing-song (absent entirely from the Summerhill I knew): 'Here you have a group of people who dance and sing because they get fun out of doing it, not with any solemn self-consciousness . . . The Summerhill sing-songs are numerous because they are always impromptu – somebody gets an "urge", and people charging down the stairs or tearing along the corridors come in and join in just for fun . . . One minute some-body is struggling with Stravinsky, or the gramophone Neill made for himself is crooning *L'Apres-Midi d'un Faune* and the next the whole school is revelling lustily in "She was Pore but she was Honest."' The plays did survive the years: some impromptu, some written by Neill, some by the children, 'but they are always wildly amusing'. In Neill humour has always been an important component, and no doubt most children find public acting a medium for fun – their more serious preoccupations being acted out in private play.

In these descriptions there is an intimidating feeling of compulsive jollity and togetherness, but the fun *was* spontaneous and the togetherness *was* optional. If Summerhill reflected Neill's personality, there was a quiet side of him which was also reflected and which is the more important side. He was never the overpowering character that so many who have not met him have imagined. His tolerance came from a positive unwillingness to force others into his mould. His sense of fun could never have taken the brash form of a cheerleader's. 'In such a community,' Ethel Mannin observed, 'you can come and go as you please, talk or remain silent as you wish.' On my last visit to Summerhill (1970) it was a hot afternoon and many of the children were in the swimming-pool. Ten yards away, a boy of eight or nine lay doodling in the sand-pit, alone and apparently oblivious to the shouts from the pool. Whether he was happy or unhappy I do not know. His ruminations were private and he was allowed his privacy; no one would try to jolly him into joining the fun against his will.

The staff whom Neill attracted were understandably of very varied character and with very varied degrees of commitment to the school. A few stayed for a long stretch of time – in some cases for the rest of their working lives, as did George Corkhill who joined Neill at Lyme Regis and remained as science teacher, a self-effacing and much loved man, for nearly thirty years. He was respected without himself seeking respect. Others came for shorter periods and having learned from Neill went to pioneer in other allied institutions. There was Lucy Francis who joined the Summerhill staff in the twenties and left to start a sister school which she called Kingsmuir, and of a later generation there was Jimmy East who became headmaster of Burgess Hill in London. Many others stayed for very short periods, some vanishing completely from the scene after a few months, others leaving but keeping contact with the school which had given them an interesting experience but to which they did not feel deeply committed. One such man who spent a year on the staff in 1927 was the historian, Leslie Morton. He came after three years' work at a grammar school at which he had never felt at home. The distance between its ideology and his own became painfully apparent during the General Strike when he shocked the local establishment by expressing sympathy with the strikers. Summerhill has attracted many who, like Morton, found themselves working within institutions based on assumptions, ethical, educational or political, which they did not share. Morton enjoyed his year at

Summerhill though he felt he had no vocation for it, and he maintained a friendly contact over a long period.

Morton described to me the late twenties at Summerhill as being the period when Homer Lane's influence was most strongly felt in the school. In 1925 Lane had been charged for failing to re-register as an alien, a minor technical offence, but the occasion was used to try to obtain a deportation order against him. The reasons for this were presumed to be connected with an official disapproval of alleged unconventional practices (particularly with regard to money and sex) in his psycho-analytic activities. At first he resisted the order, but in the course of the hearing he surrendered in a way that suggested that there were other ramifications and pressures that Lane felt he must submit to. He went to France and died later the same year. His friends and 'pupils' were dismayed and baffled by this turn of events and many of the circumstances remain unexplained still, even after David Wills's patient researches.

Wills's biography has removed many of the other obscurities of Lane's life, though some persist. What is clear is that he produced a powerful impact on a large number of people and even changed the course of the lives of many who encountered his influence. But the nature of this influence varied enormously from one person to another and there seems no agreement even on what kind of man he was. As J. H. Simpson put it, to different eyes Lane appeared 'an adventurer, or nothing remarkable, or just an educational reformer ahead of his time, one of the greatest influences in a life, a genius of intuitive understanding of human motives, "a creative artist in human character" (Nunn), "simple, good, generous, modest, trusting, happy, great" (Lytton).'[11] Neill was one who has repeatedly declared that Lane was a dominant influence for him. Another was a young anthropologist, John Layard, who was transformed through his contact with Lane from a powerless, drug-dependent neurotic to a man of idiosyncratic strength who himself became a psychotherapist of rare quality. Layard's part in editing the only authentic collection of Lane's lectures (*Talks to Parents and Teachers*) has never been acknowledged. On the other hand, his conversion of W. H. Auden to the Lane doctrine is recorded by the poet in *Letters from Iceland*: 'I met a chap called Layard and he fed / New doctrine into my receptive head / Part came from Lane, and part from D. H. Lawrence; / Gide though I didn't know it then, gave part. / They taught me to express my deep abhorrence / If I caught anyone preferring Art / To Life and Love and being Pure-in-Heart.'[12]

This conversion took place at a chance meeting in a Berlin café shortly after Lane's death when Layard was frantic to tell the world of the Christ it had quietly crucified. In his characteristically whimsical fashion, Isherwood has described the effect on Auden: 'His whole vocabulary, I found was renovated and revised to include new catchwords. We hadn't been together a quarter of an hour before he was reproving me for harbouring a "death wish". I had admitted to feeling ill: "You've got to drop all that," said Weston.* "When people are ill, they're wicked. You must stop it. You must be pure-in-heart."

'"What nonsense!" I retorted. "How can I stop it? There's nothing the matter with my heart. It's my tonsils."

'"Your tonsils? That's very interesting . . ." Weston's consulting-room manner was excessively irritating. "I suppose you know what *that* means."

'"Certainly. It means I've caught a chill."

'"It means you're telling lies."

'"Oh indeed? What have I been telling lies about?"

'Weston looked down his nose, provokingly mysterious. I could have kicked him: "You're the only person who can answer that!"'[13]

Whatever the trouble, tonsilitis or cancer or wars, it was due to a failure to be pure-in-heart. Whether it was Lane or Layard or Auden who invented that 'annoying and priggish-sounding phrase' Isherwood was not sure about, but it seemed indispensable and he too was soon using it freely. 'The pure-in-heart became our new ideal. He represented indeed our picture of Lane himself. He was essentially free and easy, generous with his money and his belongings, without worries or inhibitions. He would let you brush your teeth with his toothbrush or write with his fountain-pen. He was a wonderful listener but never "sympathised" with your troubles . . . He was entirely without fear: therefore he would never catch an infectious disease. And without sexual guilt: therefore he was immune from syphilis. Above all, he was profoundly, fundamentally happy.'

The psychosomatic nature of diseases is something that the medical profession is chary to accept but a poet is likely to find it a meaningful metaphor. The heroic company in which Auden placed Lane certainly suggests so:

Lawrence, Blake and Homer Lane, once healers in our English land.
These are dead as iron for ever; these can never hold our hand.[14]

The cause of the human malaise, showing itself in crime and disease and like unpleasantnesses, was held to result from a disobedience to the 'inner law' of our own nature, a transgression induced on us as children by our educators. As Isherwood reports the idea: 'it is the fault of those who teach us, as children, to control God (our desires) instead of giving him room to grow . . . Lawrence, like Lane, exclaimed against the conception

* Isherwood used pseudonyms so that he could retain a novelist's freedom in elaborating character. Weston is based on Auden, and Barnard on Layard.

of the "right" kinds of feeling invented by professional moralists – meekness and forbearance and consideration for others . . .'[15]

Such a point of view with its clear Nietzschean roots appeared in the philosophy of other young writers of that time. John Lehmann, for instance, recalls in his autobiography that for writers in his periodical *New Signatures* 'the ideas of Freud and Lawrence – and perhaps Groddeck and Homer Lane as well – were as important as the new revolutionary awareness.'[16] Auden seems not to have shared any revolutionary optimism. He was aware of approaching doom and was terrified at the isolation which followed the death of the men who had offered hope – two of them having been killed, it seemed, by the society they were trying to help – Lawrence by the 'smut-hounds', and Homer Lane 'killed in action by the Twickenham Baptist gang'. He prophesied the approaching convulsion of civilization, a powerless poet cowering in dread:

Have things gone too far already? Are we done for? Must we wait
Hearing doom's approaching footsteps regular down miles of straight;

Run the whole night through in gumboots, stumble on and gasp for breath,
Terrors drawing closer and closer, winter landscape, fox's death;

Or, in friendly circle, sit and listen for the crash
Meaning that the mob has realised something's up, and starts to smash;[17]

Lane seems to have left a sizeable but scattered band of disciples, many uncomfortably dependent on his vanished genius and baffled by his apparent capitulation to the authorities at his trial. Neill had to some extent disentangled himself from such dependency by his years on the Continent and by the establishment of his own school, though much of his thinking was moulded by Lane's mesmeric message and much of his practice mirrored the way in which Lane had worked in the Little Commonwealth. Summerhill was in fact seen by the disciples as one concrete continuation of the dead Master's work, and at times during the last years of the decade they would meet at Leiston for week-ends and Neill would hold informal seminars based on some notes of Lane's that he had inherited. The staff of the school would be present at these gatherings and so the doctrine would be fed back into the conduct of the school. Leslie Morton was among them and he attests to the forceful impact of Lane even at second-hand – which, of course, was how Auden had come to him.

It is possible to recognize in Neill's shifting ideas of this period the same strands of Lane's teaching that in the Layard–Auden–Isherwood version are bandied about with such boyish enthusiasm. There is a difference of emphasis and of expression. The Pure-in-Heart image, which for them was a moral and aesthetic precept for personal application enjoining them to be obedient to the 'inner law' of their own natures, is discernible in Neill's doctrine of freedom. This does not postulate some system of 'laws' of human nature but rather asserts the value of naturalness, sincerity, genuineness, of avoiding the automatic adoption of social conventions, manners and morals which have no origin in personal feelings other than the fear of nonconformity. Though Neill seems not to have accepted the more fanciful ideas about the psychic origin of diseases, he did at least recognize an affinity between the psychic and somatic. The more natural foods he regarded as the healthier; he attributed Summerhill's extraordinarily clean bill of health to the freedom and happiness of the children as much as to their diet. Such views probably had their origin in Lane's influence and they were reinforced by the theories of Reich which Neill met and embraced later.

The most striking, basic and debatable of Lane's tenets was his affirmation of 'original virtue'. It is on this that the most important characteristics of Neill's educational practice rest too, although when taken in the context of his apparent rejection of an absolute moral standard the concept entails some obvious philosophical difficulties. It is necessary, however, to emphasize the two words 'apparent' and 'absolute' for neither Neill nor Lane (and especially the latter whose puritanism was never very deeply buried) was an amoralist; and though both were at pains often to point out the relativity of accepted moral codes they also implied absolutes at times.

It may be possible to distinguish two meanings in the phrase 'original goodness'. In one sense Lane used the term in a non-moralistic way, rather as a dentist might describe a tooth as 'good' or 'bad'. Original soundness might have been a better term, but he was trapped into using the language of religion in order to controvert a religious doctrine. A neutral position postulating neither a natural goodness nor a natural badness would not have been strong enough, for it would have implied the possibility of an unguided child developing either way and would thus have sanctioned adult interference. Lane's thesis was that such interference was a perverting factor. If a child were not persuaded one way or the other it would choose the good, but the efforts of persuasion create internal conflicts, disturbing the original soundness or balance, and thus actually cause the child to become bad. 'We shall continue to produce this type of mind [that is, one in the anxiety of internal conflict] as long as in the nursery we under-value instincts and over-value conscience. The creative impulse [see below] gives the true happiness; but we disallow it by teaching children that man is bad by nature and can only be made good by an effort of will. This gives them a choice between a painful life in hell and a dull one in heaven. ("Heaven," as the proverb says, "for climate; hell for company.") . . . what we have to achieve is a synthesis of good company and good climate.'[18] That is, we have to restore the original balance, or 'goodness'.

The second sense in which the term 'original virtue' was used is prescriptive: what is instinctual is good and what is imposed is bad. 'Human nature is innately good; the unconscious processes are in no way immoral,' Lane declared.[19] And Neill used this sense more commonly and more explicitly: 'The child brings with him a life force . . . He obeys the will of God. But to the adult the will of God in the child is the will of the devil . . . So that the original voice of God meets the voice of instruction. The church would call the first voice the voice of the devil, and the voice of moral instruction the voice of God. I am convinced that the names should be reversed.'[20]

These two senses, however, may not be properly distinguishable, for the prescriptive meaning turns an empirical corner. Neill's conviction as to the diabolical nature of moral instruction, for example, rests on his observation that 'I find that when I smash the moral instruction a bad boy has received he automatically becomes a good boy.'[21] Or again: 'My strong conviction is that *the boy is never in the wrong*. Every case I have handled has been a case of misguided early education.'[22] He thus distinguishes between bad actions and badness, making much the same distinction that Christian theology does between sinning and being sinful, between a breach of rules and a state of being. Neill dismisses the possibility of a child being himself bad; at most he may be temporarily perverted from his true state.

It is at this point that prescriptive definition of goodness and badness joins with Lane's notion of the synthesized man, the man who is true to his nature. 'Man is the embodiment of the master-wish for perfection of the universe, and is therefore essentially good. The motive-power of goodness is love, and love is compulsory. If a man does not love mankind and the universe, he is not true to his nature. Man does not choose to love; he must love.'[23] Lane is here walking on the brink of an idealism from which Neill kept well away. But lying behind it is a formulation whose importance Neill accepted and tried to assimilate in his educational practice. It concerns the creative functioning of man.

Lane told a curious parable in this connection: a dog is chasing a rabbit across a field. The dog is happy in his hope of catching the rabbit, but the rabbit's fear causes him to be unhappy. However, when the rabbit reaches his burrow *he* is then happy because he is safe while the dog is unhappy because of his frustrated hopes. Lane draws attention to the two kinds of happiness – the one stemming from the escape from danger and the other based on the hope of fulfilment, and asserts that 'the antagonism of these two pleasure systems, which we all have, is the basis of most nervous disorders.' He then advances the story by introducing 'the moralist or schoolmaster' who stops the chase, waving his stick and crying 'That's not right', stopping the dog's activity and speeding up the rabbit's. Thus the moralist 'lessens the capacity for happiness based on hope and increases the capacity for happiness based on fear. The problem of education is to avoid developing the "rabbit" in the child and to allow the "dog" free development. Therefore we must get rid of education based on fear.'[24]

I think we should take it as not unintentional that Lane chose to identify the pleasure system which he valued more highly – he called it 'creative happiness' – with the villainous character, the cruel, voracious dog, while the defenceless, lovable, fluffy rabbit embodies the lesser 'possessive happiness'. The image is in line with Isherwood's reporting of the Nietzschean rejection of the 'soft' virtues – meekness, forbearance, pity – and may be associated in some respects with Neill's impatience with the higher-lifers. The love which Lane saw as the motive-power of goodness was no sentimentalized coddling: it was an almost aggressive love, unblinkered and forcing, and because of this, creative.

Lane followed the parable with a more literal description of the ways in which the child's instinctive impulses from infancy become associated with fear so that 'it becomes possible for a person to enjoy unhappiness.' At weaning, the child is forced to find substitute pleasures but he is then deprived of these as they are labelled sexual and sinful, and he is threatened with both immediate and distant punishment. He is thus encouraged either to regress to the untroubled womb, or to postpone living until he is safely in heaven – both doors of retreat from himself. Lane argues that this retreat can be avoided only if the child 'is allowed, as the instinctive desires unfold from the unconscious to "grow up" and not be "brought up". Morality is spontaneous.'[25] Thus goodness (morality) is equated with trueness to the inner law.

Neill followed Lane faithfully in this. Much later Wilhelm Reich provided him with a corroborative prescription though based on a different and, for Neill, more easily assimilable metaphysic. It seems that he was never too confident with the harsher aspects of Lane's philosophy. Yet intellectually he appreciated the importance of the point that Lane was making and in reviewing the first edition of *Talks to Parents and Teachers*, Neill picks on this point as illustrative of the depth of Lane's insight.[26] He recounts the description from the book of the infant who is struggling to guide its hand to its mouth. The original impulse would have been occasioned by the accidental arrival of its fist at the source of pleasure to date – the mouth. The realization that it might be possible to repeat this event then produces an intense interest, not so much in the event itself but in his gaining power to control the movement of his hand. This is a spiritual activity, Lane maintained. However, the mother seeing the infant's struggles seeks to help him by actually putting the hand in the mouth. She is surprised to find that this makes him cry still more. 'Originally all he had wanted was the pleasure of having the fist in his mouth. But he found the unsuspected source of a still greater interest in the task of getting it there. His cry was from divine discontent with the difficulty of the job. By assisting him his mother deprived him of success and his creative energy had been baulked.'[27] Lane considered that in adults, the creative impulse having been weakened, possession is generally prized above creation. The mother is thus setting the material before the spiritual and that is the start of building 'original sin' in the child, 'the conflict in them, that is, between what they rightly want and what other people, whose attitudes of mind they will soon adopt and make their own, think that they ought to want' – or in other words the conflict between creative and possessive happiness.

In recounting this story at length in his review, Neill tries to represent it as a deeper penetration into the Oedipus situation than the Freudians had managed. He suggests that the conflict is really between activity and creativity symbolized by the father, and security and possession represented by the mother. Lane did not make such a formulation, and in fact it seems rather to weaken the image than to add to it. It seems also an unnecessary elaboration, and raises the suspicion that Neill was transplanting the idea into the personal experience of his own childhood. However that may be, it is arguable that in Summerhill there has been rather more security and possession than activity and creation. In a different connection Neill wrote: 'In the main it has been the mothers more than the fathers who have chosen to send their children to my school.'[28]

REFERENCES

1 *The New Era*, vol. 5, No. 17, January 1924.
2 *The Problem Child*, p. 209.
3 *Id*, No. 16, p. 3.
4 *Id*, No. 3, p. 4.
5 *Id*, No. 3, p. 4.
6 *The Problem Child*, p. 212.
7 Ibid. p. 212.
8 *The New Era*, vol. 5, No. 20, October 1924.
9 *The New Era*, vol. 9, No. 34, April 1928; *The Problem Parent*, p. 207; *The Problem Child* (5th edn.), p. *vii*.
10 E. Mannin, *Confessions and Impressions*, pp. 212–17.
11 J. H. Simpson, *Schoolmaster's Harvest*, p. 139.
12 W. H. Auden and C. Isherwood, *Letters from Iceland*, p. 210.
13 C. Isherwood, *Lions and Shadows*, p. 302.

14 W. H. Auden, *Poems 1930*, XXII.
15 Ibid, p. 301.
16 John Lehmann, *The Whispering Gallery*, vol. 1, p. 253.
17 W. H. Auden, *Poems 1930*, XXII.
18 H. Lane, *Talks to Parents and Teachers*, p. 129.
19 Ibid. p. 130.
20 *The Problem Child*, p. 6.
21 Ibid. p. 7.
22 Ibid. p. 3.
23 H. Lane, op. cit. p. 177.
24 Ibid. p. 121f.
25 Ibid. p. 124.
26 *The New Era*, Vol. 9, No. 35, July 1928.
27 H. Lane, op. cit. p. 21.
28 *Hearts not Heads in the School*, p. 126.

7 Freedom: Experiment or Demonstration?

'Visitors come to see my "experiment". But there is no experiment. There is only a demonstration. In an experiment one tries to see what will happen; in a demonstration one knows what will happen.'[1] Thus Neill wrote in 1928: by that time what he knew was that children coming to him as problems would 'in a very short time become normal and happy (the terms are synonymous)'.

Apart from expressing his confidence Neill was here raising issues that are crucial to the politics of change in education. They are issues which are still unresolved. In 1965 a colloquium was held at Dartington which was intended to explore the common ground between state and independent schools. The discussions, as reported by Maurice Ash, ended in a 'distressing, perplexing and ominous irreconcilability of attitudes',[2] and one of the controversies centred around the suggestion that the independent progressive schools should be absorbed into the state system as experimental schools. It was a suggestion which displayed a deep misunderstanding of the position of these educational pioneers. Mr King Harris tried to correct the misapprehension: 'We may do experimental work,' he said, 'but we do it when we are absolutely convinced that it's the right thing to do. Other people may call it "experimental"; we don't call it experimental. We call it the right thing.' He added that he considered it ethically dubious to experiment with 'live, genuine children'.[3]

To the true experimentalist such prior conviction might actually invalidate an experiment. He might prefer those who were to administer a teaching programme not to have any strong investment in the results if it is the programme itself that is to be tested – rather than the teachers' belief in it. But, ethics apart, it is very doubtful whether it is at all realistic to talk about 'the programme itself', for the human interventions in administering and receiving the programme are inescapable in any individual case even though the experimenter may try to remove their effects by statistical manoeuvres. And in this case there is the implication that it is not individual, but overall, effects that are of prime importance in education. This raises another set of ethical questions to which the progressives' attitude is fairly clear. Certainly the individual has always been a prime concern of Neill's.

'When the individual and the social interests clash,' he declared, 'the individual interests should be allowed to take precedence.'[4]

In his report of the Dartington Colloquy, Maurice Ash draws attention to an important concept that lay behind the discussion of these issues. 'The progressive schools are concerned with a form of education, called Progressive Education, which is distinct from orthodox education and not at variance with it merely in the minor degree which is permissible to experiment, before experiment disqualifies itself by establishing too many variables.' Ash elaborated this notion by suggesting that experiment with a form itself is a possibility only if it is undertaken with 'a shared conviction of its participants in the validity of the form, in its meaningful potential – not if they treat it as a variation of some other form wherein their convictions still vest.'[5]

This is a crucial point which both the participants in, and the critics of, the progressive schools are apt not to appreciate. Perhaps a lack of this understanding was an important contributory factor to the collapse of Michael Duane's 'experiment' at Risinghill. Neill himself acted in the main as though he understood it, but because he had not articulated it he seems to have been unaware of the points in his practice which contradicted the implications. Most noticeable was his failure to accommodate an appropriate form of learning (in the conventional sense). He attempted merely to graft on lessons of the kind common to the morphologically distinct traditional schools. But Neill was an intuitionist, and his intuition did not function where his interest was lacking.

Neill closed his book *The Problem Child* with two chapters which are important to an understanding of what made his education a distinctive form. These chapters, 'The philosophy of freedom' and 'The practice of psychology', also provide an extended definition of his practice of freedom at that time, revealing a quite different conception from that of most other New Educationists.

He admitted that his interest in freedom began as a protest against the authority that restricted his own childhood. The manner of his identification with the children at Gretna bears this out. However, in the intervening ten years he had met Homer Lane, undergone psychological treatment both with Lane and, briefly, with Stekel in Vienna (neither course was very successful therapeutically, apparently, but they were important intellectually); he had studied Freud, Jung and Adler, and had read many of the psychological books of Pfister, Frink, Nicoll, Ferenczi, Healy, and others; he had had much deeper contact with many children; he had been lecturing on psychology and education, and had been discussing these matters with numerous teachers, parents, psychologists and educationists. So he could justifiably claim that he had advanced from the primary springs of motivation to a more soundly based 'appreciation of freedom for its own sake'.[6]

As in most discussions of this kind, Neill faced the issue of the freedom of the individual in the context of the demands of the society in which the individual lives. In doing so he defines the limitation on this freedom much as did John Stuart Mill who wrote in his essay 'On Liberty': 'The only freedom which deserves the name is that of pursuing our own good in our own way, so long as we do not attempt to deprive others of theirs, or impede their efforts to obtain it.' There is the important difference that Mill specifically excludes children from the right to such freedom while Neill, of course, was demanding freedom for children, and insisted that the community should refrain from interfering with the child's actions so long as those actions did not encroach on the freedom of others. Further, discussing civilized adult societies, Mill would have allowed all efforts of persuasion even in areas of private action, but Neill ruled out persuasion and suggestion as vigorously as he resisted compulsion.

Thus, if Jimmy is throwing stones, other children will try to stop him, and Neill is content that they should do so only because theirs is a counter-persuasion to Jimmy's attempts to impose his will. This would be a lesson in social education. So long as Jimmy is interfering with the freedom of others the crowd is within its rights to restrain him, but it would have no rights to influence, for instance, Jimmy's decision as whether he should go to lessons. That is entirely his affair, and however he chooses he will not be infringing the liberty of others. To compel a child to learn Latin was on a par with forcing a man to adopt a religion by Act of Parliament, Neill thought. And he added that it was equally foolish, because the child would learn much more efficiently through his own volitions than as a result of compulsion. However, Neill was not proposing some subtle form of manipulation. It was the child's right of decision that was his passionate concern, and he was genuinely unworried as to whether or not his pupils learnt Latin – or anything else, for that matter. They would learn something because they were human beings, but precisely what they learnt did not matter and did not have to be prescribed.

The definition of social and individual interests was not always so clear-cut however. Neill considered another situation in which a young boy wants to make mud-pies but his mother is alarmed lest the neighbours criticize his dirty clothes, and he concludes that 'in this case, the social claim – what society thinks – must give way to the individual claim – the joy of playing and making.'[7] The case could be argued the other way, of course: perhaps the neighbours' aesthetic sensibilities should be considered, or the effect on the neighbours' children who might have been encouraged to similar 'unsavoury' play. Neill was not concerned with such matters, nor did he consider the feelings of the mother who might want to protect herself from her neighbours' criticisms, or even from the possibility of social ostracism. In such a light, the conflict appears to be between two sets of individual interests – mother's and son's – and Neill seems to be suggesting that generally the child's need to play should be given a higher priority than the mother's need to protect herself from neighbourly disapproval. In other words, he was differentiating the case for freedom for the child from that for freedom for the adult. 'We adults have to make sacrifices,' he wrote;[8] and though he sympathized with fathers coming home from a busy day in the office he thought that teachers (and by implication, mothers) should be prepared to endure the wear and tear of freedom.

The education which Neill was developing was directed towards the child 'living his own life' – designing his own way of living and following through the implications of his design. This contrasted with the orthodox form of education whose main aim was to get the child to adopt a prepared adult pattern of life. In Neill's form it is the process that is important: the child's present living is valued for itself as an act of self-creation. In the traditional form the criterion of success is the product, and the pupils' benefits are measured by what they acquire at the end, both in terms of paper qualifications and behaviour reflexes.

The distinction is much the same as that between the two forms of happiness, the creative and the possessive, as defined by Lane (see Chapter 6). The renunciation of intentional and specific influence on children most clearly distinguishes Neill's form of education not only from the orthodox but equally from that of other progressives of that time. He chided them for their 'godlike desire to save souls, the resolution to make the world better.' He wanted freedom for his children as a context of their living, but for the progressives generally who wished to school children in their own ideals it was either a method of instruction or a barely attainable goal.

In 1927, the year of Pestalozzi's centenary, the New Education Fellowship held a conference with the title 'The True Meaning of Freedom in Education', which was fairly fully reported in *The New Era* (No. 32). In style this report is very different from Neill's writing. His arguments were in terms of stone-throwing and making mud-pies: the New Educationists enunciated principles which leave the practical implications obscure. The most obvious substantive difference perhaps arises from the New Educationists' concern to define the relation between freedom and discipline, a connection which never occurred to Neill. A leading French delegate to the conference, Adolphe Ferrière, declared: 'The only way to freedom is through discipline.' It was no new proposition, of course. Professor Bovet quoted Pestalozzi: 'What is error? Where is truth? Freedom is a good thing; obedience is likewise a good thing', and he did not expect the conference to produce any resolutions very different from Pestalozzi's. It was a religious approach, with some psychological elaborations, that was being expressed, and it assumed much the same puritan ethic that Neill had found so trying among the *Jugend* Movement in Germany. 'The winning of freedom for ourselves is a religious, a spiritual act,' declared another speaker, Dr Elizabeth Rotten. For her, freedom was not a condition in which a person may live but a state of his soul to which he might aspire after a lifelong struggle with external and internal limitations. We should 'thirst after' these limitations since they were means by which freedom might be attained, and it was for the teacher to provide just that right degree of limitation with which a child could contend in his own personal quest. This required that the teacher should take the responsibility of adjusting the relationship of his pupils to their surroundings and to their contemporaries – a task which Neill specifically avoided and forbade his staff to attempt.

What these ideas meant in practice can be seen in an account given in *The New Era*[9] of the school Frensham Heights which, headed by Mrs Ensor with a Miss King as co-principal, was seen by these ladies as 'a laboratory in which they may test the conclusions to which they have come' – and in view of Mrs Ensor's position in the N.E.F. these conclusions may be thought of as 'official'. It was established as a co-educational boarding-school with fifty-six pupils aged from three to eighteen years. These children were allocated to 'companies' each under the care of a staff 'adviser' and a 'sub-adviser' who was one of the older pupils. Each company had a title, a motto and a hero. The 'Mountaineers' whose motto was 'Perseverance' had Mallory as hero; 'Les Chevaliers' followed the example of St George under the banner of 'Courtesy'; and thirdly there were the 'Co-operators' under Lincoln's heroship and with the motto, 'Co-operation'. The pupils worked for matriculation, intermediate and university entrance examinations, their work being organized under a modified Dalton Plan. 'They arrange their own timetables subject to the approval of their advisers, and subject to those broad unwritten laws to which every child conforms if treated as a reasonable being.'(!) The social pressure to conform appears to have been quite marked: one boy is quoted as saying that though it was quite possible to 'slack' no one did so for long: 'they found it did not really pay and that they were regarded as nuisances by the rest.' There was non-sectarian religious teaching, and the day began with an Assembly which included always the reading of the Lord's Prayer. On Sundays 'the children go to whatever church their parents wish them to attend, and in the evening they have a service of their own in the school.' There was a friendly relationship between pupils and staff. A Council of children and staff met two or three times a term when questions of discipline and administration beyond the powers of the advisers came up for settlement. There were games between the two houses – the greys and the greens – into which the school was divided just for that purpose. The whole school turned out every morning for a run at seven o'clock followed by a cold shower. 'The emotional side is satisfied by the cultivation of definite musical appreciation; they hear and are taught to understand and to love good music . . .'

As with the philosophy, the practice held little in common with that of Summerhill where Neill maintained that 'No man is good enough to tell another how to live. No man is wise enough to guide another's footsteps.'[10] Perseverance, courtesy and co-operation were only for those who felt perseverant, courteous or co-operative – 'free children have manners but no etiquette. They seldom say "Thank you" but they would never imitate a stutterer or tie a tin to a dog's tail.' There were house-mothers who darned socks, patched cut knees, and in the evenings opened their rooms to their small group of children; but they could not be called advisers supervising, approving or disapproving of, the way the children used their time; nor would they deal with any 'disciplinary' matters – for there were no such matters to be dealt with. If children broke rules it would not be called a breach of discipline; it would be called breaking rules. At Summerhill the whole school would meet each week to talk about such things: 'They make laws and keep them . . . The rules made by their peers are sacred to children.' That at any rate was his verdict when the school was relatively small, when the *Schulegemeinde* was held every Sunday following the practice started in Hellerau. This generally worked well though there were sometimes difficulties as when one rebellious girl, Ansi, caused all rules to be cancelled and then set out with a few friends armed with axes and saws on what was to be an orgy of destruction. Neill dug his potato patch, and an hour later the rules were reinstated at a meeting called by the rebel. A clothes-pole had been sawn in two, but otherwise all was as it was, except perhaps for Ansi, who had learned that it was not chaos she wanted. More serious disruptions occurred later when the school grew in size and these resulted in a prolonged period of anarchy ended only by strenuous staff insistence on some form of government, and an elected cabinet was instituted. At the end of his postscript to the fifth edition of *The Problem Child*, Neill confessed that he had had to thrust self-government on the children who 'are but mildly interested in government'. But it was the staff's only hope of peace. 'After all,' he concludes, 'any living together of adults and children must be a compromise. Their values are not our values, and their manners are not our manners.'

Such compromises were kept to a minimal necessity, the adult values and manners being intentionally thrust forward only where the plain mechanics of living seemed to demand it. This did not include early morning runs or cold showers, nor did it include any religious observances. At this time Neill was not the outright atheist that he was later to become. He recognized 'a force in man that seeks religion', but his loathing of the contemporary form of the Christian religion, particularly its conception of sin and the resulting image of God as an object of fear, caused him to screen his pupils from religious worship and instruction. It was the introduction of this kind of fear into a child's life that he stigmatized as 'the worst of all possible crimes'. At the same time, he hoped for the growth of a new religion which would refute the idea of man being born in sin and return to the life, not the death, of Jesus Christ, and would eliminate the antitheses of Body and Spirit and of God and the Devil. 'The religion that makes men good also makes men bad, but the religion known as Freedom makes all men good, for it destroys the conflict that makes men devils.'[11]

Neill may have derived some satisfaction from his solitary position at the extremity of the progressive wing, but he may have found it lonely too. At any rate, when Bertrand Russell with his wife Dora opened his school, Beacon Hill, in 1927, Neill was quick to claim him as an ally. This was the only school in England besides Summerhill that was 'demonstrating complete freedom in choice of work and behaviour,' he declared.[12] In fact the identity of principle was not nearly so complete as Neill supposed.

Unlike Neill, Russell elaborated his educational theory before he started working with children. His book *On Education* was published in the year before he opened his school. Neill then wrote enthusiastically to the author, marvelling that two men, working from different angles, should arrive at 'essentially the same conclusions'.[13] It seems equally remarkable that he should have thought them 'essentially the same'. This is partly explained by the fact that his own ideas were not fully developed – he disclaimed first-hand knowledge of infant-rearing, for instance, and approved Russell's advice on this though it conflicts with Homer Lane's ideas and certainly with Neill's own later system of self-regulation. (In fact, Russell himself later considered that the methods he had proposed were 'unduly harsh'.[14]) But it is not possible to account for the whole of Neill's blind eye by his ignorance or uncertainties. He was quite dogmatic, for instance, in not only rejecting the Christian doctrine of original sin but, like Lane, in asserting his faith in original goodness, whereas Russell, in rejecting the religious doctrine added that 'there is an opposite error . . . far less pernicious, but still scientifically an error, and that is the belief that children are naturally virtuous. . . . They are born only with reflexes and a few instincts. Out of these, by action of the environment, habits are produced which may be either healthy or morbid.'[15] It was a model which was made for the application of a behaviourist psychology in which Russell put much more faith than he did in the other 'new psychology' – psycho-analysis. This he respected but found much in its detail 'too fantastic' to accept and consequently he refrained from weaving it into the fabric of his educational theory as Neill did.

Again in contrast to Neill, Russell listed a number of virtues that he thought children should be encouraged to develop: vitality, courage, sensitiveness and intelligence. It was for parents to cultivate these qualities in their infants so that further virtues would later be developed spontaneously as a result of good habits already existing and ambitions already stimulated. Behaviourist psychology suggested the means by which these basic attitudes could be fostered, and by way of illustration Russell described his efforts to condition his own son to be fearless of sea-bathing. Neill disliked this and suggested that the daily immersion might have made a more introverted boy think that 'Daddy wants to drown me.' (Russell himself was also ducked up to his neck as a child – but upside-down, held by his heels. He recounts this without, however, recommending it.) Neill thought it quite unimportant whether or not a child overcame a fear of the sea. 'One of my best friends,' he wrote to Russell, 'old Dauvit in my native village, is 89 and never had a bath in his life.'[16] Dauvit appears frequently in the Dominie books, an endearing figure of native wisdom and unschooled independence, and in citing him in this context Neill seems to be trying to deflate Russell's exalted conditions for human excellence. In any case, Neill could have no truck with behaviourism, insisting as he did so uncompromisingly on the child's being left free of adult manipulations to make its own decisions and form its own values.

Bertrand Russell was a rationalist, but far from an unfeeling one, yet in writing about education, especially in contrast to Neill, he seems coldly clinical. He disapproved of punishment, for instance, only because it seemed an ineffective instrument of education. He praised Montessori for finding the 'technical means' of embodying the idea that 'the right discipline consists, not in external compulsion, but in habits of mind which lead spontaneously to desirable rather than undesirable activities.' He quoted her technique of isolating a recalcitrant child and placing him where he could observe his more conformist companions earning their teacher's approval by their industry.

To call this a technical method rather than a punishment and to ignore the probability that it was a habit of conformity rather than of industry that was being taught makes for a thin argument, but in commenting on it Neill ignored such refinements and countered with a characteristically passionate thrust to the main issue. In a letter to Russell he wrote, 'I cannot agree with a system set up by a strong churchwoman with a strict moral aim. Montessori wants to direct a child. I don't.'[17] But Russell did. He wanted children to acquire the moral and intellectual virtues that he himself admired and to this end he would mobilize the most effective techniques he could find. Of his list of intellectual virtues – curiosity, open-mindedness, a belief that knowledge is possible though difficult, patience, industry, concentration and exactness – only the first two are qualities that Neill ever enthused over. The acquisition of these virtues demanded a long education, Russell thought, and he conceived of this in terms of the conventional school studies. Neill despised these; and he compelled no child to attend lessons because he considered that the process of choice and the activities which a child himself chose were more important to that child than anything he might learn in compulsory subject-lessons. Russell's pupils were to enjoy a similar freedom, but for a different reason – that they would learn more efficiently if they felt that they were not being coerced into learning. But so that they would choose to learn what he wanted them to learn he added: 'Those who do not want it (instruction) should be allowed to go without, though I should see to it that they were bored if they were absent during lesson-time. If they see others learning they will presently clamour to be taught: the teacher can then appear as conferring a benefit which is the truth of the situation.'[18] He goes on to describe the large bare room in which this boredom would be provided; it would be to this room also that pupils who 'behaved badly in lesson-time should be sent as a punishment'.

These ideas were formulated before Russell had had any practical experience with children beyond seeing his own boy and girl through their infancy. His own childhood was of scant help for it had been a solitary one, and his only experience of school had been of a crammer when he was sixteen. Yet his book purported to give practical advice. It acquired the respect that properly belonged only to its author; but its sales enabled Russell with his wife to open their own school. One reason for their doing so was to provide their own children with the society of others of the same age without involving them in 'the prudery and religious instruction and a great many restraints on freedom which are taken for granted in conventional schools'.[19] Russell added that they could not agree with 'most modern educationists' in thinking scholastic instruction unimportant, or in advocating a *complete* absence of discipline. The comment seems not to apply to any of the modern schools of 1927 – King Alfred, Bedales, Frensham Heights, St Christopher's, for instance – except to Summerhill. It suggests that already, even to so discriminating a mind as Russell's, the New Education and A. S. Neill were becoming identified.

There was, however, another reason for Russell's establishing his own school: he wanted to test the validity and practicability of his ideas on education. Four years after Beacon Hill opened he withdrew from it, and in a press interview at that time he explained: 'It was an experiment on my part. I wrote a book on education and [wanted to] try out my own theories ... To my surprise the theories have worked out well.'[20] This implies an objectivity of a kind which neither Neill nor most of the other new educationists would have wanted. Probably Russell was also convinced that his was a correct approach, and his surprise at the way his theories worked may relate just to the detailed effects. Yet the scientific flavour of his phrases suggest a greater universality for his conclusions than actually seems justified. Some of these conclusions (which were detailed in the press report quoted above) do not match Neill's experience, for instance. Russell found that the children 'still come to lessons, all of them' even when told that they were not bound to. Neill had some children who stayed away from lessons for years and many whose attendance was spasmodic. Summerhill children did not stop swearing, as the Beacon Hill children did when they found that no one tried to control their language. Russell said that 'the children are a jolly sight better behaved when I am not watching them', while at Summerhill the behaviour did not seem to depend on the proximity of staff. Perhaps this last observation is the clue to the divergencies: quite different effects may result from not obvious variations in staff behaviour and attitudes.

In his *Autobiography*[21] Russell dwells more on the difficulties that he encountered than the successes of Beacon Hill that he understandably advertised to the press at the time. Like Neill, he found the initial financial problems could only be solved by his, and his wife's, supplementary earnings which they acquired by lecture-tours of America. His consequent absence from the school during its first term, and Dora's during the second, may partly explain their second difficulty – the failure of his staff to act in accordance with the principles which Russell enunciated. His expectation that a meticulous exposition of these principles should unfailingly result in the appropriate actions by his staff is paralleled by similar misconceptions of human behaviour in Russell's construct of children's thought which he supposed would follow the same rational pattern as his own. It is a major weakness in his educational theory, and accounts in part for his consternation in face of the third great difficulty at Beacon Hill – the fact that he was sent an 'undue proportion of problem children'. He thought that this was because parents who are having difficulty with their children are most apt to choose an unconventional school. This is certainly true, but it is also the case that children who behave tolerably in a controlled and disciplined environment may well act in very different, and often difficult, ways when accustomed restraints are removed. Had he realized this, Russell might have seen that his neat model of well-conditioned infants did not do justice to the complexities of human behaviour, but he remained painfully baffled to find the children giving vent to an intolerable degree of violence and cruelty towards one another.

Neill also found more problem behaviour among his pupils than he had bargained for, though he reports less bullying than Russell. There is some evidence to suggest that there may have been more of this at Summerhill than Neill was aware of, but even so there are reasons for the Russells having found it more of a problem. Firstly, Neill was probably more skilled, and obviously more experienced, at dealing with behaviour problems than were either Bertrand or Dora Russell at this time; secondly, because he had older children in the school, Neill was able to mobilize the resources of the *Schulegemeinde* to help regulate the relations between children; and thirdly, it seems that Russell presented his children with a confusingly ambiguous situation. 'There was a pretence of more freedom than in fact existed,' he confesses, though he claims that this illusion was not of his making but was created by 'foolish people, and especially journalists, in search of a sensation'. The result was that children who came expecting a complete absence of restraints and compulsions would test the situation by 'seeing how far they could go in naughtiness without being stopped'.

These words betray a quite different attitude from Neill's; they suggest underlying authoritarian assumptions. Russell's own formulation of his attitude (made at the time that Neill was writing *A Dominie's Log*) retains a deliberate element of authority which, he considered, is unavoidable in education. 'Those who educate,' he wrote, 'have to find a way of exercising authority in accordance with the *spirit* of liberty.'[22] For this a teacher must have 'reverence' – an 'unaccountable humility' in the presence of children – which will cause him to question when it is necessary to limit the freedom of the children by exercising authority, rather than asking at what points he might safely curtail his authority by giving the children a measure of freedom.

There is little doubt that Russell himself acted with such reverence. He exercised his authority for four reasons: for the safety, for the health, for the social security, and for the intellectual development of the children. Neill also secured the children's safety by use of his own authority. As regards health, he was probably more prepared than Russell was to let the children's freedom of decision run if necessary at the temporary expense of their physical health – though Summerhill's health record was actually extraordinarily good. He was also able to use the processes of self-government to order such things as bed-times, and he relied on it almost entirely in the question of the children's social security intervening himself only when particularly difficult children were involved – and then as a therapist, not as an authority figure.

Most obviously Neill differed from Russell in his attitude to the intellectual development of children. If Neill was not aware of this difference, Russell certainly was. In a letter asking H. G. Wells to sponsor an appeal for funds for Beacon Hill he wrote: 'You will realise that hardly any other educational reformers lay much stress upon intelligence. A. S. Neill, for example, who is in many ways an admirable man, allows such complete liberty that his children fail to get the necessary training and are always going to the cinema, when they might otherwise be interested in things of more value.'[23] In recommendation of his own school he went on to draw attention to the absence there of 'opportunity for exciting pleasures'. There is no doubt that Russell does here identify Neill's most vulnerable point even though it may be felt that he distorts the issue by talking just in terms of intellectual development, as an inveterate rationalist is apt to do, and even though his recipe of organized boredom may not seem the happiest method of dealing with the problem.

Teachers in modern primary schools are now developing more promising formulations based not on the simple dichotomies of intellectual and emotional activities or of authoritarian and permissive structures. Such extensions of educational theory must be considered later (see Chapter 13), but at this juncture it is convenient to look at the work of one of their early pioneers, Susan Isaacs, whose experimental school was a contemporary of Beacon Hill, and to compare some of her ideas with those of Neill.

If Russell considered himself an experimentalist, Susan Isaacs had even more explicitly scientific intentions. Her school, Malting House at Cambridge, was too much of a laboratory, according to Dora Russell – 'a fundamental experiment, leaving children very great freedom in order to see what they would do and what they would find out for themselves'.[24] The school was founded, in the words of its eccentric financial sponsor Geoffrey Pike, 'as a piece of scientific work and research', and Susan Isaacs came from a career in psychological research to conduct it. But she herself was at pains to emphasize that she was also a trained teacher of young children and sympathetic to Dewey's educational theories,[25] and that she 'by no means approached the work of the school solely or primarily as a psycho-analyst'. Rather she took it up 'in the deliberate hope that a greater degree of freedom in the children's relations with one another . . . would prove a benefit to them both in their intellectual and in their social development'. Her hopes were apparently not disappointed: the change 'from fear and peevishness and active hostility to calm and friendliness and freedom in play and cumulative activity' was remarkable in many of the more difficult children. Those who had suffered from insomnia and night-terrors from babyhood began to sleep the whole night through – though significantly they tended to relapse within a day or two of the beginning of the holidays. Like Neill's problem pupils they were becoming 'normal and happy'.

Susan Isaacs declared in the light of this and in spite of much parental disapproval and a number of calumnious stories about the school that were circulated in Cambridge, that she 'saw no reason for departing from my general educational methods'. But according to one of her assistants, Evelyn Lawrence, she was moved to make a number of modifications largely as a result of her observation of the children's aggression, physical and verbal, towards one another. 'She realized increasingly the young child's need for order and stability, for adult support of his loving and constructive impulses against his own hate and aggression.'[26]

This conclusion differed from Neill's and there was a corresponding theoretical divergence regarding the development of the super-ego. While Neill took the earlier Freudian view that the super-ego was the result of the child's internalizing of parental (and other) moral training, Susan Isaacs adopted a formulation, first put forward by M. N. Searl, that the child's parent-self begins to form earlier, the mental incorporation of the parent being based on the physical experience of taking the mother's breast into the mouth. If, as is almost always the case, the infant has to cry to attract the mother, this is felt as painful; and if he is left to scream, the experience is both one of attacking and of being attacked. The child's own attempts to control this situation are the first glimmerings of the super-ego which, if necessity demands, may become a dominant feature of his psyche. The super-ego 'is in essence intrinsic and spontaneous to the child's mind'.[27]

Supporting evidence for this theory Susan Isaacs claimed to find in her interpretation of children's fantasies which, she considered, showed that the apparently amoral, anti-social child was not lacking a conscience but had too severe and overwhelming a one, and that such children's delinquent behaviour was 'an outcome of the need to ease the internal pressure of their sadistic super-ego by proving that the worst does not in any case happen in reality, that it is safe to be bad'.[28]

Neill was also familiar with this phenomenon of anti-social children with a severe, though hidden, conscience, and equally he cites examples of the child who behaves sweetly while entertaining murderous fantasies. One such angelic little girl, so tender in her feelings that she could not bring herself to eat meat, was playing with Neill one day when he found her punching him quite hard. '"Do you want to kill me?" he asked. "Yes!" she cried passionately.

'"Anyone else you'd like to kill?' Promptly came the answer, "Yes, mother and Flora and Betty, but Betty first." (Betty is the oldest sister.) "I'd do it with a big knife," she said, "and then I'd make a hole in her leg and drink her blood."'[29]

Neill relates this incident in a commentary at the end of *A Dominie's Five*, which is the write-up of a long tale that he told to a group of five of the Hellerau children – or rather, it is a story he told *with* them, for as its chief characters they supplied many of the ideas, and Neill turned the plot in response to their comments. It is a bloodthirsty yarn awash with killings and tortures. Such inventions were of a similar nature to those uncovered by Susan Isaacs, but while she felt that 'the task of the educator is not to reinforce but to dissipate such fantasies',[30] Neill wanted actively to participate in them so as to legitimize the associated feelings and thus help the children to accommodate to them, rather than merely repress them. 'To kill savages and wolves in a story is to be sadistic without guilt. Helga wouldn't hurt a fly, yet her face used to shine at the description of a battle.'[31]

A similar disparity is evident in their recommendations as to how the sexual curiosity and excremental interests of children should be dealt with. Susan Isaacs argued, as Neill did, against any strong 'verbot' on mutual exploration, exhibitionism, and sexual play, but she favoured diversionary activities and mild prohibitions of the kind, 'I shouldn't do that if I were you. Come and do this.' She considered it both unwise and unnecessary to reproach a child for masturbating, which would 'gradually pass away' if he were supplied with plenty of play materials, occupations and social contact with other children. As to what she calls 'verbal exhibitionism', adults should simply refrain from joining in with younger children's playful or defiant use of 'references to excretary processes', though with the over-fives definite requests to refrain from such language should be made.

Neill must have regarded this advice as quite specious. In order to help children escape from 'the diseased attitudes to sexuality and bodily functions' that almost inevitably they would have acquired, he wanted the whole subject to be kept in the open and he would have regarded diversionary activities as merely obstructing a child's release from a fixation of interest. He cites children who were able to take an interest in lessons only when he had arranged opportunities for them to exhaust a preoccupation with excrement or water-closets.[32] Above all Neill wanted not only to avoid, but actively to destroy, all traces of moral interdictions. He would certainly have disliked Susan Isaacs' 'mild prohibitions', and in order to help eliminate the child's experience of a moral training he wanted the adult sometimes to join in the child's games and to use the language that the children delighted in.

Thus Neill's attempts to undo any moral training a child might have received derived from his conviction that this was the source of the child's conflicts. Susan Isaacs, believing the super-ego to be inevitable and intrinsic, considered the conflicts to stem from the child's uncertainty as to his own destructive potential and she wished to reassure him with a firm but benevolent control by the parent and parent-figures who 'should represent to him a stable and ordered world of values'.[33] She added, more-over, what appears to be an explicit refutation of Neill's practice: 'It will be clear that these facts as to the early developments of the super-ego lend no colour to the theory that the little child needs, and can make use of, complete and absolute "freedom". This view has had a certain vogue in recent years ... There have been educational reformers, and today there are some schools for children, making a serious attempt to do away with literally every type of restraint or limitation upon the child's impulses.' There is no record that Susan Isaacs ever visited Summerhill or met Neill, and if she was relying on hearsay she might well have thought that in this passage she was accurately describing Summerhill, for Neill has often had to refute the idea that his school offered 'complete and absolute freedom'.

There are other remarks of Susan Isaacs' that may be taken as oblique, and uncomplimentary, references to Neill. For instance, after describing the 'shock and horror' with which psycho-analytic ideas were initially received, she observes that latterly 'there has been an eager concern on the part of many teachers and educational theorists to absorb all the so-called "new psychology" and apply it to their daily labour with children. Many popular expositors of psycho-analysis have arisen to meet this demand, the esoteric doctrine being thinned out and watered down in this way and that ... And two or three "experimental" schools have arisen which make open claim to apply certain supposed psycho-analytic notions ... These schools stand for extreme doctrines of freedom ...'[34]

But whether these disdainful strictures were intended to apply to Neill is a moot point. Two of the people who knew her well have suggested that Susan Isaacs was very sympathetic to Neill's work. Evelyn Lawrence, who worked at the Malting House, feels that though Susan Isaacs 'would have felt that he lacked a rigorous theoretical background' they did share a 'similar child-centred approach' and that her remarks (quoted above) are not likely to have been directed against him.[35] Miss Gardner is more emphatic. She writes: 'I always heard her refer to his [Neill's] work with respect and I think that she sent her students to visit him at Summerhill as she did to Dartington Hall. She was *very* keen on progressive schools when they were the result of genuine conviction, but there were some (less well known) very "odd" places ... Susan may possibly have disagreed with Neill on this or that issue, but I'm certain she had a very real respect for him and would have sympathised with many of his beliefs and many of the features of his school even if not *everything*. But I don't *know* of anything in the school of which she was critical and if she had been very critical I think I should have known it. Her ammunition was I'm sure directed at a lower level than Neill ...'[36]

No doubt many early lay interpretations of psycho-analytic theory were not only inaccurately based but very alarming to the professionals who, possibly on this account, were mostly inclined to protect their 'esoteric doctrine' by withdrawing from the social implications of their theories. This, coupled with their jealous protection of their professional boundaries, led many of them to attack Neill quite viciously. When he was lecturing in London he would find the front rows filled with prominent analysts who would bombard him with questions which were clearly designed to diminish him. It appeared to Neill not as a reasoned disagreement, but an irrational hostility; this pained him, for to his mind they agreed on the basic things. But it was not only these attacks that he regretted; it seemed to him that the doctors would do nothing outside their consulting-rooms to correct the evils which psycho-analysis had uncovered. He saw none of the leading analysts 'on platforms advocating a new social attitude to sex'; none were campaigning 'to abolish fear and authority in the school . . . they are doing little to alter society. Psycho-analysis is in great danger of becoming academic. If it fails to join the social movement it will be major tragedy, for Freud's genius was too salient to remain in the consulting-room at a guinea a session.'[37] However, he added that there were some exceptions: 'Women like Anna Freud and Susan Isaacs are earnest workers who are a long way outside the consulting-room . . . But one or two Freudian swallows don't make a summer.'

REFERENCES

1 *The New Era*, vol. 9, No. 34, April 1928.
2 M. Ash, *Who Are the Progressives Now?*, p. ix.
3 Ibid. p. 56.
4 *The Problem Child*, p. 216.
5 M. Ash, op. cit. p. 57.
6 *The Problem Child*, p. 214.
7 Ibid. p. 216.
8 Ibid. p. 47.
9 *The New Era*, vol. 7, No. 26, April 1926.
10 *The Problem Child*, p. 217.
11 *The Problem Child*, p. 125.
12 *The Problem Parent*, p. 107.
13 B. Russell, *Autobiography*, vol. 2, p. 181.
14 Ibid. p. 182.
15 B. Russell, *On Education*, p. 24.
16 B. Russell, *Autobiography*, vol. 2, p. 182.
17 Ibid. p. 182.
18 B. Russell, *On Education*, p. 95.
19 B. Russell, *Autobiography*, vol. 2, p. 152.

20 *News Chronicle*, 16 March 1931.
21 B. Russell, *Autobiography*, vol. 2, pp. 154–5.
22 B. Russell, *Principles of Social Reconstruction*, p. 102.
23 B. Russell, *Autobiography*, vol. 2, p. 181.
24 *Anarchy*, 71, January 1967.
25 S. Isaacs, *Social Development in Young Children*, p. 18 ff.
26 D. E. M. Gardner, *Susan Isaacs*, p. 68.
27 S. Isaacs, op. cit. p. 416.
28 Ibid. p. 417.
29 *A Dominie's Five*, p. 250.
30 S. Isaacs, op. cit. p. 419.
31 *A Dominie's Five*, p. 255.
32 *The Problem Child*, pp. 36–7.
33 S. Isaacs, op. cit. p. 420.
34 Ibid. Part II, Ch. 1, *passim*.
35 Letter to author, dated 13 August 1969.
36 Letter to author, dated 5 August 1969.
37 *Hearts Not Heads in the School*, p. 23.

8 Retreat from Freedom

Neill's criticisms of the psycho-analysts quoted at the end of the last chapter were made in 1944 when his own hopes for social change had been reinvigorated by his association with Reich. He had embarked on his progress towards educational reform quite strongly motivated by the same kind of compassion for the depressed and degraded working-man (and the children of working-men) that led others to radical political actions. He hoped that a new education would lead to wider social change. Homer Lane does not appear to have had similar socio-political interests, and his influence had led Neill to concentrate his attention much more on the psychology of individual children.

Those who came to Summerhill were mainly of the middle-classes and had experienced none of the difficulties which stem from economic hardships, but Neill's political sympathies remained firmly on the Left. In fact, he declared (in a Preface written in 1934 to a later edition of *The Problem Child*) that socialism was a 'psychological necessity'; there was, he thought, no chance for 'creative love' to find expression under capitalism which valued possession above creation. However, he saw little hope from the British Labour Party whose early ideals had been perverted by the Old Men who had captured it. The Communist Party demanded too much submission to official policy for an individualist such as Neill, and although he had many communist friends during the thirties he never actually joined their ranks. He came close enough to it, however, to cause the United States' Government to refuse him a visa in 1951. At that time he commented to the press: 'I am a communist with a small c in the sense that the early Christians were communists.'[1]

In the inter-war years the Communist Party was largely guided and sustained by the progress of socialism in Russia; and in the twenties it seemed that Russia, for all its confused tribulations was mounting a social revolution of momentous significance and of a character that must have excited Neill's admiration. Of course, news from the socialist outcast came only slowly, and then unreliably: perhaps the first credible and comprehending account of the changes that were being initiated came in Maurice Hindus' books. His *Humanity Uprooted* was published in 1929. It is an extraordinary account of the feverish re-birth of a civilization. 'She wants a society without religion, with sex freedom, with external compulsions removed from family and love, with mental and manual workers reduced to the same level, with the individual depending for his salvation not on himself but on the group. A whole generation is being reared in the belief that religion is a monstrous unreality, that the accumulation of material substance is the grossest of wrongs . . .'[2] Two of Neill's darkest *bête-noires* – bourgeois sex morality and the superstitions of organized religion – were being swept aside. Moreover, as Hindus reported the events, it was being done with the joyous approval of a majority of the population. He was astounded at the ubiquity of the change; he had been born in Russia and was returning to a country in which he had spent most of his childhood, so that he was familiar with the repressed pre-revolutionary Russia. The regulation of sex-life had been removed from the judgements of the law (except in cases of rape) and now 'the gist of the new sex morality is freedom of personal judgement and action . . . The Russians will have none of the old strictures and the old precepts . . . Religion has likewise been cast aside . . . The Russians will have no God commanding or terrorizing them into a prescribed mode of conduct.'[3]

A necessary part of this social and sexual liberation was the obliteration of the economic and moral distinctions between men and women. They were replaced by 'an all-pervading spirit of comradeship between the sexes', the barriers between them having been 'Hewn down with feverish energy'. The 'ancient doctrine of virginity topples like a heap of snow struck by a rock . . . once for all they are done with enforced chastity for women.' Birth control and abortions were legalized, and information about them was freely available. 'No half measures; no step by step experimentation; no piece-meal reforms . . . no mere half-covert freedom such as Mrs Bertrand Russell is seeking.'(!)[4]

It was true that there were some voices of restraint within Russia, 'older men with stern views on sex', and Lenin himself (though apparently approving of the liberation – 'Communism must bring the joy of life and the vigour which comes with the completeness of love-life,' he had said) did not want the country merely to wallow in an orgy of excesses. The aesthetic aspects of sex must not be forgotten. 'Does a normal man,' he asked, 'under normal conditions drink from a glass from which dozens of others have drunk?' In the early years of the Revolution the new freedom had 'pushed open the floodgates of sensuality . . . [but] with the coming of political stability and a modicum of economic security, the wave of riotous indulgence has been subsiding.' Yet although there was a restraining propaganda campaign 'old standards and conceptions have remained in discard. The basic philosophy of the new sex morality has remained unshaken. Personal liberty is still its cornerstone.'[5]

Co-education was the almost invariable rule. 'From their earliest days in and out of school, boys and girls in Russia are constantly thrown together, far more so than in any land in the world. They study together, play together in parks, club-houses and theatres. They swim together, exercise together, frolic together. They are fed on the same sentiments. They are being impregnated with the ideas of devotion to the social purpose of the Revolution. When they grow up they work side by side in shop, factory and office.'[6]

This assiduous impregnation was the only fault that Neill saw in what he read. The rest he welcomed enthusiastically. He thought Russia 'the most wonderful country in the world'. While Britain's values in morals and economics were unchanged as though the war had never destroyed 'ten million men and as many traditions, Russia alone of all the belligerents began life again and began it differently'.[7] She was providing the economic solutions and it would be Russia who provided the answer to the moral question. She had, he considered, given the lie to the Nietzschean theory of a slave morality. 'The only country in the world that has a chance of making a new God of Love is Russia, for she is the only country that has seen that the churches have become the enemy of human progress and happiness. When a Russian village turns its church into a cinema or a reading-room it is doing what Jesus Christ would have approved of and applauded.'[8]

The direction of the educational developments in Russia also met with Neill's approval. After the Revolution the Bolsheviks had repudiated all the major features of Tsarist education and, as Scott Nearing put it, had 'begun combing the world for suggestions'.[9] The Eighth Congress of the Communist Party had decreed in 1919 'co-education for both sexes [*sic*] free from religious influences in a school where teaching is closely connected with socially useful labour.' Scott Nearing commented that 'the Soviet Union is at this moment the world's largest, and most important, educational laboratory'.[10] That was in 1926, and two years later Dewey visited this educational laboratory which was putting so many of his ideas into practice on a scale which dwarfed the tentative trials of progressives elsewhere. He reported on what he had seen in the *New Republic*.[11] Although he deplored the ubiquitous indoctrination, he was obviously impressed by, and rather envious of, most other aspects. 'The Russian educational situation,' he wrote, 'is enough to convert one to the idea that only in a society based on co-operative principles can the ideals of educational reformers be adequately carried into operation.' The pace at which educational change was being attempted astounded most observers, and shamed those with progressive aspirations when they compared it with the timidity of advances in their own countries. At an N.E.F. conference, for instance, John Lister reported his own observations: 'The New Education debates co-education: it is axiomatic in Russia. The new education debates self-government: in Russian schools self-government is practised to a degree that would be positively indecent to the Etonian mind ... New educators debate constantly the question of corporal punishment. Soviet Russia has made corporal punishment illegal by national edict, and a teacher has been dismissed for even slapping a child ... Every Soviet school is an activity school.'[12]

Reports of self-government in Russian schools must have interested Neill greatly, even though he would have found some aspects distasteful. The rationale was stated in a report (quoted by Scott Nearing[13]) by the Scientific Pedalogical Section of the State Council of Education. With their critique of the authoritarian ethos Neill would certainly have agreed: 'The bourgeoisie places before the school as objective: raising a citizen who is docile and little disposed to change the essential forms of the established order. This object determines the character of the work and the internal structure of the school ... The instructor plays the part of an absolute master ... A system of punishments and other devices are added – among them rewards, that are aimed to assist the instructor to reach the desired end. The children are at his mercy ... They struggle against his rules, violate them deliberately, form groups for this purpose. The teacher is the representative of State power, and in fighting him, the pupils are fighting against the orders of the State.' The passage suggests that 'in combing the world for suggestions' the communists may have come across some of Neill's writings, for it reads like a paraphrase of his ideas. In 1919 he had written, for instance: 'It has long been recognised that the function of State education is to turn out obedient and, if possible, efficient, wage-slaves. The manner was by means of authority which is, in the last resort, fear.'[14] His articles on the subject in *The New Era* voiced the same criticisms which the Soviet report went on to level against the way in which self-government (or student autonomy, as they called it) had been introduced in some schools of capitalist countries. Either it was used simply to 'eliminate the struggle between the teachers and students, to raise the prestige of the teacher' or it had the purpose of giving a training in the institutions of the 'bourgeois democratic republic'. In Russia, the report claimed, 'self-government is not a means to governing the students more readily, neither is it a practical method for studying the workings of the constitution. It is a means by which the pupils may learn to live and work more intelligently.'

These are sentiments which were well in tune with Neill's ideals, but he would not have been happy with the way in which they were understood. If there was no intention to give a direct training in the mechanics of citizenship, it yet seems clear that insistent efforts were made to rear the children in the ideology of the socialist state. 'The object of our schools is this: to raise a useful member of human society, joyous, vigorous and able to work, alive with social instincts, accustomed to organised activity . . . an able constructor of communist society.'

This spectacle of an uprooted humanity refashioning its educational methods along lines so close to the ideals of the New Education forced the bourgeois progressives into a disturbing ambivalence. The reports of those who had visited Russia – *The New Era* devoted one of its issues[15] to the subject in 1928 – showed clearly that all the main ideas of the movement were being applied in that vast educational laboratory. And it seemed as if they were being applied with conviction and understanding. And yet this whole apparatus of activity and discovery methods, the new ways with science and history, the mechanisms of self-government and communal living, the humanized relationships between staff and pupils, the co-education, the sex education – all of this which seemed so promising in the context of liberal humanism or administered by the gentle Theosophists and Quakers, seemed to take on sinister aspects when appropriated by those whose ideals were of Marxist materialism. They could hardly accept this as an appropriate context for the application of their cherished principles and yet it was not so easy to reject out of hand: when Professor Dewey took a Russian worker to the mountain-top of American affluence and asked him if he would not like to own a motor-car the reply was: 'Yes, if all the rest of the people can have one.'

Neill was not faced with the same dilemma for from the start he had condemned the character-moulding of the 'Higher-lifers' as being just as criminal as that practised in any public school – or, as was now becoming apparent, in any communist school. It made no difference to him whether it was a 'good' or a 'bad' ideal that was the inspiration: the act of persuasion diminished the freedom of the child. 'Communist teacher friends blame me because I refuse to teach my pupils Communism, but die-hard friends might just as reasonably blame me for not teaching Fascism. I hold that moulding of the young mind is criminal, whether the moulding is moral or religious or political. Free education must allow a free open mind.'[16]

With this uncompromising attitude on Neill's part, it is not immediately clear why so many English communists were attracted to Summerhill during the thirties – teachers, parents and visitors. One of these, Leslie Morton, explained to me that although there was no actual communist teaching there, at least there was none of the religious and social indoctrination that was inescapable in State schools and in other private schools. Whether the superficial similarity between Neill's practice and that of the Russian schools of the twenties added strength to Summerhill's attraction for them is not clear. In any case it would have soon subsided, for with the Stalin era the trends in Soviet education were quickly reversed. In 1931 the Central Committee of the Communist Party passed a resolution ordering elementary schools to apply themselves more seriously to formal instruction, backing the motion with sentiments akin to those which characterize the backlash against English primary schools today. The committee declared that 'unfortunate results showed that the project method and Dalton Plan do not provide sound and profound knowledge and do not train children to work systematically.'[17] This was followed in 1932 by another resolution which was directed against the secondary schools: special stress was laid upon the strengthening of discipline and the restoration of the teacher as 'leader', and it had the effect of ending any form of student autonomy. Textbooks were to be re-written 'to impart a more systematic knowledge of the subjects', and the grading system that had been abandoned since Tsarist days was restored. The resolution condemned the science of pedalogy – the study of child development which had given the lead to child-centred education – and with the dismissal of its chief exponent, Blonsky, in 1936, any hopes of a reversion were eclipsed.

Communication from inside Russia has always been notoriously unreliable and slow, so that in spite of the actual turn of events it is not surprising that the older image lingered. Neill retained his qualified admiration of Russian education until after 1943 when co-education there was reported abandoned. Actually this applied only to the ten-year schools in the larger cities and was presented as a wartime measure though the decree was not revoked until 1954 after Stalin's death, by which time few people in England saw Russia as the birthplace of a new civilization – with or without co-education!

The collapse of Russia's moral revolution was as disappointing to the libertarians as it was reassuring to the more conservative. To many it seemed in retrospect inevitable. G. D. H. Cole, for instance, described it as 'the picking up of what was inescapable in the moral traditions of the older Russia – inescapable, whether it be in the abstract "good" or "bad", because men cannot change their morality very fast without destroying it.'[18] There have been more profound explanations of the Russian people's acquiescence to this abrupt withdrawal of their liberation and Wilhelm Reich's is one that is relevant to this study and this will be examined later.

There was a parallel retreat from the promise of moral liberation in England though of course there had been no revolution to spur dramatic changes as in Russia. We have come to know the post-war period as the Gay Twenties, and they were gay for some, but dirty for others – perhaps for most. Homelessness and poverty, unemployment, hunger marches, the General Strike were reasons for a bitterness that was demanding a different kind of freedom from that indulged in by middle-class flappers. Yet between the frolics and the misery there was an intellectual and artistic flourish which exploited with talent and vigour the breakthrough that had been one of the few helpful side-effects of what Neill insisted on calling the Great Civil War. 'The forces of intelligence and enlightenment were winning,' David Garnett has written of these years; there were 'rearguard actions fought by the Victorians' – as, for instance, the persecution of D. H. Lawrence for the alleged obscenity of his books and pictures – but mostly 'the twenties were years of joy, of freedom and of enlightenment. They closed in America with widespread ruin and disaster which soon spread to Europe.'[19]

There is little evidence that the main protagonists of this movement of joy, freedom and enlightenment had any great sympathy for the progressive wing of educationists. Bertrand Russell was perhaps the only representative of this intellectual flowering who showed any active understanding of it – and he really belonged to an earlier generation. D. H. Lawrence might have given the movement additional vitality, but there seems no indication of interest from either side.

Fairly typical of the uncomprehending nature of the reactions of the other intellectuals of the time is a short article by Aldous Huxley entitled 'On Making Things Too Easy' that was printed in *The New Era*.[20] 'Children should be happy – we are all agreed on that,' he wrote. 'But in their laudably humanitarian desire to see that they are happy many "advanced" educationists seem to forget that they should also be intellectually efficient and well equipped with knowledge ... When you meet a boy who knows little Latin and less Greek, and none of his multiplication tables, you may hazard a guess that he has been brought up at an "advanced" school.' Huxley went on to use an it-didn't-do-me-any-harm sort of argument for the reversion to the forced intellectual marches on which he had been brought up. 'For it is a poor kind of virtue that has not been trained in the school of effort and sacrifice.' True, this was written in 1930 at the beginning of the decade in which there was a general withdrawal from the advanced positions that had been occupied in the twenties. For all the cold-shouldering that they received, the New Educationists certainly thought of themselves as a part of the process of intellectual and moral enlightenment and they too followed the retreat to safer positions.

In making this retreat (which was to leave Neill in such isolation that he could not even be regarded as the progressives' left-wing) they struggled, but found it not easy, to persuade themselves that they were not deserting their old idealism. Partly this shift may be attributed to their long-standing aspirations towards internationalism: when this had been directed towards dispelling the jingoism that had lingered in education since the nineteenth century they were on firm ground – they were still English educationists but seeking to pull their profession away from the parish pump, particularly in regard to the teaching of history. They had also done much to open Britain's educational thinking to foreign influence: many of the great names in progressive thought had not been English ones – Rousseau, Froebel, Pestalozzi, Dewey; and the two dominant influences in the twenties had come from overseas – Montessori in the elementary schools and the Dalton plan in the secondary field. These influences had been on educational techniques and had been used to implement a more home-grown philosophy. In their internationalism there was also a more political strand of thought to do with the part that education might play in promoting peace through understanding – laudable indeed, though with roots quite different from those of their other ideals. However, this side of their ideal featured only in their lecture notes and articles. Few had actually done anything in this direction beyond teaching to a revised history syllabus so that they remained innocent of the kind of practical difficulties of international education that Neill had experienced in Germany. The New Education was essentially about personal relationships, and it was child-centred. Neither of these features is intimately concerned with a League-of-Nations ideology, which was organizational and to do with the adult world.

Nevertheless, this other idealism was so seductive that the progressives allowed themselves to be overwhelmed by it. They became involved in a series of international contacts, and from 1921 onwards their conferences at Calais, Montreux, Heidelberg, Locarno, Elsinore, Nice, Cape Town, Cheltenham became a dominating feature of their activities. Perhaps it was the need to present a more powerful intellectual front at these conferences that occasioned the infiltration and virtual takeover by a number of professors of education and Oxford dons: men like Fred Clarke, Percy Nunn, Wyatt Rawson, Michael Sadlier became constant contributors to *The New Era*. Blameless liberals they all were, but too respectable to be militant, and their balmy influence soon diverted the radicalism of the New Education so that as the thirties proceeded it took on a much less challenging aspect than the deceased voices of Edmond Holmes and Homer Lane had promised.

Fred Clarke initiated the swing away from radicalism in an article that was printed just before the Nice conference of 1932 and was evidently intended to point the way for the British contribution to that conference. It was the first of a series of articles that ran under the title 'The Key to Tomorrow', and Clarke's opener was carefully subtitled 'The reconstruction of discipline'.[21] He claimed that 'the movement towards criticism and re-synthesis of current concepts of education gathers strength' though he contrived still to appear progressive by insisting that his reconstruction applied just as much to rigid systems of discipline common in public schools as to 'self-government, free-discipline and all the other features of modern methods'. But which of these two extremes he was the more troubled by (though, to be sure, it was in *The New Era* that he was writing) he made plain: 'I should be content to define it [his purpose] in terms of freedom were I not convinced that I should be misunderstood . . . I am concerned with the question of *emphasis* and it is wiser and more urgent to begin with discipline and interpret in terms of freedom than to take the reverse order.'

This was a striking *volte-face* for the progressives to endure and Clarke's justification was strangely similar to that put forward by the founding fathers for the emphasis to be put on freedom. 'Little more than a glance around the world is needed to realise how urgent a new disciplinary interpretation is needed. Lawlessness is, everywhere, its distinguishing feature.' When the New Ideals had first been formulated, a glance round the world had shown even more lawlessness than was apparent at a glance in 1931. Hitler was then on the way but was not yet a publicly recognized barbarian: the international anarchy to which Clarke referred (as the first of three anarchies) presumably alluded to Manchuria and to the financial breakdown that led to the great depression. He did not of course attribute such events directly to the progressive educationists (in the way that some of the recent Blackpaper backlashings lay anachronistic charges on the contemporary innovators) but he did seem to make a notional connection. He suggested that these anarchies arose from a 'ferment of indiscipline' in the face of which education should achieve a philosophy of its own. The early pioneers had achieved this, of course: in the face of the hatred and destructiveness of war they had sought a philosophy of love and creativity. Clarke dismissed this: as he saw it 'discipline is the need: a discipline of ideas deriving from a Science of Man and . . . a Philosophy of Society. . . . Questions of curriculum and teaching method must occupy a central place in the whole discussion. For it is the re-making of man's *mind* with which we are pre-eminently concerned.'

Previously it had been the children's souls, or at least their hearts, with which the New Education had been concerned. The return to their minds would obviously have satisfied Aldous Huxley and it may well have been a relief to others. In her editorial of the issue of *The New Era* in which Fred Clarke's article appeared, Mrs Ensor underlined the point, declaring that all action must have its source in the world of *ideas*, that much of the chaos in the world was due to faulty and superficial *thinking*, and that it was the prime duty of education to put this right. She affirmed a belief in the League of Nations' attempt to bring together 'self-disciplined nations' to seek the welfare of the world as a whole but pointed out that before we could hope for self-disciplined nations we must have self-disciplined individuals. The key to world stability, she thought, lay in the 'right education of individuals. Our Fellowship since 1915 has steadily had this end in view . . . But rapid changes have made it necessary to expand our philosophy. Then we were only dimly groping for terms in which to formulate the spiritual basis of the New Education. Now we hope to secure at Nice a fundamental formulation of a philosophy of life.'

It was a defeating time for the idealists who had heralded the new era so hopefully only a dozen or so years earlier. 'In politics,' Mrs Ensor wrote, 'despite the League, Treaties, Covenants, Pacts, we are confronted with a world armed to the teeth . . . In economics bedlam reigns. Plenty of food and millions starving. Plenty that needs doing and millions unemployed. . . . Haggling continues over Reparations and War Debts . . .' She refers wistfully to the 'open conspiracy' that H. G. Wells had proposed in 1928. He too had observed this crisis in human affairs when, in spite of the great promise of abundant life, men were haunted by a sense of profound instability and discontent. He called for intelligent people to band together in an 'open conspiracy against the established things – an intellectual rebirth'. He too considered that 'a revolution in education is the most imperative and fundamental part of the adaptation of life to its new conditions'[22] and he wanted 'schools which would become laboratories of educational methods and patterns for new state schools' to produce a social *élite*, children who 'will learn to speak, draw, think, compute lucidly and subtly, and into their vigorous minds they will take the broad concepts of history, biology, and mechanical progress, the basis of the new world, naturally and easily'.[23] The New Educationists no doubt saw themselves as a spearhead of such an open conspiracy but although Wells claimed in his revised 1933 edition that the conspiracy had 'broken out all over the place' (thanks largely, he said modestly, not to his own book, but to 'the mental stimulation of the Russian Five Year Plan') the initial zeal of the New Education Fellowship was losing its conviction, and the revisions of principle which were now being foreshadowed were not of the kind likely to re-stimulate it. In fact, its older adherents may have had similar feelings to those of the faithful beasts in Animal Farm when they found that the Seven Commandments of the old revolution inscribed on the wall of the barn had been amended to the single Commandment: 'All animals are equal but some animals are more equal than others.' In the case of the N.E.F. the commandments – or rather, the principles – were printed on the back cover of each issue of *The New Era*; they, too, disappeared with no explanation. In their fairly detailed history of the N.E.F. Rawson and

Boyd (both of whom were involved in these events) give the statement of principles which were drawn up after the Calais conference in 1921 and which were, they say, 'printed in every number of the three main magazines of the Fellowship up to the Nice conference in 1932, when a new statement took their place'.[24] But the authors do not print the new statement, nor do they explain the reason for the revision. There is the same omission from the book which Rawson edited, *A New World in the Making*, which reports the Nice conference in detail.

In fact, the principles and aims disappeared from *The New Era*, not after the Nice conference, but two years earlier when the magazine changed from being a quarterly to a monthly publication. There had been seven principles and three aims. In summary form the principles were as follows:

(1) To train the child to desire the supremacy of spirit over matter.
(2) To study and respect the child's individuality which can develop only under a form of discipline which ensures freedom for the child's spiritual facilities.
(3) That education should give fresh rein to the innate interests of the child – i.e. those which arise spontaneously within him.
(4) To foster individual self-discipline, tending to self-government.
(5) That a spirit of co-operation should replace the spirit of selfish competition.
(6) That there should be co-operation between the sexes.
(7) To develop not only the future citizens ready and able to fulfil his duty towards his neighbours, nation and humanity as a whole, but also the man conscious of his own dignity.

The three aims were:

(1) To introduce the principles into existing schools and to establish new schools specifically to put those principles into practice.
(2) To promote co-operation between teachers and between teachers and parents.
(3) To promote relations and a solidarity among like-minded teachers of other countries.

In the light of these high-minded sentiments it is not surprising that Neill should have wanted no part in it he had never actually joined the N.E.F. and had been only to the first conference at Calais where he had shocked the continentals with a talk on 'The Abolition of Authority'. The year of the Nice conference also saw the publication of Neill's second 'problem' book, *The Problem Parent*, in which he showed himself to be still as uncompromising as he had been at Calais. Discipline, he insisted, is a projection of self-hate and makes the victim a hater. Self-hate is at the root of militarism and anti-semitism, of our criminal code and our prison system.

It causes men to make perfection the aim of life when happiness should be the goal. There were people now, he said, who were rejecting such idealistic philosophies of life and were refusing to force their values and standards on the young. If we could divert our perfectionist ambitions just on to mechanical things then self-hate would disappear, and with it other hatreds and punishments and wars. 'The abolition of character-moulding will mean the beginning of a new free and happy world.'[25]

This extremist voice was not heard at Nice. There was a bitter division on a fundamental issue at one remove from Neill's point. This was reported by Harold Rugg in *The New Era*. There was one group who 'would create a portrait of an ideal society . . . and deliberately use the curriculum and the method of the schools to indoctrinate a new society'. The opposing group would use a 'more objective approach': not feeling themselves competent to 'predict surely the outlines of that society which will succeed ours' they would content themselves with 'formulating educational goals in terms of the traits of the individual man or woman desired: in terms of "independent judgment", scientific attitude, respect for the personality, and the like'.[26] In Neill's terms, however, both groups were character-moulders. There seemed little place for him in the Movement.

He did, however, make one last gesture towards uniting the progressives on a progressive course by writing an article for *The New Era* on the proposed inspection of private schools.[27] This was a threat, he argued, and he urged others to close their schools and sell matches in Piccadilly rather than agree to compromise on the basis of an inspector's recommendations. 'But can we unite?' he asked. Their ways seemed so diverse that there seemed little prospect of unity, and he held out only one tenuous hope. If they could arrange for informal social contacts this might promote a mutual understanding. 'If a man smokes the same baccy as I do I have a bond with him.'

But many of the progressives smoked no baccy at all, and moreover strongly disapproved of those who did. There were annual meetings of the heads of progressive schools but far from achieving a cementing *bonhomie*, for Neill at least they seemed only to accentuate his apartness. When a discussion on self-government was revealing a paltry lack of understanding, for instance, W. B. Curry (of Dartington) urged Neill to 'get up and tell them what self-government is.'

'What's the good?' he asked wearily. 'They don't want to believe self-government can succeed.'[28] This particular issue was crucial, for in reporting the incident Neill adds, 'The school that has no self-government should not be called a progressive school at all. It is a compromise school.'

The fact was that even without inspectors the progressives were compromising. 'We are now veering back to a middle way,' Mrs Ensor wrote after the Nice conference.[29] Curry was perhaps the only man who stayed anywhere near to Neill, but his too-calm rationality was suspect. As Dora Russell has observed: 'Curry's pupils used often to quote him as saying to them, "I think we are all reasonable people," whereas they felt themselves to be very much the reverse.'[30]

The isolation in which Neill was left perhaps helped to throw his image into sharper relief, and he began to be regarded as something of an authority, particularly in the treatment of difficult children, and many people on the fringe of education saw him as a man of courage and talent pursuing answers to questions that others chose to ignore. The sixteen years of Summerhill experience that Neill could now claim marked him as a seasoned practitioner, no passing cheapjack, and his evidence could not be so easily shrugged off.

The many and full reviews of his book *That Dreadful School* indicate the esteem that he was earning; with *The Problem Child* this was probably the most widely read of his books until the compilation *Summerhill* was published. Professor Joad, writing in the *New Statesman*[31] affectionately recommended Neill for a peerage and suggested an endowment for that dreadful school from the Board of Education. But though Joad dubbed Neill a genius, he was no convert, and held that children needed discipline to control their 'inevitable dose of original sin'. *The Times Educational Supplement*[32] gave a brief and schoolmasterly admonition to Neill for his childish desire to show off his own naughtiness. The *Observer*[33] too thought he was often trying to shock but admitted that 'Mr Neill seems to be collecting more and more evidence in support of the theory that children, given freedom from restrictions, threats, punishments, sexual misinformation and other manifestations of adult neurosis will develop spontaneously a strong social and community sense.' The *Spectator, Listener* and *Time and Tide*[34] were among other periodicals to accord the book substantial and respectful notices, and back in Neill's homeland the *Scots Magazine*[35] gave it their three-page lead review, asserting that it 'goes to prove how false is the usual argument against freedom for children'. The reviewer complimented Neill on his courage and added: 'It takes courage to read it properly, and to confess at the end that you missed much by not having had the chance to be educated yourself at Summerhill.'

It is equally interesting to find the popular press paying lengthy attention to Neill. The *News Chronicle*[36] ran a serialized digest of *That Dreadful School* with half-page quotations over five consecutive days, and the *Daily Herald*[37] too gave Neill publicity in the form of a lengthy notice of his book (which reveals, incidentally, that he was also getting some from a revue song about the school where 'We never say "Yes" and we never say "No"'). Not surprisingly the *Daily Herald* highlighted what were then the more sensational aspects: 'The children are allowed to swear, smoke, skip classes if they feel like it, know all about sex, and call the headmaster "That silly ass, Neill" to his face.' But the review was written approvingly, with sneers at the 'orthodox' who would shudder at that dreadful school. It concludes: 'You may think "I doubt if I'd let my child go there." But, if you are honest, you will probably admit "As a child I should like to have gone there." And Mr Neill would say "Exactly!"'

This extension of the debate did not alter the fact that the issues were in any case relevant only to a small minority of children. For the majority education was still conceived of in terms of basic literacy and discipline, though the Hadow Report (1931) certainly foreshadowed the development of more child-centred thinking, particularly in relation to primary schools; tentatively, this committee suggested that there are occasions and purposes for which 'the well-tried methods of corporate teaching' may not be so suitable as other methods which 'leave the pupil reasonable scope to ensue his own special interests, to learn in his own way, and to acquire the priceless habit of independent purposeful work'.[38] How tentative this suggestion was is illustrated on the following page of the Report where handwork is discussed and there is a plea that the exercises should be so graded that at every stage a child can 'put something of himself into them'. And then comes the most daring suggestion: 'Here and there, there should indeed be scope for invention and artistic creation.' In the secondary sphere the ideas were not so advanced. There was some discussion of the issue between what was referred to as 'two opposing schools of modern educational thought', one of which attached primary importance to the individual pupils and their interests while the other emphasizes the claims of society as a whole seeking 'to equip the pupils for service as workmen and citizens'.[39] But it turned out that the issue was only one of curriculum and the committee came down firmly in the middle of the road combining, it hoped, the two ideals 'in the single conception of social individuality'.

It was a nice example of a placating compromise, too reasonable to be meaningful. The committee knew of course that they were talking of things that concerned a minority – only one child in five had any secondary education at that time – though they were arguing for an expansion. But the expansion which followed was largely a continuation of the development of grammar schools at which there were about half a million children in attendance by the end of the decade.

It was on the playing-fields of these grammar schools (according to G. M. Trevelyan) that the Battle of Britain was won, though until 1938 the nation as a whole was not at all preoccupied with the threat of war: it indulged largely in various forms of domestic escapism – youth hostels and week-end rambling, Test matches, football pools and double-feature film programmes; but the intellectuals were deeply affected by the advancing fascist irrational, dramatized by the Spanish Civil War which gloomed over the earlier adventure of ideas. Now with Auden they were for sure 'Hearing doom's approaching footsteps regular down miles of straight'. It seemed unreal to think of new worlds, and yet equally unpromising to leave things as they were. In education the effect was to bring the orthodox and the progressives closer together.

An interesting booklet by W. H. Auden and T. C. Worsley,[40] brought out in 1939, illustrates how the intellectuals had by that time absorbed some of the lessons of the educational radicals (they cite Curry as 'one of the prime practitioners') but had finally rejected them in a mood of somewhat regretful social realism. Earlier certainties, they admitted, were no longer absolute, but too few new certainties had appeared: individual teachers were changing but generally the old methods persisted, and this for four main reasons. Firstly, tradition: the public-school model was still powerfully to the fore as the educational pattern which the rich handed down to the poor. Secondly, the strait-jacketing of progressively inclined teachers by the examination system. Thirdly, the size of classes: Curry was quoted as saying that a class of seventeen was too large for his purposes; and fourthly, the cost of the larger number of teachers and the expensive equipment (Dartington Hall was again the model that Auden and Worsley had in mind) made the methods impracticable for adoption in state schools. The authors went on to contrast the social assumptions of medieval education (and its adaptation by first the Renaissance and then the Reformation) with those of Rousseau and what they called 'Romantic Anarchism'. The latter had introduced some questionable assumptions on top of the medieval conception of a static society, but at least it had caused people to study children, and as a consequence was mainly responsible for such improvements as there had been in educational practice.

However, education had had little effect on the behaviour of adults or of nations: its products always reverted to the norms of the society in which they found themselves. 'This is not to say that school society ought to be no better than society outside, but to say that it cannot be; different schools imitate different sections of society. The State School imitates the mass-production factory, the Public School the army and the Colonial Civil Services, while the progressive school community resembles that of the *rentier* who is free to devote himself to higher things and is under no obligation to develop his courage or cunning.'[41] It was as pessimistic a message as the social realist with no commanding ideology is apt to purvey. 'Every teacher knows in his heart of hearts that . . . he is working largely in the dark, that on most of his pupils he has no effect at all and probably a bad effect on half the rest.'

If the booklet was more effective in de-bunking the ideas of others than in presenting constructive alternatives this was not untypical of a decade characterized by 'an incorrigible *immobilisme* in State and society ... exasperated and despondent by repeated experience of an inability to impose any effective control on policies'.[42] Yet there was a strong desire for direction and control by the state, and proposals for planning the economy came from various political sources. Education would have to serve this economy, based as it would be on a developing technology; and perhaps also it would be an education for democracy in defence against an infiltrating fascism. It was here that the progressive and the orthodox found a meeting-ground.

The orthodox advanced to the extent suggested by the Spens Report which admitted in effect some of the more obvious social inequities and proposed correcting them by the application of the advancing science of psychometrics. Intelligence testing seemed to offer an impartial way of rationing resources for a projected expansion in education and Spens presented the notion as though it were a scientific structure for tailoring educational provision to the needs of individual children. It thus seemed to fit the progressive ideology well. Equally interesting to the progressives was the liberalization of the curriculum which Spens seemed to promise.

From the other direction the progressives' continued modification of their dogma brought them towards the orthodox. They were worried mostly by the question of freedom – or at least not so much by the question itself as by how they could rationalize a practice of control without seeming to betray their early radicalism. The N.E.F. 1936 conference had this objective and the conference report[43] records much grandiloquence about the spiritual freedom that must be fought for. Personal freedom is the flowering of our personality: personality is an achievement, a conquest of the self, a second birth, that required control of the body, of the passions, of the intellect. They were formulations that lent themselves to widely varying interpretations which the Report displays, yet as Fred Clarke pointed out in his Introduction there were indications of a common point of view. In his words, 'there was an increasing disposition to see in Discipline, rightly interpreted, the art of maintaining and extending the necessary *conditions* of Freedom'. Later, under the stimulus of war, he felt confident enough to be more dogmatic about this, for the war was, he said, a kind of shock treatment that helped us to move out of a period of hallucination into sanity – from 'a self-deluded belief in unreal freedom to a realization that freedom had to be *trained for* under specific discipline ... No apology,' he added apologetically, 'need be made for the use of that ominous word.'

Like the Russians in the early years of their Revolution, we had had our fling: now our rulers were to take control and plan our freedom for us. 'You must take the trouble to *organize* freedom if you really want it', and he suggested the substitution of a Ministry for a Board of Education 'designed to care for the growth of the young from birth to maturity . . . So in our planned society we shall have to learn lessons about obedience and authority as conditions of freedom and get rid once for all of anarchical notions.'[44] Thus the organ of radicalism in educational thought gave its sanction to the new era of bureaucracy.

REFERENCES

1 *Daily Express*, 28 July 1950.
2 M. Hindus, *Humanity Uprooted*, p. 11.
3 Ibid. p. 94.
4 Ibid. p. 98.
5 Ibid. p. 100.
6 Ibid. p. 134.
7 *The Problem Parent*, p. 42.
8 Ibid. p. 187.
9 Scott Nearing, *Education in Soviet Russia*, p. 8.
10 Ibid. p. 15.
11 *New Republic*, November and December 1928.
12 W. Boyd (ed.) *Towards a New Education*, p. 86.
13 Scott Nearing, op. cit. p. 117.
14 *The New Age*, 4 December 1919.
15 *The New Era*, vol. 9, No. 33, January 1928.
16 *The Problem Parent*, p. 132.
17 Pinkevich, *Science and Education in the U.S.S.R.*, p. 40.
18 G. D. H. Cole, *Essays in Social Theory*, p. 79.
19 David Garnett, *The Familiar Faces*, p. xiii.
20 *The New Era*, vol. 11, No. 44, December 1930.
21 *The New Era*, vol. 13, No. 2, February 1932.
22 H. G. Wells, *The Open Conspiracy*, p. 21.
23 Ibid. p. 86.
24 W. Boyd and W. Rawson, *The Story of the New Education*, p. 73.
25 *The Problem Parent*, p. 44.
26 *The New Era*, vol. 13, No. 8, September 1932.
27 *The New Era*, vol. 13, No. 9, October 1932.
28 *That Dreadful School*, p. 31.
29 *The New Era*, vol. 13, No. 9, October 1932.
30 *Anarchy*, 71, January 1967.
31 *New Statesman and Nation*, 8 May 1937.
32 *Times Educational Supplement*, 20 March 1937.
33 *Observer*, 25 April 1937.
34 *Time and Tide*, 10 April 1937; *Listener*, 25 August 1937; *Spectator*, 30 April 1937.
35 *Scots Magazine*, May 1937.
36 *News Chronicle*, 12–16 April 1937.
37 *Daily Herald*, 1 April 1937.

38 *Report of the Consultative Committee on the Primary School* (Hadow Report), p. 153.
39 *Report of the Consultative Committee on the Education of the Adolescent* (Hadow Report), p. 101.
40 W. H. Auden and T. C. Worsley, *Education – Today and Tomorrow*.
41 Ibid. p. 37.
42 D. Thompson, *England in the Twentieth Century*, p. 181.
43 W. Rawson, *The Freedom we Seek*.
44 *The New Era*, vol. 21, No. 9, November 1940.

9 Planned Freedom

The east coast of England was a possible invasion area during the war and consequently Summerhill was evacuated to Wales. The five years they spent there were difficult ones for Neill, the more so on account of the collapse and prolonged illness of his wife. She died before the school returned to its proper home.

Even when he did return, to buildings more damaged by the army's occupation than by a dozen years of reputedly destructive children, Neill could not hope to re-occupy the place of esteem that he had earned in pre-war days. England wanted a planned society, security, fair shares and economic stability. Education was an important part of the social blueprint and the 1944 Act set out the appropriate meritocratic path that it was to follow. The country was in no mood to listen to Neill's ideas or to face the questions which he posed. It was too anxious to believe the promises that its plans implied.

Neill's book, *Hearts not Heads in the School*, published in 1944 'to suggest a few points that are apt to be overlooked by the planners' was quite out-of-tune with the current preoccupations. It was in any case a weary book, repeating well-practised formulae with little of his earlier fire and humour. He ended the book with a tribute to his once stalwart Mrs Lins: for her epitaph he proposed, 'She belonged to tomorrow, to youth, to hope.' His book was about tomorrow but there is little feeling of convinced hope about it. Its reviewers found varying reasons for rejecting it, mostly in a rather ill-tempered fashion. T. C. Worsley,[1] for example, disliked its 'provoking title' and seemed to find nothing important in the substance of the book. In the *Tribune*[2] Colin Horne brushed it aside with the significant but unhelpful comment that 'our community ... is not ready or able to allow its citizens ... the freedom that Neill insists on.'

If the purpose of the book had really been to persuade the planners to question their priorities then Neill's skill as a propagandist had clearly deserted him. He wrote a book that they could ignore. But it does not seem that he thought he would be heeded and more than once he suggests that he was writing not so much for tomorrow as for the day after. As he saw it, the planners were going to produce pre-Freudian schools for a post-

Freudian world, by which he meant not that psycho-analysis was an available tool for educationists but that its revelation of the importance of the unconscious made it futile to think only in terms of increasing children's conscious knowledge. The latter certainly seemed to be the basis of the emerging education in which, even for young children, the examination rituals put a weighty premium on academic learning – or rather, on prescribed learning, for most of it was a travesty of true academicism.

Even Professor Clarke, who had persuaded the progressives to plan their freedom, began to have doubts that he expressed in a little book *Freedom in the Educative Society* in which he tried to reconcile the idea of planned freedom with the reality that was beginning to emerge. It is a very different kind of book from Neill's: Clarke's thought was rooted in orthodox Christian theology (he added a postscript commending the doctrine of original sin) laced with a fashionable sociological perspective, while Neill was now firmly anti-Christian and spoke in terms of depth psychology; Clarke's thesis was undemonstrated theory while Neill had twenty-five years of practice to back his ideas; Clarke respected an obligation for reasoned argument, but Neill did not try to hide his own illogicalities and his tentative or brazen self-contradictions. And of course their contrasting styles embodied widely differing concepts of freedom.

For Clarke, the current pursuit of prosperity had replaced the threat of anarchy in his anxiety-structure. To achieve both prosperity and freedom, order and discipline were still essential, he argued; but on the other hand, freedom would be lost if compulsion proved necessary to secure that order. Only by 'intelligent, cultivated conscience' could we steer safely through the obstacles. Prosperity was something that Neill had never thought worth discussion – and this is an indication of how much he was out-of-tune with contemporary ambitions. But more important, the idea of freedom growing out of order and discipline was quite foreign to Neill's thinking. They might, probably would, develop out of freedom, but never the reverse. 'Freedom can order itself, but it cannot be ordered by an external authority.'[3]

This may correspond to Clarke's warning that compulsion is the knell of freedom but that was an ambiguous warning when coupled with his concept of a 'cultivated conscience'. The cultivation must involve some form of indoctrination. We should not be squeamish about this, Clarke argued, for a child cannot even learn its mother-tongue with being indoctrinated. But it is clear that his programme of indoctrination would not end there: 'It is the first business of education to induce such conformity in terms of the culture in which the child will grow up.'[4] This conformity is important to the social ethic: 'To do skilled and faithful service for a fair reward, and to accept the common discipline which this entails is then seen as the first duty of citizenship.'[5] This is the stuff of that conformity we need 'before we can even begin to be freed'; and because the intention of the educator will be to ensure the child's freedom, the required indoctrination is justified.

Such conformity is a necessary condition of freedom because, Clarke argues, freedom is a human attribute and only by becoming the bearer of the culture into which one is born can one be genuinely human. Clarke was writing at a time when an awareness of sub-cultures was not so clear as it is becoming now: even so, he might have questioned whether the 'culture into which the child is born' is identical with the idealized version he was blue-printing. He was aware of the discrepancy for he referred to the 'acute disharmonies' between the social values that children actually experienced and those that were recommended at school. Indeed, if the conformities he required were really a part of everyday culture no special effort of indoctrination would be needed. Clarke admits as much when he suggests that the extreme form of libertarian education which he is at pains to refute could only have gained credence in such a secure culture where 'conformity could be ignored in theory just because it could be taken so completely for granted in practice.'[6] Now, he seems to be saying our culture had lost this security and needed a measure of internal defence.

The argument would not have impressed Neill since he evinced none of Clarke's hopes to preserve this insecure culture. He thought it was corrupt, diseased and self-destructive, a culture dominated by the Old Men who sacrificed their youth in war, and in peacetime kept them in subjugation by the devitalizing effects of sexual repression. 'Parental and school discipline have the deep motive of keeping youth from power, and the sex morality imposed on youth is but one aspect of this motive.'[7] Neill was not trying to promote any specific social organization, but he had no interest in bending his education to preserve the existing one.

Clarke's valuing of the present social order was, however, only in part a fear of the anarchy that might fill the vacuum left by its disintegration. In part also, it was a concession to the prevailing desires for security and prosperity; but mainly and most positively it was a valuing of its culture – that is, of its higher culture. For the preservation and extension of this culture he argued for the deliberate cultivation of an *élite* to replace its declining aristocratic guardians. This new *élite* would not form a class nor would it have any distinctive social or political place (though he did not explain what measures would be taken to avoid its assuming one, unless it was that the 'intelligent informed conscience' was sufficient guarantee of such self-abnegation); but it would be recognizable and respected, and to ensure this education 'at the lower levels' would have to aim at a degree of 'awareness' in the masses, while for their part the *élite* would need to develop 'a sympathetic sensibility towards the tastes, the amusements and the day-to-day habits of the common folk'.[8] The condescending paternalism of these words may seem embarrassing today but it was a part of the philosophy of the emerging meritocracy. Clarke was not to know that the amusements and day-to-day habits of the common folk would include rock 'n' roll, teddy boys, mods and rockers battling out their frustrations on the beaches, Hell's Angels and skinheads, nor that so many of the carefully chosen young *élite* would be driven to a revolt committed to the destruction of society and the forging of a counter-culture designed to replace work by play, duty by love, money by flowers.

Neill was certainly no *élitist* and no great defender of our cultural heritage; nor did he consider it a proper function of education to attempt to guide the future cultural development. He preferred a do-it-yourself culture. The average age of curriculum-makers should be about seventeen, he suggested. He would rather children enjoy dance music uninhibitedly than that they should be made to practise Chopin or listen to Bach. The idea that the 'lower levels of education' should inculcate a respect for the cultural attainments of an *élite* would have been repugnant to him. 'We "educated" men have managed and still manage to impress the great public. I want an end to that era.'[9]

It may be true that, like the sergeant he met in the army who had been 'bowled over' on discovering that Private Neill was an M.A., Neill too felt an awe for the high culture that he had never properly absorbed, and perversely this may have led him sometimes to imply that most culture-worship, if not culture itself, was a sham. But even without such suspicions he would have wanted to shield his children from culture-appreciation courses. The personal freedom of each child included its right to a self-determined value system. Of course this had to be constructed within a social environment, but not a loaded one – the children should be screened from what seemed to be a pre-packed, morally-based, authority-backed value system. Such insistence on individual freedom led Neill to avoid serious consideration of the social consequences of his education: he was prepared to let these evolve in their own way. On the individual level, he was saying that if the emotions were right the intellect would look after itself, and as regards social structure he seemed to be assuming that, given emotionally healthy individuals, their culture could safely be left to develop. Certainly, any education affected the future development of society, but it should not presume to prescribe this development beyond saying that society should become what a community of free individuals might decide it should be.

Man was born free and education had to preserve that freedom, largely by a preventative programme – preventing, principally, sexual conflicts that would be used by society to perpetuate many of its ills, preventing feelings of inferiority, preventing residues of hate and aggression resulting from early frustrations. He was confident that the culture of a society of individuals thus free of internal conflict would flourish healthily. He would point to the painting and drama of Summerhill to illustrate the children's creativity, and he claimed that a higher proportion of them than normal found jobs in the Arts. Even in regard to the appreciation of traditional culture Neill considered that his pupils were better equipped than the average, and he quoted the opinion of a visiting Polish headmaster who considered that of the forty-five English schools he had seen only Summerhill had reached his idea of a proper academic standard. What had impressed him had been the analysis of the characters in *Macbeth* that the senior pupils had given him and their appreciation of the effects of the French Revolution on English culture and philosophy. Neill's claim was that it was because this group of pupils had mostly come to Summerhill as infants, at intervals skipping a lot of lessons, that they brought to the studies that they eventually chose more wisdom, originality, sincerity and creativeness than the students of a disciplined school would have resource to. Not all would choose the subjects that children in other schools would be compelled to attend to, but 'there will always be people who will delight in Chaucer or Keats: the hope is that those whose ideas of culture are nearer to tractors and films will not feel inferior in the presence of the classically cultured as they do today.'[10]

Such an attitude would have been more in tune with the comprehensive ideology which replaced the frustrations of the meritocracy, but at the time *élitist* philosophies such as Clarke's were more in vogue. To some extent Clarke's emphasis on freedom was combating the contemporary dangers from social engineering, but he seemed more concerned with those stemming from what he called the 'popular doctrine' which regards the attainment of freedom as a 'free and comparatively smooth "development" of inner potentialities, unfolding as it were from within'.[11] This was to ignore the cultural influences, he maintained – inner potentialities may determine what a child *can* learn, but the prevailing culture and the child's actual and prospective place in it largely determine what he *does* learn. (This does not seem unreasonable, except in so far as it implies that a child's freedom is dependent on what he learns. A more promising formulation might be that what a person makes of his freedom, how he uses it, is dependent on what he learns.)

Clarke further distinguished between freedom as a doctrine or technique and freedom as an objective. Of the first he had little to say except to imply that he thought it generally a good technique. He quoted Rousseau's dictum: 'Never command him to do anything whatever, not the least thing in the world', and suggested that the weight should be in the word 'command', as though Rousseau was merely purveying tips for teachers. Freedom as an objective he also approved of – but that was quite a different thing, to be attained only after years of disciplined learning for it involved a sufficiency of knowledge and was intimately connected with responsibility. This was not an existential responsibility but a social one, an acceptance of the duty of a citizen to work honestly and faithfully in return for promised rights to employment and social security. Clarke did not expect by any means all the citizens to complete the 'conquest' of freedom: many would never grasp it, and many, having grasped it would decide that they did not want the burden of it. In fact this freedom would be the distinguishing characteristic of the *élite*, though 'it is the business of the national education system to produce them in the greatest possible numbers.'[12]

Clarke's was a joyless concept of freedom and it is sometimes difficult to see why it should be called freedom at all. The answer is perhaps to be found in his observation that 'The man who can swim is more free in the water than the man who cannot'.[13] But this only provokes further questions: one might want to know, for instance, who is the more free – the swimmer, the trapeze artiste, the Greek scholar or the teenage jiver? It would seem to depend on whether they were in the water, or flying through the air, or deciphering an ancient document, or in a discotheque. If they are in the water then we might ask how and why did they get there. The experience of the Gaderene swine might suggest that freedom resides not so much in the ability to swim as in the ability to decide whether or not to plunge into the water.

Clarke's puritanical version of freedom led him to point to the parable of the Pharisee and the publican, the one 'left unconscious of his own utter flabbiness', the other crazed with a realization of 'the gulf between the majesty of his human calling and the ignominy of his achievement'.[14] To Clarke the moral tension implied by this sense of inadequacy and sin was the mark of 'full sanity', and he complained that a lack of tension was one of the main faults of the 'development' theory of education. Educational thought should recognize the bipolar nature of the process – spontaneity and discipline, pupil and teacher, action and reflection, individual and society, impulse and principle, liberty and leadership . . .

Neill's attitude to freedom was much more hedonistic. He concluded a chapter on 'Freedom in Education' with the words: 'Frankly I don't know why I am writing about freedom; it all seems so natural and delightful to me after twenty-three years of life in a community of free children.'[15] Education was not for him a hard struggle, a painful conquest, but rather something to be enjoyed; yet this is not to say that he wished to subside into a flabby, tensionless lotus-land. It is true that the Summerhill children were able to opt out of studies they found irksome but of course even the traditional form of education has its drop-outs and its slide-outs. This is not the same as saying that the education is flabby and tensionless in either case. Neill's remark about the natural and delightful quality of freedom came as a comment on an incident in which he had gate-crashed the birth-day-party of a five year old who, seeing Neill, had cried out: 'Here, you weren't invited. Get out!' The unstructured relationships, child and child, adult and child, adult and adult, have their tensions just as much as the formalized relationship of pupil and teacher; and these tensions are felt by both sides – for as Neill points out the adult at Summerhill has often told a child to 'Buzz off' as a child ejected an adult or another child from a party or a private room. On the other hand it seems that in the case of a form-alized relationship the tensions are irreducible, because another of Clarke's recommended bipolars – action and reflection – is generally absent. In the Summerhill situation the effects of interpersonal actions were continuously reflected upon and debated rather than being mainly observed and felt, possibly with resentment, possibly with gratitude. The act of reflection was most assiduously pursued in the Summerhill school meetings and dis-cussions.

Others of Clarke's suggested bipolars are also discernible in the Summer-hill model, though because it was a different form of education to the traditional one they strike less familiar accents. Most obviously felt was the tension between the individual and society. In the usual school setting (at least at the time when Clarke was writing) the cards were stacked for the benefit of society and the degree of conformity usually demanded of a pupil was such that the tension was certainly there but its implications were left largely unexplored: it would manifest itself occasionally in sad little squabbles between a headmaster and his sixth-formers who did not want to wear their school caps! In Summerhill it is not easy to say which way the cards were stacked, if at all: from the outside, they would seem to favour the individual – it was the do-as-you-please school, according to the pop-ular press, but many times Neill has tried to repudiate this naïve judge-ment. In replying to T. C. Worsley's review of *Hearts not Heads*, for instance, he wrote: 'A self-governing school is full of authority, an authority that sincerely tries to balance the rights of individual and community.'[16] The tensions were tensions of balance rather than of suppression and con-flict. It is probably the case that while tensions are a necessary feature of an educational process (of a living, that is) conflict is actually anti-educational.

The form of education exemplified in Summerhill attempts to avoid conflict (not always successfully) but to explore tensions. These are not endured in any spirit of ascetic hardiness but are recognized as being implicit in the process (in that sense they are 'natural' rather than being artificially introduced); and because the process is enjoyable – the experience of the tensions may be, too – 'natural and delightful'. Neill's aim was that his children should be happy, but he also said that happiness is interest.

With some justification it might be said that Summerhill did less than it might have done to provide sufficient stimulus of interest but this was not because it relied on 'the idea of the free development of inner potentialities'. 'Such an education,' Clarke wrote, 'has the function of providing suitable nurture and of removing obstructions. It is not, in any real sense, directive or formative. The inner potentialities take care of that.'[17] This simple developmental model that he wanted to foist on some unnamed 'modern educationists' does not fit Summerhill. Education there was non-directive, it is true, and this by very deliberate design; but it was formative in the sense that it tried to compel the pupils to create themselves through their choice of action. The obstacles that were being removed were obstacles to the apprehension of the I-Thou-It triangle, and educationally the freedom that Neill extolled might be reduced to that – the freedom from obstacles to self-knowledge and the concomitant freedom to explore relationships. It was Neill's claim that under such freedom 'children acquire something that no compulsory system can give them, a sincerity that stands out bravely, an attitude to life that is independent and fluid, an interest in people and things that all the textbooks in the world cannot give them.'[18]

How far this was the case can only be judged by the impressions of independent witnesses. Herbert Read has agreed with the verdict in declaring that Neill, in the forty years of Summerhill's existence, had 'proved one simple truth – *freedom works*'. This affirmation is quoted in the publisher's blurb to *Summerhill*, a book that also carried an approving foreword by Erich Fromm who in his *Fear of Freedom* had produced his own analysis of the problem of freedom in modern society. The book was published in England in 1942 and was a significant contribution to the debate that accompanied the establishment of the post-war society. His approach was very different from both Clarke's and Neill's, but he reached conclusions which might have provided Neill with a supportive rationale. For various reasons, however, Neill appears to have ignored his arguments.

Fromm brought a revised, some would say a watered-down, Freudian perspective to examine the rise and present state of western civilization. From the Middle Ages on, this history has been characterized by growing individuation and growing freedom, though at the expense of personal security. Capitalism brought about a clamorous affirmation of the individual though it also led to a self-negation and asceticism. On the economic plane it became man's fate to toil for the growth of the economy, to amass capital not for his own happiness or eventual salvation, but as an end in itself. He became a cog to serve a purpose outside himself. Parallel to this, or almost in preparation for it, the teaching of Luther and Calvin reduced man to an evil and sinful being whose purpose was 'exclusively God's glory and nothing of his own'. Thus in both spheres, economic and spiritual, man was abased into personal insignificance and powerlessness by the imposition of extrapersonal purposes.

As capitalism developed, man became even more fully an instrument of his own society: technology freed him from his powerlessness over natural forces only to subjugate him to equally brutal social forces. Relationships became increasingly instrumentalized: those between competitors were based on human indifference, employer and employee became mere instruments of economic gain and a man became a commodity even in his feeling for his own self as his self-esteem became dependent on his saleability. The freedom of capitalism thus results in a bewilderment of aloneness and reification, and the monopolistic phase in both economic and social organization has so accentuated this insecurity of isolation and personal insignificance that people have come to fear the freedom they once sought, and now seek one or other of a variety of escape-routes from it. The most common of these in the democratic societies is what Fromm calls automaton conformity in which the individual ceases to be himself by adopting all the socially required patterns thus dissolving the discrepancy between the self and the world and with it the conscious feeling of aloneness and powerlessness.

Fromm's analysis suggested that there may be an inevitable circle that leads from freedom into a new dependence: the fear of isolation may compel the individual to seek a new bondage. To break this circle Fromm suggested a two-fold need: the individual needs to achieve a full realization of his self, and he needs to be capable of loving relationships which involve neither the dissolution of the self nor the possession of another. An essential characteristic for the fulfilment of these needs is spontaneity – activity of one's free will, which entails the acceptance of the total personality and the elimination of the split between 'reason' and 'nature', between heads and hearts, in Neill's terms. In such spontaneous realization of the self 'man unites himself anew with the world, with man, with nature, and himself. Love is the foremost component of such spontaneity . . . work is the other component.'[19]

The prescription comes close to Neill's ideal of an education based in freedom, happiness ('which is interest') and love. Fromm had little to say in *The Fear of Freedom* about the way in which these qualities of spontaneity and work-interest might be achieved, but he did point out that at present education was working in the opposite direction. It was a process of suppression, making continuous demands for conformity, insisting on the avoidance of expressions of the emotions and cultivating the expression of unfelt emotions; likewise 'original thinking is discouraged and ready-made thoughts are put into people's heads'. It was, he declared, an education 'in insincerity by insincerity'.[20]

It is therefore not surprising that when he later discovered Summerhill, Fromm should have been so approving that he felt able to write such a warm foreword to Neill's most definitive book, *Summerhill: a Radical Approach to Education* (or to *Child-rearing*, as it appeared in the American edition). Neill, on the other hand, makes little reference to Fromm; the reason is perhaps partly that he had no taste for the theoretical type of writing that was Fromm's medium, but more potently the fact that by this time he had become strongly wedded to Wilhelm Reich's analysis which differed markedly from Fromm's in placing a total emphasis on the social effects of sexual regulation. Fromm himself realized that this was the main point on which he differed from Neill. In his foreword to *Summerhill* he faulted Neill on just two counts: he thought that Neill underestimated the 'importance, pleasure, and authenticity of an intellectual grasp of the world' and that he overestimated the significance of sex 'as Freudians tend to do'. It was not really 'as a Freudian' that Neill made this emphasis. He had departed from the orthodox Freudian theory quite early on – suggesting, for instance, that the Oedipus situation was more a power conflict than a sexual one. Most strongly he was critical of the Freudians' reluctance to join the struggle for sexual liberation, of their timidity in failing un-equivocally to recommend the avoidance of the repression of infantile sexuality, or the freeing of adolescent sexuality, or the abolition of an anachronistic moral code governing adult sexual behaviour. He really ceased to be a Freudian when, in Marcuse's words 'it became clear to what extent psycho-analysis was still committed to the society whose secrets it revealed. The psycho-analytic conception of man, with its belief in the basic unchangeability of human nature appeared as "reactionary". Freudian theory seemed to imply that the humanitarian ideals of socialism were humanly unattainable.'[21] Reich attempted to counter this pessimism by putting even more emphasis on the effects of sexual repression, Fromm by removing much of the emphasis in order to accentuate the effects of the suppression of other drives. 'Although I believe that the discouragement of sexual joy is not the only important suppression of spontaneous reactions but one of many, certainly its importance is not to be underrated.'[22] Yet in the whole of *The Fear of Freedom* there are only two or three paragraphs devoted to its discussion.

In spite of this crucial difference there remains a considerable common

ɪ

ground between Neill and Fromm. The light which Fromm's thesis sheds on Clarke's attempt to reconcile freedom and discipline is also interesting. Clarke's main worry was the threat he saw to social stability in the abandonment of a socially controlled discipline – controlled, that is, not by the actual society of the child but by the wider society through its more or less authoritarian intermediaries, the parents and teachers. He proposed a defence of the existing social order by first ensuring a ground of conformity before releasing the individual towards freedom. The recipe was, in Fromm's terms, the very contrary to what was needed; for it was society's insistence on conformity that led to the individual's inability to establish a self sufficiently integrated to withstand the fear of freedom, and that led progressively to the automaton's escape-route. The release to freedom would probably not be taken. Clarke admitted this in effect when he suggested that only a minority – his *élite* – would accept the challenge of the 'conquest' which he proposed for them; the rest would be educated to respect the lead of this *élite*. They would become the automata, or at least the submissive mass, and it does not seem an unlikely corollary that the *élite* – with their identities also undermined by the conformist discipline to which they would have been subjected – would assume the dominant role in a symbiotic partnership. An equally basic objection to Clarke's plan is against his mapping of the characteristics of freedom: the most important condition is 'to be able to swim' – 'trained capacities of thought and action'. It is a freedom for power, for control of man and nature, and this, in Fromm's analysis, is the very impetus that inspired the rise of capitalism and led western civilization in its as yet unbroken circle of personal isolation and dependence.

REFERENCES

1 *New Statesman and Nation*, 12 January 1946.
2 *Tribune*, 1 February 1946.
3 *Hearts not Heads in the School*, p. 105.
4 F. Clarke, *Freedom in the Educative Society*, p. 29.
5 Ibid. p. 32.
6 Ibid. p. 17.
7 *Hearts not Heads*, p. 122.
8 Clarke, op. cit. p. 48.
9 *Hearts not Heads*, p. 51.
10 Ibid. p. 52.
11 Clarke, op. cit. p. 53.
12 Ibid. p. 58.
13 Ibid. p. 58.
14 Ibid. p. 62.
15 *Hearts not Heads*, p. 108.

16 *New Statesman and Nation*, 12 January 1946.
17 Clarke, op. cit. p. 53.
18 *Hearts not Heads*, p. 103.
19 Fromm, *The Fear of Freedom*, p. 255.
20 Fromm, op. cit. p. 213.
21 H. Marcuse, *Eros and Civilization*, p. 190.
22 Fromm, op. cit. p. 210.

10 Sexual Freedom

Looking back on his fifty years of Summerhill, Neill remarked to me that he counted himself extraordinarily lucky in having known well two great men – Homer Lane and Wilhelm Reich. It had not been just chance, though. In both cases he had heard of their work before meeting them and had sought them out and asked each to accept him as a student. They had both agreed to this very readily, and in each case the relationship ripened quickly into an intimate friendship. There seems to have been a strong element of hero-worship in Neill's attitude to both these men, though it is also clear that he realized his urge to idolize them and he consciously resisted the temptation to lapse into the dependency of a discipleship. It is striking, however, that he attributed to both Christlike qualities – to Lane on account of a capacity for selfless love, and to Reich because of his vision of, and work for, the sustenance of Life. Neither of them was quite immune to the temptation which this tribute concealed. There was an occasion when Reich, hearing a woman lauding the virtues of Krishna-murti, growled out his envy: 'If this man is so Christlike, why has he not been crucified?' And David Wills's quoted Lane's remark to the effect that the only difference between Christ and himself was that Christ was crucified.* But as things turned out both men eventually had themselves crucified. Lane died within six months of being cast out of this country on an unsubstantiated pretext – 'killed in action by the Twickenham Baptist gang,' as Auden put it – and Reich died in the prison to which he had been consigned for his failure to comply with a judicial directive to destroy, and thereby to renounce, what he himself regarded as the culminating material products of his life's work. Thus each died following their trials on charges obliquely connected with their doctrine, and their practice of it, though in both cases their judges refrained, Pilate-wise, from actually condemning those doctrines. Neill employed the ideas of both men, and built on them, but he never allowed obsessions to blind him to practical politics. So he survives, feeling no need to be crucified. As he remarked to me in conversation, 'You can tell I'm not a genius: I have not gone mad!'

By the mid-thirties he had virtually exhausted the vein that Lane had

* This remark was reported through John Layard. But Layard told me that Lane had not claimed this as the *only* difference between himself and Christ.

located for him. He had fairly well mastered the therapeutic techniques into which Lane had initiated him and he had established a school for both normal and difficult children which was based on Lane's guiding principles – freedom, a belief in original goodness, aiming at happiness and with an emphasis on the emotions that derived from psycho-analytic theories about the Unconscious. The school was well established and shown to offer a viable form of education, and Neill himself was acknowledged as an authority at least by those who were similarly inclined to see the inadequacies of the traditional forms. It was as such an authority that he was lecturing in Oslo in 1937 when he learned that Wilhelm Reich was in his audience. Neill had only recently been reading Reich's book *The Mass Psychology of Fascism* which had impressed him so much that he telephoned to suggest a meeting. They talked together into the early hours of the following morning and, as at the end of his first meeting with Lane, Neill asked if he might become a student of Reich's. So for the next two years he went back to Norway each vacation to renew the friendship which quickly developed between them, to study Reich's ideas and, not least important, to undergo a course of Reichian therapy.

Neill had been disappointed with both of the two courses of psychotherapy that he had had earlier in his career – one with Lane, and the other with Stekel. They had been 'all head-talk and symbolism' which, he complained, had never really touched him. Reich's technique – vegetotherapy, as it was called – was the first major outcome of what was to be Reich's lifelong quest for a biological basis of psychic functioning. Vegetotherapy was essentially an attack by the therapist on the muscular 'armouring' of his patient – a more or less permanent state of muscular tension or 'stiffness' in which, according to Reich, the neurosis resided. Neill was at first sceptical about this, but became convinced of its truth partly by his own experience under treatment and partly by his observations of young children at Summerhill. The locking of suppressed emotions by muscular tensions is not an unfamiliar idea: the experience of aches of various kinds resulting from everyday stressful situations is common enough to support the credibility of such a connection, though of course Reich's methods were based on rather more sophisticated observations than this. Neill gives an instance of the kind of situation that arose in the course of his treatment: he recounts how in one session he discovered his jealousy of Reich's achievements and his unconscious dislike of learning from a man fifteen years his junior being expressed in tensions in his neck muscles, the intense pain from which dissolved when he gave vent to these feelings. The therapeutic attack on the muscular tensions would normally start with the face and head which held the more superficial characterlogical armouring and proceed down the body towards the genital region where the most deep-seated inhibitions would be located. Particularly significant was the region of the stomach whose stiffness would be both inhibiting the full use of the diaphragm in breathing and retracting the pelvis in an attitude of sexual fear. Returning from Norway, Neill examined the children in the kindergarten at Summerhill. 'I was astonished to find that the ones who had been brought up without morality had soft stomachs, while the children of the religious and the moral had stiff stomachs.'[1]

The muscular tensions were thus both the expression and the lodging of neuroses; they contained the character structure of the individual and Reich's treatment combined the freeing of muscular tensions with an assault on the characterological defences of the patient. Neill's own Christlike pose by which he was repressing his hate come in for such an assault, for instance.[2]

The validity of this treatment, as of other techniques, has to be judged by its success, though generally there is not universal agreement as to what is to be counted as the success of a psycho-analytic treatment. For Reich, however, the issue was clear-cut: his criterion of success was the establishment of what he called orgastic potency,[3] and this he defined with precision, if possibly with some arbitrariness. Correspondingly, he considered sexual repression to be the major primary source of psychic disturbance, the 'rings' of muscular tensions being the physical seat of the disturbance in so far as they blocked the discharge of (bioelectric) energy in the orgasm reflex, and he made the goal of his treatment the elimination of such sexual malfunctioning.

Neill had never been as unequivocal as this in any of his speculations as to the origins of the disturbances in problem children, though by the time he met Reich he had fairly decided views as to the importance of sexual freedom to a child's healthy development. In his early days at Gretna, his reading of the 'advanced' writers like Shaw and Ibsen, had made him dimly aware that there was something wrong with conventional attitudes to sex: he wanted his pupils to develop a 'rational, elemental view of sex instead of a conventional hypocritical one',[4] but he excused himself from helping them to this by protesting that he would lose his job if he mentioned the subject in school. This may have been true, but it was probably also a projection of his own internal censorship implanted by his very inhibiting upbringing. Even if he had had his own private school he decided that until they reached the age of nine the children would be encouraged to believe in the stork theory of birth. Then they would get the naked truth.

This was before he had heard of Freud; when he did, he amended these naïve views. In *A Dominie in Doubt* he advocated full sex instruction: 'The child should be told the truth about sex whenever he asks for information.'[5] But he *was* in doubt: he saw no set of persons – teachers, doctors or parents

– whose own attitudes were free enough to give this information in an unadulterated form. He concluded that the matter could best be tackled negatively by teachers in the sense that the sex instinct was identifiable with the creative instinct, and that the teacher's job was 'to provide ways and means for creation'. He realized this was only a second-best, but at least it would guard against the danger of the child's regressing 'to what is called auto-eroticism'. Co-education too could help in affording a 'harmless and unconscious outlet for sex interest', but it was no panacea.

By the time he wrote *The Problem Child*, however, he had adopted a more forthright view, recognizing the harm done by the moral prohibitions which fixated children in infantile sex and caused them to grow up with perverted tendencies. Such moral training and inadequate, or actually false, sex instruction resulted in all children who came to Summerhill having 'a diseased attitude to sexuality and to bodily functions'. But though he abhorred such practices and such results he was still quite far from recognizing sex as a fundamental component in the child's psyche. The hatred of the flesh which moral training taught had the effect, he thought, of giving to sex 'a prominence out of all proportion to its importance'.[6] It was not Freud who should be blamed for 'putting sex into everything' but moral education, by making the forbidden fruit so enticing.

Neill acquired the reputation of being in the vanguard of sexual liberation, but a reading of these earlier books suggests that this was based on the open way in which he discussed questions of sex education rather than the actual doctrine he preached. What he was saying was concerned almost exclusively with the handling of early sexuality – and even in that sphere, while abominating all forms of moral training he did not accept a full Freudian account of the sexual proclivities of young children. In many instances, for example, he favoured the Adlerian model of power struggles as a more satisfying explanation of the origins of many of the conflicts in young children. Much later, after his meeting with Reich, he indirectly criticized these earlier opinions by warning the 'problem teacher' that 'his own repressed attitude to sex may make him overvalue the psychology of Dr Alfred Adler, a doctrine that is apt to attract the timid ones whom Freud scared away with sex theory'.[7]

It was not until he wrote *That Dreadful School*, that Neill declared his attitude to adolescent sex. The implication had always been that he would raise no barriers to the full enjoyment of sexual freedom by adolescents, but it now appeared that he accepted the barriers which society erected. At Gretna he had refrained from any form of sex instruction for fear of losing his job; at Summerhill he would not countenance adolescent sex for fear of losing his school. He explained his attitude by recounting his warning to a boy and a girl who had both come to Summerhill late in their adolescence. They fell in love. (The words are Neill's: significantly he attributes to them full adult emotions.) He met them together late one night. '"I don't know what you two are doing." I said, "and morally I don't care, for it isn't a moral question at all. But economically I do care. If you, Kate, had a kid my school would be ruined."'[8]

In all other aspects of sex it seems that the Summerhill pupils were not denied complete freedom, and they appeared to have none of the normal inhibitions; they shared the same bathrooms, they would occasionally bathe in the nude, they used sexual swear-words freely, there was no censorship of their reading. They would fall in love perhaps, but 'pairing off is seldom seen', Neill commented.[9] In fact, his account of his adolescents' sexual activity was at this date strikingly reticent considering his reputation as one who was eager to shock. It seems probable not that this was an area in which he did not have the courage of his convictions, but one in which he did not have the convictions. His contact with Reich cleared his doubts and his subsequent books became increasingly forthright on the question.

Is Scotland Educated? appeared shortly before his meeting with Reich although it does contain a short reference to that 'brilliant psychologist' and he used Reich's theory that 'sex repression is unconsciously planned and carried out by the Capitalist class' to underpin a sustained attack on contemporary sexual mores. The suppression of sex in Scotland, he declared, must be called obscene, cruel, narrow, un-Christlike. In his next book, *The Problem Teacher* (1939), he was arguing for the necessity of more healthy attitudes to sex on the part of teachers and for their own need of a satisfying sex-life. He also expanded on Reich's theories about sexual repression, and for the first time he argued openly, if mainly by quotation from Reich, in favour of a full and free sex-life for 'our proletarian youth'. He accepted more personal responsibility for these views in *The Free Child* (1954). He now distinguished between the 'free child' who had been reared from birth according to the principles of self-regulation (another concept which Reich's teaching enabled him to clarify) and the 'semi-free child', as he described most of the Summerhill children who were living in a free environment but who had had the usual 'anti-life' conditioning in infancy. Such conditioned children he said were 'incapable of loving' – a remarkable assertion which, he added sarcastically, should save the heads of many co-educational boarding-schools from sleepless nights. Mutual interest between the sexes might appear spasmodically in the so-called latency period and this might involve some 'gentle genital play', but too often it takes the form of sadistic horseplay'[10]– another indication of the effects of early conditioning in marring the loving capability.

More interest is evidenced just before and during puberty, though here again he found that only one in three boys was able to have love affairs – a proportion one might think still high enough to cause those heads of schools some sleepless nights. The fact was, however, that no Summerhill girl had become pregnant in all the school's thirty-odd years. 'Every older pupil knows . . . that I approve of a full sex-life for all who wish for one, whatever the age.' There was no supervision of the pupils to keep them out of each other's beds, yet Neill could still not bring himself actively to facilitate the sex-life to which he believed these adolescents had every right – he did not, for instance, make contraceptives available to them ('a matter of bad conscience in me') for he judged that to do so would be a sure way of having the school closed. From the first, Reich had tried to move him on this point:

> We often had long discussions about the sex question. 'Neill,' he said, when I first knew him in Norway, 'you are wrong. You "dulden" adolescent sex where you ought to "bejahen" it.'
> 'Dulden' meant tolerate while 'bejahen' meant active approval. I argued that I was running a school while he wasn't. I told him that to allow a full sex-life to adolescents would mean the end of my school if and when the government heard about it. He was not convinced, but one day when driven into a corner, he smiled and said: 'I guess if I'd a school I'd have to be a damned coward, too.' 'Reich,' I said, 'you couldn't run a school. You are far too impatient and dictatorial.'[11]

But although Neill never crossed this particular line he was now quite explicit as to his own beliefs: he declared roundly that no argument against youth's love-life held water – all were based on 'repressed emotion or hate of life'. He consoled his bad conscience with the reflection that in the non-moral attitudes sustained at Summerhill some, at least, of the perverted factors in sex lessened or disappeared – 'the voyeur element, the purely pornographic, the guilty leering element'. He had no evidence as to the quality of his pupils' sex-life after they left school though he knew that many married – sometimes old schoolmates but more often they found partners from other schools; he thought that they brought up their own children in a more enlightened way than most* – though he did not give them a blameless report on this for some, he thought, had not grasped the difference between freedom and licence.

Reich seems never to have had any of Neill's caution in facing these issues. As early as 1919 he had written in his diary: 'From my own experience, and from observation of myself and others I have become convinced that sexuality is the centre around which revolves the whole of the social life as well as the inner life of the individual.'[12] For Reich it was to be the centre around which the whole of his life's work was to revolve. In the

---

* There is now some independent evidence on this point (see Chapter 11).

early twenties he became one of the youngest members of Freud's inner circle, but though for some time he was one of the Master's favourites he soon became something of an embarrassment to the psycho-analytic movement as his political activities increased and as he tried to persuade other members that socio-political thought and action were a vital concern of theirs. The coupling of his left-wing social doctrines with an insistence on an extreme form of the theory of the sexual basis of neuroses was not the kind of mixture that the conservative-minded doctors wanted any truck with. He was expelled from the German Psychiatric Society in 1933 and from the International Association the following year after the publication of his book *The Mass Psychology of Fascism*.

These expulsions were painful to Reich. They seem to have been handled in a rather devious fashion, and to have partly been instigated by some internecine vindictiveness: but they probably were a correct recognition that Reich was, to put it gently, no longer an orthodox Freudian. To Reich, though, it appeared as though he was remaining true while the movement defected from itself. He maintained that he was extending Freud's theories rather than developing an alternative. His ideas no more rivalled Freud's, he said, than Newton's theory of gravitation rivalled Kepler's laws of planetary motion. He probably intended all the obvious implications of this casting, for he was not inhibited by any false modesty; but as he tells it the story is not implausible. It is true that Freud fancied the idea of finding a biological basis of neurosis and this is the ambition that Reich set himself and claimed finally to have achieved. Freud concentrated his interest almost entirely on the 'psychoneuroses' (which had their origins in childhood, in incest fantasies or castration fears, and were the psychic expressions of these distant, but living, conflicts) and largely ignored the 'actual neuroses' which, lacking a psychic etiology, were relatively uncomplex, present-day disturbances caused by the misuse of sexual energy; he considered that they could be dealt with by the simple elimination of harmful practices. Reich, however, made the 'actual neuroses' his particular interest. He had noted a passing remark of Freud's to the effect that every psychoneurosis probably centred on an actual-neurotic core, and he took a literal interpretation to Freud's speculation that an actual neurosis was a misdirection of biological energy. This concentration of interest led him to the development of his technique of character analysis (which directed the analytic attention to the patient's present-day gestalt) and culminated in the breakthrough that resulted from his discovery of the orgone which, he claimed, was that biological energy about which Freud had speculated.

But even before the advent of the orgone he was developing his notions of what he called sex-economy. 'The safeguarding of the distribution of goods requires a rational economic policy. A rational sexual policy is not different if the same obvious principles are applied to sexual instead of economic, needs.'[13] What these sexual needs were Reich learnt partly through his clinical experience but also as a result of his work at a number of sex-hygiene clinics that he had opened first in Vienna and later in Berlin. At these clinics he gave lectures to many thousands (he claimed) of men and women of working-class origin, and in listening to, and answering, their questions he formed the impression of widespread unhappiness and anxiety stemming from the inability of these people to make effective adjustments to their sexual functioning. These difficulties were so widespread that he felt justified in coining the term 'the emotional plague'. In his judgement, about 70 per cent of those who came to his clinics needed treatment, and for the majority of these two or three years of intensive therapy would have been required. Obviously this would be impossible to supply and so he concluded that prophylaxis, rather than therapy, should be his major concern, and he turned his attention to the possible origins of the plague.

Most obviously it seemed to him that 'the authoritarian, sex-suppressing family upbringing' was the immediate cause, but he also recognized this upbringing as an integral part of the organization of industrial society: it was the means by which children were brought up to be characterologically submissive and thus be ready to occupy the subservient role that society required of them. Their parents unwittingly colluded with the capitalist masters. Education was harnessed to the life-repressive regime that society required, and the system was self-perpetuating since children reared in this anti-life fashion would grow into parents who could rear their children in no other way.

This analysis was one which had an obvious affinity to Neill's point of view: he too had formed the impression of ubiquity of diseased attitudes to sexual functioning among the children who came to Summerhill, and he too had attributed this to the authoritarian – or, as he called it, the moralistic – upbringing that almost all children were subjected to. He too expected that their liberation from such training would result in their wanting to rear their own children in different ways and would thus enable them not only to break free from the compulsions imposed by the 'Old Men' who control society but also to break the chain of transmitted neurosis. But while Neill chose to create a small demonstration of this process of liberation, Reich attempted to harness political action for the promotion of a large-scale prophylactic programme.

He had been a member of the Social Democratic Party in Vienna and he joined the Communist Party in 1930 when he moved to Berlin. He hoped to persuade the policy-makers within the Party that beyond the economic misery, which was manifest, lay the psychological conditioning by which the system was maintained and that unless this was replaced by a life-positive education the revolution could not sustain its liberating aspirations. He wanted to establish a Freudo-Marxian synthesis. Freud – or at least Reich's adaptation of Freud – focused, as Marx had done, on the concrete needs of a humanity suffering under the yoke of its own society; like Marxism, psycho-analysis was essentially dialectical, its theme being psychic, rather than economic, conflict; and both concentrated their attention on the inherent contradictions within existing society that threatened its own destruction – Reich maintained that bourgeois morality was repressive to the point that it created neurotic disorders on such a scale that they could not be contained but must at some point explode in revolutionary action.

He did not disagree with the Marxist economic analysis but he questioned its revolutionary validity by pointing out that revolutions had in the past always reverted to authoritarian ideologies – and, he argued, inevitably so, for such ideologies were anchored in the character structures of individuals and any purely socio-economic change still leaves this basic ideology imbedded in individuals. If it is to last, then, revolutionary action must dislodge the grip of the patriarchal authoritarian family and institute a programme of sexual reform.

Reich failed to persuade the Party to accept his analysis. In 1930 he published his own manifesto, *Die Sexualität im Kulturkampf*. He extended it in a second edition in 1936, and the English edition came out in 1944 under the title *The Sexual Revolution*. Had he produced this work ten years earlier he might have had more success; but it first appeared at the beginning of the Stalinist phase of Russian communism which spelled the end of the hopeful adventures in socialist sexual freedom (see Chapter 8). Reich was expelled from the Party in 1932, almost at the same time as he lost his membership of the Psycho-analytic Society, and he gradually abandoned hopes of helpful political action. 'Politics has definitely played out,' he wrote in the preface to the English edition of *The Sexual Revolution*, and by then he had pinned his faith to science as the means by which humanity would be led to a happier social condition. He went to Oslo to lecture particularly on his technique of character analysis which was then recognized as an important contribution to psycho-analytic method. In Oslo he also had the use of a laboratory, and it was here that he made his discovery of orgone energy and of the bion (a microscopic vesicle charged with orgone energy). In the years that followed this initial discovery he claimed far-reaching consequences ranging from a cancer-cure to weather-control; unfortunately, no one outside his own laboratories seems to have been able, or as he would have said, inclined, to rediscover this life-energy, and most authorities have dismissed all of his biophysics as a set of insane imaginings – 'the wild and fantastic hobbies of Reich's later years', as Marcuse has put it.[14]

Neill did not commit himself on this issue, explaining that he did not have the scientific expertise to judge this part of Reich's work and that in any case what he was interested in was the psychological side on which he felt that Reich had made immense contributions. But he did incline to believe that Reich had made genuine discoveries in his biophysics – he reported for instance seeing a motor running in Reich's American laboratory apparently by orgone energy and he kept at Summerhill, and used, an orgone accumulator – the device by which Reich focused and concentrated the free orgone energy in the atmosphere. On one occasion he sent one of Reich's books to H. G. Wells hoping to get an independent assessment but received only a curt and unencouraging reply. In the face of almost universal disparagement it is difficult to retain any confidence in this later work of Reich's, and his wife's biography of him shows with little doubt that he was overtaken with paranoid delusions in other respects. On the other hand, there are two sides to a state of paranoia. As early as 1930 Reich had experienced calumnious attacks on his character and moral integrity and he had understood them to be the almost inevitable reaction of the victims of the emotional plague to one who attempted to unmask the disease. 'I knew that nothing could compare in hatred and bitterness to this reaction, nothing in the world could match this reaction in its silent murderous instigation of human suffering,' he wrote.[15] Since that time Reich had been continuously attacked, and had been rejected by his professional colleagues, by his political associates, and by the orthodoxy of science. Not so surprisingly, the Nazis had banned his books, but when finally the American administration did the same it is at least understandable that he felt this as the final blow in a world-wide conspiracy against him. He died in prison, sent there for his refusal to comply with this last instruction for self-suppression.

It does not seem realistic to regard Reich's madness as belonging to him alone. As R. D. Laing observed: 'The extent to which Reich is ignored cannot be explained rationally, and invites an explanation along his own lines – viz. the [emotional] plague is no respecter of professional boundaries, and psychiatrists suffer from it as much as anyone else. One of its symptoms is an inability to see that one suffers from it.'[16] Neill put the point another way: 'Doctors and scientists stormed against his orgone theory, but one does not usually storm against what is called a crank theory. Folks do not hate a man who believes the world is flat. They laugh at him. They did not laugh at Reich; they dismissed him as a paranoic. All I can say is that if Reich were mad, and, say, the men in the Pentagon and Westminster are sane, the world is an odd sort of place.'[17]

Neill's first indebtedness to Reich was on account of the personal therapy he received. Their association developed into a long and mutually supportive friendship. On the professional side Neill's ideas expanded in two main directions as a result of this association: on the matter of adolescent sex, and on the question of infant-rearing. In the preface to the English edition to *The Sexual Revolution* Reich declared that 'the suppression of infantile and adolescent sex-life [is] the basic mechanism by which character structures supporting political, ideological and economic serfdom are produced'. His clinical observations of patients whose vegetative energies were released from their fixation in muscular armouring suggested what was possible. Their total behaviour changed once their infantile fixations had been dissolved and their genital inhibitions and anxieties had been eliminated. They became able to establish 'natural contacts' in place of the previous 'unnatural pseudo-contacts' with both their own impulses and with their environment. A 'visible development of a natural spontaneous behaviour' in the patient was accompanied by a capability for 'regulating his life and solving conflicts in an un-neurotic way'. As the natural impulses regained their realm so a 'natural' morality took over from the familiar compulsive morality, and the anti-social impulses were eliminated.

Reich realized that individual treatment could never produce changes on a mass scale and he looked for ways by which more widespread effects might be made possible. He rejected the Freudian view that instinctual repression was a necessary condition for man's cultural achievements and he maintained that the conflict between instinctual and cultural man was inevitable only for what he called the patriarchal authoritarian society with which Freud had been familiar. The dissolution of the authoritarian family unit was the first essential in Reich's revolutionary programme for this was the main breeding-ground of a conservative ideology. It was also, he maintained, the origin of much misery engendered on the one hand by its enforced life-long monogamy and on the other by the triangle situation between a child and his parents. The familiar oedipal tensions were aggravated for the child by his being forbidden the release of masturbation or of sex-play with other children. Adolescents had to face the dual problem of the after-effects of their family-rearing and the tension caused by their sexual maturity contained by the social demand for sexual abstinence. Reich's experience of proletarian youth in Europe convinced him that their impulses led them to deviate from the social demands in ways which led them only to further misery and dissatisfaction. He compared this situation with that revealed in Judge Lindsay's book *The Revolt of Modern Youth* which described the wide extent, and the unsatisfactory nature of, the sexual activities of the relatively well-to-do American adolescents. Both situations were, he concluded, chaotic.

Reich insisted that this intolerable family structure was maintained by, and for, the economic arrangements of society. So long as the family was dependent on the male wage-earner he was both tied to the family and given a dominance over it. In revolutionary Russia this was changed for a while partly by edict and partly by the institution of such things as factory creches and youth communes and schools which were not based on orthodox authoritarian assumptions. But the absence of any clear formulation of principles and the lack of guidance in finding satisfactory modes of regulating domestic and sexual behaviour led inevitably, as Reich saw it, to the regress which came after a decade of confused experimentation. By the thirties the regress was complete: divorce laws were tightened, abortions again made illegal, the family whose patriarchal structure had been loosened was re-instituted, children were disciplined as before and made subject to moral demands as stringent, or more so, as those in any bourgeois society.

In America and other western countries the weakening of the patriarchal family seems to have been effected by increasing national affluence, but it is doubtful whether the adolescent is any better placed now to carry through a sexual revolution than the young communards of the early Soviets. Reich is frequently quoted by the young revolutionaries of today but in many ways his demands are too stringent for them and it may be that what is developing is merely the chaotic situation that he feared; what he graphically described as 'a free-for-all fucking epidemic'[18] may be replacing the original form of the emotional plague. He had always recognized a danger to his revolution from the young revolutionaries themselves who would have been perverted in infancy. He therefore wanted a period of controlled change analogous to the temporary dictatorship of the proletariat envisaged in classical communist theory. He argued, perhaps quite reasonably, for the necessity of a censorship prohibiting 'pornography and mystery stories as well as gruesome fairy tales for children' to protect them against the implanting of sexual anxiety and guilt-feelings. But there are stronger undertones of paternalism when he writes, in what seems to be more of an instruction than a prediction, that youth must be made to feel that they can build their own lives but 'this will not induce them to neglect their general social tasks'.[19]

It is this strain in Reich's make-up that causes some of today's young radicals, in spite of their general approval of him, to chide him as an 'old fuddy-duddy'.[20] As Neill had told him he was impatient and dictatorial, and his role as an apostle of freedom did not fit as easily as it did Neill. Yet even he could not avoid assumptions that seem to be a residue of a 'bourgeois morality'. He observed, for instance, that children who came late to Summerhill showed a tendency 'to be promiscuous in desire if not always in practice, and here I mean changing partners too often'.[21] Of course, he would argue that this was not a moral criticism, that promiscuity was evidence of a weakness in psychic structure that precluded fulfilling relationships. But this is a dangerous kind of argument. An adolescent may need a period of promiscuity for quite straightforward reasons and is no more to be criticized for it than an infant who is promiscuous in his sex-play.

However, Neill cannot be accused of any great degree of inconsistency of this kind. He was much more concerned with getting his educational practice right than with prescribing behaviour. He persevered with his conviction that the human organism was capable of appropriate self-adjustment so long as its power in this regard was not atrophied by continuous other-adjustments. He was providing a demonstration of the kind of prophylaxis that Reich sought, and from the mid-forties on his major preoccupation was with infant-rearing.

In 1947 he had his first and only child, Zoe, who was brought up from the start according to the principles to which Reich had given the term 'self-regulation'. Neill first began to write about this in *The Problem Family* and he described it fully in *The Free Child* which he wrote when Zoe had lived her first five crucial years.

Self-regulation is the extension of the freedom that is Summerhill into the years of infancy, to the first minute, in fact, of a child's life. Neill has tended to give all the credit for the idea to Reich, though in fact Homer Lane had spelled out the principles twenty-five years earlier. The chapter on Infancy in his only book is written entirely in the spirit of self-regulation but Neill's work with children of school age had led him to overlook this. However, as his experience increased, he became more and more aware of the limitations of the benefits of freedom: there was always a residue of ill-effects from faulty treatment in infancy. The child who had had the usual controlled feeding schedules as a baby, who had been subjected to early toilet-training, who had experienced unnecessary frustrations and fears and who had unwarranted restrictions placed on its play, particularly on sex-play – such a child coming to Summerhill at four or five and staying there until about sixteen would be only a 'semi-free child'. There were few truly free children – but Zoe was to be one.

In describing Zoe's development Neill tried to suppress the natural partiality that a father could not avoid and he described her short-comings as well as the overwhelming catalogue of satisfactions. He mentioned her tetchiness after an occasional short night's sleep, for instance; he discussed the fact that at five she was still wetting her bed; and he was worried by her refusal to decide sensibly on the clothes she should wear. This was the only point on which her parents interfered with Zoe's own decisions on a matter that concerned solely her own welfare. If they had allowed it, she would have run about naked all day in all weathers. As it was she would shiver with blue nose and cheeks, resisting all attempts to persuade her to put on more clothes, so that they felt they had to 'bully her into wearing what we think she ought to wear'. This was the one apparent failure of the theory on which self-regulation is based – that the human child will respond intelligently to its biological needs if it is allowed the freedom to do so. Neill maintained that it did not disprove the theory so much as demonstrate the lack of courage on the part of himself and his wife to act according to their convictions.

In other matters they were content to let Zoe follow her own decisions. Perhaps this meant that she did much as the Neills' would have wanted her to do, but this was because their ideas were based so firmly on an assessment of children's wants: her decisions were often not the ones that most parents would have made.

There was no potty-training, and this delayed her acquisition of bladder-control which most parents would expect from children at a much earlier age. From birth she was fed whenever she seemed to be hungry and this meant frequent feeds for the first two months of her life after which she took larger quantities at longer intervals. As in other matters, Neill counselled parents to follow a child's expressions intelligently, and though insisting that a baby must never be allowed to 'cry itself out' he did not want parents to assume always that a crying baby was hungry. After she was weaned, she would choose, from what was available, the food she wanted and this worked well, although she ate less than her parents would have expected. In fact, at five Zoe showed little interest in eating: she would leave a box of chocolates untouched at her bedside for days, and if she was called to play by another child in the middle of a meal she would leave her food and never return to it. But her parents were not worried by this for she was obviously in good health. Neill was particularly interested to notice that when she had a cold Zoe would feed just on fruit-juices. To Neill with his interest in nature-cures (for years he regularly visited a Dr Thompson in Edinburgh) this was a significant indication of his belief in an untrained child's capacity to respond to its bodily needs.*

* Dr Carl Rogers in a quite different context also credits infants with what he calls 'an organismic valuing process'. He refers to an experiment in which young children had a score or more dishes of natural (i.e. unflavoured) food spread in front of them. Over a period of time they were found to 'value the foods which enhanced their own survival, growth and development'. They might gorge themselves on starches but would balance subsequently with a protein binge. If one selected a diet deficient in some vitamin he would later seek out foods rich in that vitamin. See *Freedom to Learn*, pp. 242–3.

In fact Zoe grew according to the best of Neill's hopes and expectations. She developed an inventive imagination and a joyful sense of fun; she was supple and 'as relaxed as a kitten'; she showed a loving disposition (mostly, it seems, her love was directed towards animals); she had an uncomplicated attitude to sex and to bodily functions in general, showing no more than a passing interest in her own and her parents genitals; she indulged in no infantile masturbation and showed neither interest nor disgust in her excreta. Much of her behaviour led Neill to doubt the reliability of many of the developmental characteristics attributed to children, and though realizing that he could draw no general conclusions from the evidence of one child he thought there was enough in his observation of Zoe to suggest that many assumptions about child nature may be valid only for a trained child.

There were few other self-regulated children in the school to provide Neill with corroborative evidence. Yet he was totally convinced of the correctness of this method of child-rearing and of its far-reaching effects. 'The observed results so far suggest the beginnings of a new civilization,' he declared. Others may not have felt ready to agree with that, yet scores of outsiders, Neill claimed, had said of Zoe: 'Here is something quite new, a child of grace and balance and happiness, at peace with her surroundings, not at war.' When she was two, Zoe appeared as cover girl to *Picture Post*[22] and under the heading 'The child who never gets slapped' Susan Hicklin gave a balanced report of the self-regulation method and its apparent results. She thought Zoe was 'bright-eyed, strong-limbed and unafraid of people. Her movements have a steadiness rare in such a young child . . . [she] has the straightest legs I have seen in any child'. Marjorie Proops, then writing for the *Daily Herald* gave a similar testimonial.[23] She reported finding Zoe happy, healthy and uncomplicated, mentally and physically in advance of many children of the same age. She was full of admiration for Zoe's parents whose 'sincere efforts have produced a lovely, lively creature, unselfconscious and never showing-off'.

The interest of the popular press in Zoe's upbringing is partly accounted for by the fact that at this time the methods of infant-rearing were being strongly influenced – among the middle-classes at any rate – by Dr Spock's book *Baby and Child Care* whose recommendations differed little from Neill's. In fact, Neill had seen the book in the States before it was published in England and had described it as the 'best book on babies I have come across . . . It is nearer to self-regulation than any book I have seen.'[24] Spock was more influential than Neill for a variety of reasons, not least of which was his very reassuring manner. He seemed to imply that if parents were not always right, at least they were so most of the time and might always be right if only they allowed themselves to follow their common sense.

Neill, on the other hand, implied that for the most part parents were lamentably wrong – not, of course, that this was their fault, but just because they had been themselves reared in an anti-life way. There is never a problem child, he had long been saying; there is only a problem parent. Now he amended this for the apparently suicidal age of the H-bomb to saying that there is only a problem humanity.[25] Thus it seemed that he could be speaking only to a minority. Spock, though, embraced all young and well-meaning (that is to say, middle-class) parents like a good-natured grandfather, telling them not to worry, but to enjoy loving their funny little kids. Moreover, he did not seem to be suggesting, as Neill may have been, that they throw all their babies out with the bath-water. Time-table feeding? Sure, the doctors and nurses will prescribe schedules (Dr Spock was an American), but it is the rhythm of the baby's digestive system that sets the schedules. The mother should follow her instinct without any hesitation, nursing the child as soon as he starts to cry. She does not have to bite her nails waiting for the clock to say it's feeding-time: she adjusts the schedule to the baby. But, Dr Spock adds, this is not an argument against reasonable regularity; we all come round to regular meals sooner or later and it is good that mother and baby should work towards a schedule. Then there is the little problem of 'handling the genitals'. But really it isn't a problem at all. Baby will explore himself whilst sitting on his potty. But it will only last a few seconds. It won't 'come to anything or start a bad habit. You can distract him with a toy if you want, but don't feel that you've *got* to.'[26]

It was all so very reasonable and reassuring – permissive for parents as well as children. It was a handbook on how to prepare for the sexual revolution without actually revolving – or at least without getting giddy – and this, at a time of a mild swell of permissiveness, made the book very acceptable. So much so in fact that it became possible to talk of the 'Spock generation', and later the genial Doctor, when protesting against the Vietnam war, could speak out in defence of 'his' children. However, whatever the extent of Spock's influence in the States, it seems fairly certain that in Britain he helped to change only middle-class practices. Neill was well aware that he too reached few parents of the working-classes, and was also aware that, especially in sexual matters, the industrial working-classes were far more tightly in the grip of repressive attitudes. This is borne out, for instance, in the extensive study carried out in Nottingham by John and Elizabeth Newson and reported in their book *Patterns of Infant Care*. The figures relating to parents' attempts to suppress genital play, which Neill regarded as a crucial measure of anti-sex training, are striking. Of the mothers who reported genital play by their children the percentages in the various socio-economic classes who attempted to check it were as follows:[27]

I and II	III (w.-c.)	III (man.)	IV	V*
25%	50%	57%	69%	93%

The severity of the actions taken by those mothers who did attempt such suppression seemed to follow a similar pattern by class. None of the mothers in classes I and II did any more than to 'take his hand away' or 'put his nappy on quickly', while a third of the mothers in class V, and 'a few' of the class III mothers who tried to stop masturbation, did so by smacking. This class-pattern of smacking did not extend to the treatment of other 'offences' except that rather fewer of the class I and II mothers smacked their children: 44 per cent of these mothers smacked their infants for 'all offences', while in the other classes this proportion ranged from 53 per cent (III, w.-c.) to 60 per cent (III, man.) with class V at 58 per cent.†

This picture of working-class mores corroborates Reich's account of the way in which the workers collude with capitalist intentions in keeping their children in submissive attitudes, though Reich can hardly be said to have had any realistic programme for changing this state of affairs. Neill too could only hope to have an indirect effect. He admitted that his school was a middle-class one, though he insisted that it was so not by choice, as he thought the public schools were, but by necessity, since its only financial support came from the fees that it earned. He accepted too the charge that his school was an island, isolated from the community in which it was set. He hoped that it would influence people on the mainland: they came to visit him frequently and he sent them his books. But though he was a critic of the larger society he did not aspire to being its saviour. His contribution was his school and his books: he was determined to protect his school and to run it according to his own ideas with as little compromise as possible.

At the same time he was obviously not just a schoolmaster – in fact, it sounds odd even to refer to him as one. 'I am interested in life, not in schools,' he wrote;[28] and the extension of his doctrine to apply it to infancy underlines this. In making that extension he completed his synthesis of freedom: the freedom of the infant in determining its own feeding habits, in enjoying its chosen ways of exploring its own body and the

---

* The classification is the usual one by fathers' occupations. That is, I and II, professional and managerial; III (w.-c.), white-collar workers; III (man), skilled manual workers; IV, semi-skilled workers; V, unskilled workers. See Newson, J. & E., op. cit. pp. 152–6.

† The Newsons note that these figures, relating as they do to the treatment of babies in their first years of life, do not give an accurate reflection of the numbers of parents who use, or approve of, physical violence on their older children, and remarks made to the interviewers suggest that many more parents would not have hesitated in chastising their three- or four-year-old children. In 1949 a Gallup poll reported that 60 per cent of parents were in favour of corporal punishment. Our society does not appear to have become any more permissive in this respect.

physical world around it, and its relations with other children and adults. The freedom of the child continuing from the self-regulation of infancy was largely a freedom in play and expression, and it developed into the freedom of adolescents in using their maturing sexuality, in finding their appropriate mode of work and in developing their own moral attitudes. From such beginnings would develop men and women fit to enjoy the freedom of what Reich rather overbearingly called a work-democracy. It would have been contradictory for Neill to have attempted a description of what this might be like, and for the most part he refrained from doing so. He said only what he thought it would not be like.

REFERENCES

1 *The Problem Teacher*, p. 68.
2 *The Free Child*, p. 11.
3 See W. Reich, *The Function of the Orgasm*, pp. 114–21.
4 *A Dominie's Log*, p. 77.
5 *A Dominie in Doubt*, p. 158.
6 *The Problem Child*, p. 23.
7 *The Problem Teacher*, p. 80.
8 *That Dreadful School*, p. 77.
9 Ibid. p. 81.
10 *The Free Child*, p. 38.
11 P. Ritter and A. S. Neill, *Wilhelm Reich*, p. 24.
12 W. Reich, op. cit. p. 44.
13 Ibid. p. 222.
14 H. Marcuse, *Eros and Civilization*, p. 191.
15 W. Reich, op. cit. p. 194.
16 *New Society*, 23 March 1968.
17 *Talking of Summerhill*, p. 78.
18 W. Reich, *The Murder of Christ*, p. 94.
19 W. Reich, *The Sexual Revolution*, p. 264.
20 Quoted in R. Neville, *Play Power*.
21 *The Free Child*, p. 49.
22 *Picture Post*, 11 June 1949.
23 *Daily Herald*, 16 May 1949.
24 *The Problem Family*, p. 144.
25 Ibid. p. 9.
26 B. Spock, *Baby and Child Care*, p. 295.
27 J. and E. Newson, *Patterns of Infant Care*, p. 201.
28 *The Problem Family*, p. 125.

11 The Bare Minimum of a School

There have been a few, but only a few, first-hand accounts of Summerhill life outside those in Neill's books. Best known, and probably most significant, is the report by two government inspectors who went there in 1949.[1] They surprised Neill by the extent to which, in his terms, they were able to adjust their usual assumptions and only in one paragraph did he think that they 'failed to rise above their academic preoccupations'. The report surprised others, no doubt, in that it accepted the school as a quite possible variant, as well as in its corroboration of so many of Neill's own claims about his school: that the children were full of life, showing no signs of apathy or boredom; that they were friendly, pleasant people with delightful (if not always conventional) manners; that qualities of initiative, responsibility and integrity were developed; that the children seemed able, when they left school, to fit into the society they then had to live in.

The inspectors' criticisms were mainly to do with the conduct of the academic work. They were not impressed with the results of the system of optional study, but significantly they condemned it not in principle but only in the way it was operated. The main defects they singled out were the lack of a good teacher for the juniors, the surprisingly old-fashioned and formal teaching methods elsewhere in the school, the poor guidance given to the children in planning their studies, and the lack of privacy available for study. Neill did not think any of these criticisms unfair but the remark which he felt betrayed the inspectors' limitations praised him for creating a situation in which the most intelligent kind of academic education could have flourished but regretted that the opportunity thus opened up was being missed because in the inspectors' view such education was not in fact flourishing.

In commenting on this Neill claimed that examination results showed that the system worked perfectly well for the child who wanted an academic education. But the passing of examinations was surely not the object that the inspectors had in mind when they wrote of an academic education 'of the most intelligent kind'; no doubt they were thinking of the more creative possibilities which were opening up in other schools at that time. Yet to import such additional aims might well have disturbed the priorities to an extent which would endanger the gains which Neill prized. His refusal to encourage his staff to develop advanced teaching methods has been due not just to lack of vision in this direction: he has also had a well-based fear of wheeling in a Trojan horse.

Professor Harry Rée has observed: 'One of the secrets of Summerhill has always been that it is – as I heard a recent visitor describe it – the bare minimum of a school.'[2] The elaborately structured and equipped school is advertised as giving more freedom because it offers more opportunities but in practice the elaborations as often act as constraints as freedoms. Neill purged his school of inessentials, stripped away all the demanding extras so as to leave, as it were, some rudimentary toy which the children were each able to use for their own discovered and changing purposes.

It may be, however, that in discouraging 'academic learning' to the extent that he did, Neill reduced his school to below the minimum. A number of his ex-pupils appear to think that this was the case. An American, Emmanuel Bernstein, has interviewed fifty of these Old Summerhillians in order to assess the various effects of this schooling.* Twenty-six of this sample complained of the lack of academic opportunity and the dearth of inspired teachers. There is such a dearth at most schools, of course, and the descriptions that these ex-Summerhillians gave of their teachers is probably no more damning than might be expected from a group of ex-pupils of any school, though certainly it was of a different kind: 'Some padded about in sandals, growing long beards, content when the children cut class. Others ran about the school grounds plucking children from trees and trying to lure them to their lessons.' Neill would not have approved of this: he strenuously opposed efforts of persuasion in this matter coming from teachers or parents or from children who tried to lure others away from lessons. Perhaps he was unaware of children being 'plucked from trees' yet the school society was so open that he could not have remained ignorant for long of such capers (if in fact they ever happened). Yet it was always difficult to know how much Neill was seeing: one ex-pupil has suggested that 'he was at once curiously aware and yet unaware of what went on in the school'[3], while another thought that 'seeing

* The results of Bernstein's study are reported in *The New Era* (February 1967) and more fully in the American magazine *Psychology Today* (October 1968). It is from this fuller account that the quotations in this chapter are taken. Bernstein comes from the University of Oregon; he seems to have been sympathetic to, but not totally convinced by, Neill's thesis. Visiting Summerhill he found it 'interesting', but felt that a knowledge of the way in which pupils adjusted to life when they left the school was lacking and that such knowledge was necessary before judgements could be made. The fifty ex-Summerhillians (twenty-nine men, twenty-one women) to whom he gave lengthy interviews were all living in London. Their ages ranged from sixteen to forty-nine years (median age: twenty-three). The average number of years they had spent at Summerhill was 4·3, with a median of seven years. (An odd distribution: unless there is a mistake in the reporting, these figures imply that a large proportion of Bernstein's sample were at the school for less than eighteen months.)

Neill at Summerhill is like seeing the tip of an iceberg. He is in touch with everything yet he seems to be totally oblivious.[4']

In a profile of Summerhill, Nicholas Tucker, an educational psychologist, described the situation as regards lessons like this: 'Pupils treat them rather as lectures, to be attended or not according to how one feels or whatever plans one may have. When they do rejoin a class it will be small enough for each pupil to be taught individually. There is no fear of being left behind by the stately march of a classroom syllabus. The lessons themselves seem fairly popular.' He adds, I think misleadingly, that 'with no other activities laid on and going beyond the grounds forbidden in school hours, it seems fairly inevitable that pupils will go to at least some lessons.'[5] The children were confined to the grounds during school-hours because of the British law of compulsory school-attendance. But within the grounds it always seemed to me that children found plenty to do. This impression is borne out by one pupil whose profile appeared in the magazine *Id*.[6] This boy, John, went to Summerhill when he was nine, having previously made 'good academic progress at a private school. However, during his first 5 years at Summerhill he rarely went to lessons as there was always too much to do outside in the grounds with a very pleasant gang. Looking back on it he feels that with very little encouragement he would have gone to lessons but they seemed unimportant at the time.' In contrast the next profile[7] told of a boy, Keith, who was at Summerhill from age five to seventeen years and 'went to most lessons and attributes this to the fact that he never went to a school where lessons were compulsory.' These two were at the extremes; somewhere between could be quoted a third pupil, a girl, Carla, who came from the States when she was twelve, something of a misfit at her previous school, unhappy and isolated. Lessons had seemed pointless to her and she spent her spare time reading, drawing and playing on her own. 'I did all the same things at Summerhill but nobody minded. One is *tolerated* there.' She found herself at last making contact with her fellow pupils: 'I spent a lot of time sitting around with other people just talking.' She went to lessons sporadically: she did some woodwork and embroidery and read 'books on theology from Neill's library'. She left when she was sixteen, determined to go to university, and studied privately for the necessary O and A level passes.[8]

Of these three pupils, the first, John, developed an interest in music and became a teacher of woodwind instruments; Keith became a doctor and Carla is equipped for university. None of them saw any reason to complain of the lack of academic opportunity or encouragement at Summerhill as so many of Bernstein's sample did.

Set against those complaints, however, is an effect which may support the inspectors' suggestion that it was not the system that was at fault so much as its application. Six of Bernstein's sample returned to orthodox schools before they were twelve years old: five of these were enthusiastic about the effect that Summerhill had had on them. Though behind in academic attainment when they started at their new schools they quickly caught up and thereafter progressed rapidly and with real pleasure in their studies. As one of them said: 'I couldn't understand why all the other children stopped working when the teacher left the room.' (The sixth one of this group had been unable to adjust to Summerhill, having absconded from there, as he had from his previous schools.) This suggests that if the Summerhill teachers had offered more interesting and meaningful lessons those children who stayed there might also have found real interests in study rather than merely regarding it as a necessary preparation for examinations.

However, it does not seem from Bernstein's reporting that his sample had been permanently handicapped in their careers. Ten of the fifty had passed university entrance examinations (though four of them had had to spend two or more years cramming). Eight had graduated from universities. Bernstein lists thirty-three different categories of occupation shared among his sample (thirty-four if to be unemployed is an occupation!). They could be re-classified as follows (the figures giving the number of ex-pupils in each class of occupation):

Professional	10	Arts and crafts	7	Technical	3
Clerical	12	Housewife	6	Student	3
Manual	8				

This does not present any obvious surprises, bearing in mind that the Summerhill intake is largely middle-class but not selected on any academic basis. The figures do not bear out the impression that Neill gives that a fairly large proportion of his pupils find work in one or other of the Arts, but the overall picture is certainly not one of a group of people unable to make their way in life through not having been compelled to go to lessons through their childhood.

This bare minimum of a school has also been minimal in its physical amenities for most of its fifty years. 'There are no carefully laid-out flower-beds, school-crests and fresh paintwork to greet you at Summerhill. The elderly redbrick mansion looks gaunt and rather shabby, odd outhouses are scattered around, including some converted railway-carriages; there are broken swings and see-saws; and the hockey pitch is covered in thick bumpy grass* . . . Inside, the building is warm and clean, sparsely furnished, and has the rather battered appearance of a well-used playroom.'9 The grounds are in reality a great adventure playground, though

* It is *many* years since hockey was played on it!

with a large well-cultivated vegetable garden in it, unfenced and generally unmolested. There are greenhouses, too, with sheets of unbroken glass, and alongside them is the 'san' also glass-fronted, which is a dormitory for younger children, the 'san kids'. Scattered about the grounds were various huts in which lessons were conducted. Bryn Purdy, a sympathetic visitor who spent three weeks at Summerhill in 1961, wrote of these huts: 'The classrooms are little more than sheds, and are drab, uninviting, and, in colder months, inadequately heated. The books are such as a modern-minded junior school might have cast out 20 years ago . . .'[10] Purdy made his visit at a time when Summerhill, with only twenty-five pupils, was in such a low state as to be in danger of closing. The inspection of 1959 reported that 'the buildings are in general need of considerable expenditure on decoration and maintenance, and living conditions both in the house and in the huts have an austerity usually associated with extreme asceticism'. The inspectors conceded, however, that what would appear 'painfully primitive' to adults might hold 'character and charm' for children.[11]

Since then the influx of large numbers of American children and the energetic fund-raising by many of the school's friends have together revived its fortunes. Some £10,000 has been spent partly on a swimming-pool, partly on some cedar-wood cabins to replace the drab sheds and the converted railway-carriages, partly on central heating, and partly on redecorating and refurbishing the main house. I remarked to Neill on the transformation when I last visited him (1970) perhaps with a tinge of nostalgic regret in my voice. 'Yes,' he said, 'it's not right. We've had to compromise with these inspectors and their blasted regulations.'

The main buildings house the most important units of the school: the kitchens and dining-room, the art-room and the meeting-hall. Upstairs there are bedrooms and staff bed-sitting-rooms and Neill's untidy and gloomy study. A staff-room leads off the main hall and near by is the 'kids' sitting-room' whose chairs are now well-upholstered though they used to display their springs and stuffing uncaringly. The dining-room too is much more salubrious than in the past though still furnished with old deal tables and uncomfortable chairs. Down a dark corridor is the squarish, panelled hall that generally stands empty by day but in the evenings and at week-ends is noisy with games, pop-music and dancing. And it is here that the school meeting is held every Saturday evening. On one part of the panelling are pinned the rules which have been argued out at these meetings. As Nicholas Tucker observed: 'Summerhill is not, and never has been, that dreary cliché, a do-as-you-please school . . . The rules are written with an engaging if occasionally ungrammatical candour; a pleasant change from the constipated style usually reserved for such matters.'

Dont hide behind the boiler. All man-holes out of bounds. After 10 p.m. no one may leave its room except to go to the bogs. You must have Neill's permission to cut large branches off trees.[12]

The rules are enforced, as well as decided, by the children, offences being considered by a 'tribunal' appointed afresh each week by the school meeting. Any member of the community may bring any other member before this tribunal either for a breach of one of the rules or for some unfair practice. There is the opportunity for appeal against the findings of the tribunal at the school meeting which may reverse a verdict or change a penalty. A reversion to primitive and sadistic retributions in the manner depicted in *The Lord of the Flies* is often feared from such a situation. That this does not in fact happen at Summerhill confirms Neill's contention that the events depicted in Golding's novel represent, not a reversion to the primitive, but an aping of adult norms which the children had observed and experienced. Children from an authoritarian school might well act vindictively against one another, but Summerhill attempts to create an atmosphere of approval and the children have no reason but to act in the same spirit.

The school meetings do not deal only, or even mainly, with misdemeanours. A meeting may last up to an hour of which generally not more than the first ten minutes are occupied with business left over from the tribunal meeting. Then other matters of communal concern will be discussed. Verbatim records of three of these meetings are reproduced in an American publication, *Living at Summerhill* by Herb Snitzer, and judging from my own experience these were fairly typical meetings. The following summary of the first of them will give an idea of the way in which the time may be used. (The numbers in brackets denote how many lines of print each item occupied in Snitzer's book.)

- (9) Tribunal report.
- (19) Appeals.
- (6) Request to keep the doors of 'the carriages' closed.
- (9) Complaint against a boy for going 'up to the balcony'. Warning.
- (28) Noise at supper-time, leading on to a discussion about the powers of the dining-room officers.
- (4) Request from staff-member to keep 'foreign bodies' out of the linen closet.
- (12) Request from staff-member to refrain from banging on the door of the hut where music (Sinatra) sessions are in process. (Neill: Who is this chap 'Sinatra'?)
- (7) Request for the return of a missing book (*A Dominie Abroad* by A. S. Neill). (Boy: Who is this chap 'Neill'?)
- (6) Request for the return of a lost pen.
- (3) Request not to leave lights on unnecessarily.
- (8) Request that boys should lift the lavatory seat when urinating.

(19) Reconstitution of the cutlery committee.

(22) A case of bullying: Toro complains of Earl and Paul. Decision to display notice: 'Earl and Paul love Toro'.

(10) Children under 15 going into village during morning. Reminder of rule.

(20) Reminder that coffee-bar in the village (where there had been a knifing incident) was now out of bounds.

(26) Discussion about the lending of money. No decision.

(10) Complaint that Cottage kids (under-7's) wake people up early in the morning. They should go to end of breakfast queue if they do. Carried.

(6) Request to stop bothering kitchen-staff for mail.

(6) Announcement about magazines being put in sitting-rooms.

The second of the three meetings that Snitzer recorded followed much the same pattern as this, but the third was unusual in that it was occupied almost entirely with the discussion of one item – the ethics of offering rewards for lost objects. It seems worth summarizing this discussion in some detail as an example of the way in which the meetings were used for the working out of what may be called the dialectic of freedom.

It was Myrna who introduced the subject by pointing out that 'certain people' were taking advantage of rewards being offered by stealing things, waiting for a reward to be announced, and then 'they queue up for the reward for finding something they stole in the first place.' She proposed that no rewards should be given for anything found. 'We should be honest enough with each other,' she said, 'so that if we find anything we should give it to Carole to post on the board, and not wait till a reward is put up.'

In the discussion that followed there was no inquiry whether this practice was in fact prevalent, no suggestion of an attempt to find out who the con-men might be who were pulling such a trick, and no moralizing beyond Myrna's original statement. That it might, or did, happen was the reality and the meeting concerned itself simply with the proposal that rewards should be banned. Brendan was the first to object to this: it was up to the person who wanted to give a reward, he thought. Myrna's proposal, he considered, was in effect an unwarranted bureaucratic encroachment on his liberty. Myrna at once saw this side of her idea and modified it to suggest that the community should decide on the size of the reward. Carole intervened to observe that the worth of a lost possession depended on how the owner felt about it, not on any absolute value. 'Why should the community decide how you feel about it?' she asked. Again Myrna amended her proposal. Now she wanted a rule that would require that anyone wanting to offer a reward to bring this to the attention of the community. 'You have to make an announcement before the community before a reward can be posted.'

The chairman, perhaps seeing a chance of cutting short a tricky wrangle, took a quick vote on this very much modified proposal. It was defeated, mild as it was. Perhaps the meeting still read into it the spirit of Myrna's original proposal. Roy asked that the vote be taken again, but Wilf intervened to say that this should not be necessary. He tried to conciliate by suggesting that 'all Myrna is doing is appealing to the community not to bring up a reward straightaway.' And Myrna agreed that that was all she wanted now.

However, Carole, not following the course of the discussion too logically, reminded the meeting that 'sometimes a reward is a good thing', and she recalled an incident when a visitor's keys were lost and the reward she offered resulted in their being found on the hockey field within a couple of hours. Myrna, in spite of her retreat, was perhaps making her point: for Carole, who had defended the individual's right to decide about a reward, seemed now to be conceding that it was only sometimes a good thing.

A move that the subject be dropped was opposed by Wilf who thought it too important an issue. Rewards *did* encourage people to steal and he thought the meeting should face this fact. Carole objected: rewards were useful, encouraging people to keep their eyes open. Wilf agreed and said he didn't want rewards to be banned: 'It is just a suggestion that before you offer a reward you appeal to the community. No one said you had to do this. You can do what you want.'

Now it was as if the meeting suddenly realized that this attempt to find a formula was leading them into meaninglessness. Everybody abruptly reverted almost to their original positions. Scott said he thought the thing was personal to whoever lost the article. 'I don't think we have a right to say that someone cannot give a reward when he or she wants to. Nobody has a right to say that. It's your life.' Myrna then withdrew most of her concessions, returning to her earlier point of view that the community should decide when a reward was necessary. If she hoped to make any headway with that, she was deluded. The first objector, Brendan, came back emphatically: 'Hell, no! If I decide I want to put up a reward, that's my business – not yours.' At that the chairman moved the meeting on to the next business. 'I think we've talked this subject dead,' he said.

We have to read this interchange in ignorance of the personal feelings that lay behind it, and because of this we are likely to miss much of the significance of the dialogue. This is an important aspect of the Summerhill meetings which it is possible to appreciate only through first-hand experience. When Neill talks of the therapy of freedom he omits to mention that the freedom of Summerhill may be effective only because the conflicts which it enables the children to act out are also articulated publicly at these meetings. It seems probable that the opportunities for self-construction that Summerhill offered were fully used only as the children heard themselves and others voicing their inter-relationships. It is the process which is harnessed in group therapy, but it is not only a therapeutic tool: it is equally a means of quite normal self-expansion and self-identification which is used to some extent in formal and informal groups which are felt to be supportive.*

It is possible that this process was sometimes hurtful particularly to the more sensitive children (and adults). The discussion quoted above cannot have been an easy one for Myrna, for instance; on the other hand, in these meetings the children generally have more choice as to how far they will expose themselves to scrutiny than in the teacher-directed situation. Furthermore, when the setting is compassionate and non-moralistic there is always someone in a group who will support one against whom the tide of feeling may be flowing too strongly. Myrna had such support in the above exchange from Roy and from Wilf.

The more withdrawn child would probably not make very much active use of these public discussions and there has been a suggestion (in Emmanuel Bernstein's follow-up study of Summerhill pupils) that the 'gregarious, aggressive people seemed to benefit most' from a Summerhill schooling and even that it had a 'negative effect on the more withdrawn, quiet ones'. The detail of this latter suggestion is unfortunately a little obscured in Bernstein's reporting of his findings: the complaint would seem to have been made by at most seven out of the fifty people in his sample, and not all for quite the same reasons – lack of protection against bullies, insufficient help in academic studies, falling into the habit 'giving up too easily'. Naturally, the school cannot be held responsible for all its failures (nor for all its successes, for that matter): for instance, Bernstein describes how he had to interview one of these seven, 'a thin, shy 24-year-old', in the presence of the mother who 'always answered for him, even interrupting him when he did start to speak'. But if there is a class of pupil for whom the school was unsuitable this cannot be dismissed simply by suggesting that it was a minority. It might also be that the meetings were dominated by an extroverted minority, but experience of groups which function over a prolonged period of time suggests that this is not so likely to happen as may be supposed. If a count is made of the contributions to the three meetings recorded in Snitzer's book, it is found that no less than thirty different people contributed at one or more of these meetings. This is certainly over half the school population – perhaps about two-thirds if the very young children, who would not be expected to speak very much, are counted out. In the course of all three meetings there were 191 separate contributions; only four people made more than six remarks. These four include the chairman and Neill, who made sixteen remarks though many

* See also A. J. Grainger, *The Bullring*, Pergamon Press, 1969.

of them incidental – humorous ones, or complaints that he could not hear the speakers. Four people besides the chairman contributed to all three of the meetings, and ten to just two of them.

Neill's definition of Summerhill's freedom as the right to do anything which does not interfere with the freedom of others is only the starting-point of a complex concept, as he must have known and as the children had themselves to discover. They explored the implications of this elementary definition through their everyday living and through the articulation at the school meetings of the tensions between individual freedom and social regulation.

Such learning is possible only when the problems under discussion are real – that is, not just in contrast to imaginary or simulated problems, but in situations where the decisions are about matters that are felt to be of vital concern and where it is known that the decisions will in fact be adhered to, untampered by adults who may feel them to be unwise. This means that the social life is regulated by those whose social life it is, rather than by a few people who consider that they know best how it should be ordered. Neill has insisted on this even when a particular group has appeared not interested in doing so, or has seemed to be finding it too much for them. Typical of his refusal to take back this responsibility is the instance recalled by one of the pupils, Barbara: 'Last term the older kids had just left and a few of us were just getting to be the older ones. And it's quite a responsibility. We got a lot of new kids – about fifteen, I think. And they were so terrible. And they would have been alright if they'd been left alone. But we had a lot of other kids who wanted to influence them, rampaging up and down the corridors, wrecking our rooms. And we went up to Neill in tears. And he said there wasn't much he could do, and we would have to try and cope as best we would. We felt, "Fuck you, Neill!" We felt some of them should be chucked out – they were too disgusting to cope with. Then we felt we really could cope if we made an effort. We wanted Neill to chuck them out because it would make our life easier. But then we felt sorry for *them*. So we thought we'd give it a try for another two terms. And in fact they've been a lot better.'[13]

The revue song of the thirties which lampooned the school – 'Everything free and easy, Do as you darn well pleasey . . .' – did not include the realization that the self-regulation of social living is no easy thing. The opposing criticism that the responsibility is too great a strain for children is not borne out by the passionate way in which they defend their freedom if it seems threatened. Barbara, quoted above, was obviously pleased that she and her friends had overcome their difficulties themselves. And to quote from another pupil (also contributing views for the book *Neill and Summerhill*, though in fact this remark was not included): 'No, I've never longed for the old autocratic Head who'd settle everything in an instant.' (He had recently come from a state school.) 'That's mainly because I felt that in the old type of school the Head never did settle anything. He just made a decision.'

All institutions require that people in them make some form of adjustment both to the institution and to the people in it. Different types of institutions encourage different types of adjustment. The most obvious feature of the adjustment which Summerhill fostered was the quality of tolerance. Bernstein reported: 'This characteristic was mentioned by 24 of the [50] former students as most typical of a Summerhillian. Their definition of tolerance was accepting people as they are, without regard to race, religion or other label.' The latter part of this definition gives it a rather formal aspect, and it is possible that some at least had a more personal quality in mind. The novelist, Leonora Eyles, also singled this out as a characteristic of Summerhill children and in fact complained that her daughter's experience there had made her 'too tolerant to people who behave badly to her and to others, but most especially to her: it is a lovely thing in her, a generous and serene thing. But it may give her unbearable burdens to carry.'[14] Mrs Eyles ascribed this to the fact that there was too large a proportion of problem children in the school to whom the 'normal children' had to adjust. Her daughter was at Summerhill in its early days, but though Neill tried to reduce the proportion he has found that there is no hard line between the 'normal' and the 'problem'. Most children, it seems, use the freedom of Summerhill at some time to express some anti-social feelings, so that most children appear to be problem children at some stage. Those with whom Barbara (quoted above) and her friends were plagued were evidently in such a stage. Neill has suggested that if he could have afforded it he would like to have had a kind of prep school for Summerhill to which all pupils would go until they seemed to have exhausted their need for anti-social expression.[15]

Bernstein's sample of ex-pupils also made frequent reference to the quality of the relationships between the sexes: the ability to form satisfying relationships of this kind and a 'healthy attitude towards sex' were, in fact, the two benefits of a Summerhill schooling most universally felt. Bernstein felt that this was confirmed by what he could learn of their present domestic circumstances. Eleven of his sample had married and most of these seemed happily married though three were divorced, two having subsequently re-married 'apparently with success'. Bernstein described their relations with their children as 'warm, free and easy'; all were raising their children in a self-directive way and 'the children appeared happy and spontaneous.' Spontaneity is, of course, supposed to be one of the main attributes of the free child: in fact, it is almost tautologous to say so. Erich Fromm singled

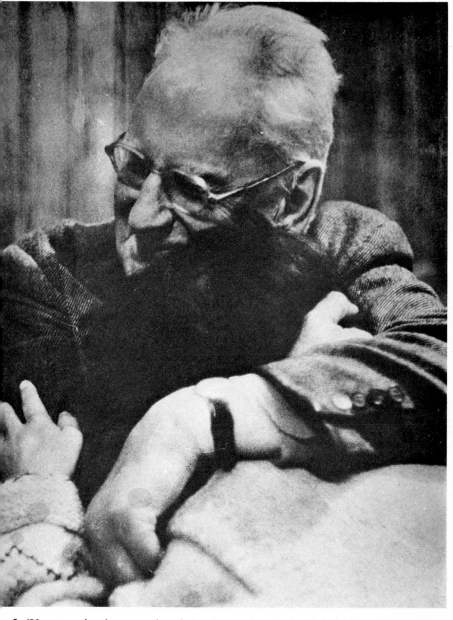

5. 'You may give them your love but not your thoughts' – Kahlil Gibran

Main house and grounds

Main house   Lesson huts   Greenhouse   'San'
Workshop

6. The Summerhill buildings, Leiston.

out this quality as the route to freedom for modern man. Neill has often described his Summerhill children as natural and sincere. The government inspectors commented in their report on the 'naturalness' of the children and this is not an uncommon judgement for visitors to make. Sincerity, after tolerance, was the second most commonly chosen attribute by Bernstein's sample of ex-Summerhill pupils when he asked them what they thought was the mark, if any, of 'the Summerhill personality'.

These fifty ex-pupils were also asked what they felt to be the main benefits of their schooling to them personally. As already stated, the two most commonly mentioned benefits were to do with their sex attitudes. Third on the list was the acquisition of 'a natural confidence and ease with authority figures'. The reverse effect is often expected from a Summerhill upbringing, as it is assumed that the ability to work within an authority structure requires a childhood training in subservience. In fact, this may often produce resentments which prevent a reasonable acceptance of authority or it may engender fears which make for too blind an acceptance. It may be prescribed by authority figures who are themselves insecure in their roles, but it is not productive. As a company manager told one of Bernstein's sample whom he was promoting to a junior executive position: 'You're the only one on this staff who is not afraid to tell me what you're thinking and how you really feel about things.'

How far the children see Neill as an authority figure it is difficult to judge. They certainly recognize him as being in charge of the school. Barbara and her friends (quoted earlier) turned to Neill for help in dealing with the rampaging juniors. They wanted him to 'chuck them out' and knew that he could have done so, even if they also knew that he would not. In the school meetings, Neill takes no special position formally, speaks not very much more than anyone else, has the same voting rights as everyone, proposes motions as others do and finds some of them accepted and some rejected.* Yet he does intervene occasionally with speeches that are obviously statements of authority. An example occurred at the end of the third meeting reported in Snitzer's book. Immediately after the discussion

---

* An example of this was shown in a television programme in 1968. A TV team was filming a feature on the school and the question arose as to whether the camera should be allowed to film the scene at the school swimming-pool where habitually many of the pupils and some staff bathe in the nude. At the meeting where this was discussed, and itself filmed, Neill spoke strongly and with obvious feeling against the idea. He maintained that the public have a perverted attitude to sex, that the sight of nude adolescents on the TV screen would be seen sensationally and misinterpreted, and that whatever else was shown of the school the nude bathing would be all that was remembered. Some pupils argued that a full and truthful record of the school should be shown and that there was nothing they had to be ashamed of. Neill's arguments were overruled in the vote, and the nude bathing was filmed and shown on the pro- gramme '24 Hours'. (After which, incidentally, the BBC was inundated with calls of shocked protest. They refused to comment.[16])

on rewards the chairman called on him to speak. His opening sentence looks in print as though it might have come from any headmaster: 'I want to say something quite serious, and I don't want any laughter about it.' He then said, 'I made a law at the beginning of this term about smoking if you are under sixteen.'* He explained why he had made this law: that because of the cancer threat, the government had told all schools to discourage children from smoking and 'Summerhill can't stand out against the whole of the schools of England'. But now he found that many underage children were still smoking 'and quite openly . . . Some of you think I'm an old softie. Neill is an easy-going guy. Well, I'm going to tell you all something'. What he told them was that they either had to stop smoking or he'd tell their parents that they could not come back to Summerhill.

Neill: I'm going to have this law carried out for my own safety and for yours as well. So don't feel you can come here, and do as you like. You can't.
Chairman: Right. We've all heard Neill. You take it from there. Is there any more business? Meeting closed, then.

I don't want to imply that this kind of intervention was at all usual. On the contrary it was very exceptional, made only because of his anxiety about the state of public opinion at the time and about possible repercussions if he failed to take strong action. (Summerhill was by this time featured fairly regularly in the press, and this particular event was reported nationally: the *News Chronicle* headlined it: 'Laying down the law',[17] though later that year the *Daily Mail* was still referring to Summerhill as 'The Smoke-and-Swear School'![18]) However, the fact that Neill felt it in order to make such a statement certainly implies that he saw himself as retaining an ultimate authority which he was prepared to use. The children too must have realized this aspect of Neill's position among them.

It is probably fair to say that where Neill exercised his authority he did so by defining the boundary conditions within which the community operated. As he said in the course of his statement about smoking, 'I can't punish you. Only the community can punish, but I can say, all right, if you don't want to live the Summerhill way, you're not coming back.' He chose to do this at a point where he saw a dangerous interaction between the school and the society outside, and he saw his action primarily as a defence of the school rather than as a sanction against individual children. In general, he tried strictly to avoid participating in any of the community's punitive actions and would always abstain from voting when such questions arose.

The relationships that the children had with Neill were public and pri-

* The phrase '*I* made a law' suggests that Neill considered this matter to belong to one of the categories for which he reserved the right of decree. It may have been a 'danger-to-life' rule, or one made to ensure conformity to national regulations.

vate. No doubt the private relationships were varied but the norm seems to have been one of a breezy friendliness, coupled with deeper resources of reliability and helpfulness at times of personal difficulty. The friendliness recognized a distance, however. He was not 'one of the gang'. He conscientiously avoided the use of nicknames, for instance. Commenting on this one ex-pupil explained that nicknames could be two-edged and could be something that a person might really hate. Neill's avoidance of their use is a small indication that despite the surface casualness of his contacts with the children he did regulate them with some care.[19] Much of this care was no doubt second-nature to him, stemming from his attitude of respect for each individual's feelings which was unobscured by any need to preserve a lofty presence. One visitor sensitively described an incident illustrative of this in a letter to the *Guardian*.[20] An article the previous week by A. V. Wood had described a Summerhill meeting at which a row developed when a boy protested that on reaching the age of twelve he had gone to re-claim a knife which Neill had earlier confiscated from him according to a law which forbade children under twelve the possession of dangerous weapons. This boy had found that Neill no longer had his knife. The letter (from Mr C. Butler) revealed that the writer had also been present at that meeting. 'The most memorable part of this incident to my mind,' he wrote, 'was when A. S. Neill trudged upstairs to his office to fetch all the penknives, then down again, and then went across the room to show them to the boy. No crooking of the finger and saying, "Come here, you!" Instead he went over to the boy.'

Neill liked to joke with the children but he preserved his own brand of humour rather than adopt theirs. It was another reminder of distance which he was not too concerned to close. 'The first thing you think of when you think of Neill is his sense of humour – which is actually highly warped, but still funny,' said one pupil.[21] They did not all understand it, but of course Neill was delighted when they did. 'He met a boy of six in the drive. *Boy:* "Hullo, Neill!" *Neill:* "Hullo, would you do something for me?" *Boy:* "I might – what?" *Neill:* "Could you fetch me the front door?" *Boy:* "O.K." (runs off; back again in a few minutes), "Sorry, Neill, someone has taken it."'[22]

The distance was there, but the children generally seem to have found it quite bridgeable and in fact many visitors have remarked on the easy way in which the children talked to him. Paul Ritter, for instance, wrote: 'It is almost unbelievable when up to this dour Scot – looking distinguished in the extreme, despite his intentions and comfortable clothes, and with whom so many visitors just cannot make conversation – up to this large, tall, grey-headed figure, whose greatness seems almost forbidding to adults, dashes a little lad, saying "Hey Neill. Seen Jane?"'[23]

The public relationship was also curiously mixed. The children seem to have had an affection for him that persuaded them to tolerate his old man's idiosyncrasies – they allowed for many years that in their Saturday evening dance every third record should be one of Neill's – which meant that the rock-'n'-roll tempo was regularly slowed down for an old-time fox-trot or waltz. 'He's a lousy teacher,' said one frankly;[24] and others have said much the same, meaning, presumably, that they found it difficult to feel that they were learning from him. Yet they went to his lessons. Perhaps it was that long ago in Germany he had decided that the 'brilliant teacher' was a bad educationist. For he was not incapable. His story-telling was an enchantment of vicarious involvement for the younger children that was so important to get right that they would become impatient with him – and be able to tell him so – if the story was going the wrong way for them. Reich's wife recalled her experience of one of these story sessions. 'The spell which Neill cast over all of us left an indelible impression. It was so real that on that same evening two little girls whose room was next to mine came up to me, and in a conspiratorial way asked me if I really had those papers [which had figured in the story] in my room.'[25]

At the school meetings he would have his effects while seeming to be ignored or even laughed at. Often he would display impatience and it would be difficult to tell whether he really felt it or whether he was trying to provoke a disorderly or careless meeting into some more constructive mood. Were his sly humorous interjections spontaneous pieces of fun or were they designed carefully to deflate the importance of some discussion? Probably the adult was inclined to read more into such casual actions than was warranted: the children often seemed puzzled and would react in silence, but at other times they would be roused to attack uninhibitedly. A striking example of this is found in another verbatim report in Snitzer's book – this one not of one of the regular Saturday school meetings but of a 'Tuesday evening discussion' in which Neill would introduce a subject of fairly general concern. On this occasion the subject he chose was swearing.

In many ways, Neill seemed to be acting out of character at this discussion, and again it is not clear (and possibly was not clear to those present) whether he was just posing as the reactionary who wanted to take away the freedom which Neill, the radical, had given. It could have been an educational ploy of this kind, but I think in fact that he was expressing genuine worries: for all his passionate conviction, Neill was very conscious of the threat which his own boldness carried and this was probably one of the times when he had to express his fears and test the validity of his teaching by hearing its echo.

He opened the discussion by saying that he thought there was more swearing currently in Summerhill than usual, and he wanted to know why.

Immediately he got a battery of stock answers. There were a lot of new kids who had not been allowed to swear at home; it's a habit; it's easier than thinking up some original epithet; here, it's sort of natural to swear; if you don't swear people here don't know what you mean; swear-words make the point; there's a lot of affection in it too. Then Neill said that he was worried because he feared that parents who hear the swearing might take their children away from Summerhill and when he pressed this point one boy perspicaciously asked him: 'Are you trying to have a discussion or are you trying to stop us swearing?' Neill: 'I'm having a discussion. I can't stop you swearing. You know that.' But the children obviously did not like it. 'It's our school,' said one. And another thought that if a parent took his child away because of some swearing, well, he was just looking for an excuse anyway. Perhaps the visitors would like the girls to wear dresses and the boys ties. So Neill threw in another argument: good manners. 'If you go into a Catholic house,' he said, 'it's not good manners to swear against the Holy Ghost.' But the visitors are coming *here*, the children objected: they can conform to *our* rules. Neill then reminded them that someone had recently said that the language of Summerhill children was a danger to the children of the village. He was told to go to the local cinema and listen to the language the local kids actually used. If you think we're bad, you should listen to them. And another boy said that at the school he used to go to the children would swear behind the teachers' backs all through the lunch-hour and playtimes ('or whatever the hell they're called'). But it was not a moral question, Neill insisted. It was a financial one. 'Am I going to lose a kid through swearing? That's my point.' The point was swept aside nonchalantly: 'How long has it been since you've lost a pupil that way, Neill?' 'I can remember one man who . . .' 'One man in over forty years of teaching, Neill?' And with that, they carried the attack to him. Would he rather have nice kids who only swear behind his back? And what about him – didn't he swear? No, he didn't swear, he said; but, when pressed, he admitted that sometimes he did say 'bloody hell'. He then took another tack: what about 'filthy sex stories'? Well, they're funny. But why are they funny? Why is anything funny? he was asked. Why do you like dirty jokes? He denied that he did; when he was a student – yes, he was famous for his collection, but he had thrown them away, except for one or two which have a point.

A girl protested: 'In the four years I've attended your lessons, you let out jokes to us every once in a while, and they've all been about lavatories, now why?'

Jerry: Oh Neill, you're finished now.

Neill: That's true, quite true. You see, I'm a psychologist, and I have to adapt myself —

Scott: Pack it in, Neill.

    Neill: — to the people who look the part. I guess all the classes you've been to have been anal-erotic. You're trying to defend your guilt by putting it on me.

Gwen: Come off it, Neill.

Marty: That's not good enough.

Millie: I guess this proves we're all pornographic slobs, so let's pack it in or change the subject.

Several voices: Hear, hear!

Neill: All I'm asking is that you be conscious of what you say, and control your tongues as much as you can when Aunt Mary's about. Okay, I think that's it for tonight.

Roy: Oh Neill, just when we get interested you always pack it in. What's on television?

Bruno Bettelheim, looking at Summerhill from across the Atlantic, considers that the changes which are effected in its students are 'all due to how they identify with him . . . From the moment they come to Summerhill, children are enveloped by Neill, by what he stands for and lives for. Everywhere there is the powerful impact of his person.'[26] This is a commonly expressed view especially by people who have not been to the school and who have not met Neill, and it is a view which is often used to discourage the spread of anything like the Summerhill form of education. It wouldn't work without Neill, is the message. Those who do go to the school, therefore, very often come away surprised to find how little Neill actually seems to figure in the everyday life there and what a quiet, unforceful personality he appears to have. 'He has the rare power of being a strong personality without dominating,' the two inspectors concluded.[27] Bryn Purdy puts it well: 'It is not that I wish to question the value of his presence, but it is not the towering presence of an Everest so much as the nine-tenths submergence of an iceberg. Neill is reassuringly *there* and the landscape of Summerhill, as it is at present, is unimaginable without him, but his main function is that of bulwark against the interference of the grown-up world into his child haven of freedom. If from such a short visit [three weeks] I can assess the regard in which he is held by the children, I should say with feelings of deep, if casually expressed, affection.'[28]

Yet it would be as foolish to deny that the contingencies of Summerhill are independent of Neill's personality and prejudices, likes and dislikes, as it is to assert that no one but Neill is capable of maintaining a school that incorporates the essentials of Summerhill, 'the bare minimum of a school'.

REFERENCES

1 *The Free Child*, pp. 162–72; *Summerhill*, pp. 75–88.
2 *New Statesman and Nation*, 17 March 1967.
3 J. Walmsley, *Neill and Summerhill* (unpaginated).

4 *Observer*, 9 August 1970.
5 N. Tucker in *Where?* No. 32, July 1967.
6 *Id*, 9, p. 7.
7 *Id*, 11, p. 23.
8 *Observer*, 9 August 1970.
9 N. Tucker, idem.
10 B. Purdy, *The Libertarian Teacher*, No. 4, Spring 1968.
11 Reported in *Times Educational Supplement*, 1 December 1967.
12 N. Tucker, idem.
13 Walmsley, op. cit.
14 L. Eyles, *For My Enemy Daughter*, p. 195.
15 *Id*, 5, p. 5.
16 *Daily Telegraph*, 20 June 1968.
17 *News Chronicle*, 11 February 1957.
18 *Daily Mail*, 10 August 1957.
19 Walmsley, op. cit.
20 *Guardian*, 22 December 1956.
21 Walmsley, op. cit.
22 Told by Lucy Francis in *Id*, 11, p. 10.
23 P. Ritter, *The Free Family*, p. 176.
24 Walmsley, op. cit.
25 Ibid.
26 H. Hart (ed.), *Summerhill: For and Against*, p. 104.
27 *The Free Child*, p. 170.
28 B. Purdy, idem.

12 Degrees of Freedom

As the machinery of the meritocracy developed its power, the fortunes of Summerhill faded. It was heads not hearts in the schools, and ever fewer parents were ready to risk their children falling behind in that competitive society for the sake of more ephemeral gains. Numbers at Summerhill dwindled so low that the closure of the school seemed imminent and his father's prophecy that Neill would end in the gutter began to look as though it would be fulfilled.

Yet ironically the press now discovered that Neill was more than just an eccentric crank who was good for titillating copy. His comments on such matters as the eleven-plus exam, the American colour bar, teenage violence, children smoking, and so on, were reported periodically through the fifties and into the sixties by both the popular and serious papers. They also kept the public informed as to the precarious state that his school was in, and seemed to do so with real concern. 'Who will help the Do-as-you-please school?' asked the *Chronicle*[1] in 1957, the year in which the Summerhill Society was formed largely for this purpose. But four years later, as the school celebrated its fortieth anniversary, the *Daily Mail*'s headline[2] – 'Unhappy birthday for that dreadful school' – and its report that there were 'only 24 boys [*sic*] left' indicates that the story had not changed. The *Mail* sympathized with Neill, pointing out that while his school seemed to be fading away, teachers elsewhere had been adopting some of his milder ideas. This was little consolation, but 'if just something created by this kindly, devoted man lives on, the lonely years of pioneering will not have passed in vain.' The *Herald*[3] expressed sympathy and quoted Neill's gloomy comment: 'I don't expect the establishment to like me, and as about 99 per cent of the people seem to belong to the establishment nowadays, I can't expect much support.'

Happily his forebodings proved to be unnecessary. Six months later the *New Statesman*[4] reported that numbers at Summerhill had risen to thirty-two, three months after that the *Queen*[5] put the number on roll at thirty-seven, and the following year Henry Fielding reported in the *Herald*[6] 'a modest boom for the "freedom schools"' in what he called 'the

---

* Burgess Hill had gone further in libertarian doctrine than Summerhill by doing away with all forms of sanctions against individual pupils. 'The community agreed to

market in happiness'. Although the Hampstead school, Burgess Hill* had been actually forced to close, Neill now had forty-five children on roll. This revival continued and security was established once and for all with the appearance in 1962 of Neill's compendium *Summerhill: a Radical Approach to Education*. Its American publisher, Harold Hart, had skilfully welded together passages from a number of Neill's books to construct a volume which gave a comprehensive view of what came to be known as 'the Summerhill idea'. Hart correctly judged that there would be a ready appetite for the book in the States, though he did so on meagre evidence. No bookseller there would place an advance order for even a single copy at its first announcement, for Neill was then virtually unknown in America. However, sales increased exponentially, until during the year 1969 over 200,000 copies were sold. It was translated into ten languages and became a worldwide best-seller.[8] It brought Neill not only royalties in plenty but also American pupils so that since its publication anxiety that the school might close through lack of support has been forgotten, though the threat of government action remained live.

In America itself the book (supplemented by a lavish article in the glossy magazine *Look*[9]) provoked an extraordinary Summerhill vogue. An American Summerhill Society was formed with the intention of opening an American Summerhill School. This did not in fact materialize, but a large number of private schools were started which advertised themselves as Summerhillian. This caused Neill more unease than satisfaction, for he had reports that many of these schools made somewhat wild interpretations of his ideas, and his alarm was such that he wrote a book specially for American consumption called *Freedom, Not Licence*.

In Britain, *Summerhill* came at a time when the revulsion against the meritocracy was finding increasingly desperate expression. Reviews of the book indicate a realization that there was relevant sense in what Neill had been saying since the war. In the *Spectator*,[10] for instance, John Vaizey asked: 'Why are parents so anxious to buy sex-segregated, academic, rigorous education to push their children through O level? To pose the question is to answer it. Mr Neill is pleased when one of his children becomes a competent motor-mechanic. We want our children to be brilliant surgeons, stockbrockers, white-coated workers.' Vaizey was talking to, and of, the middle classes, of course – the only section of society which could have patronized a fee-demanding school – and they were the last who would want to pull their children out of the rat-race to which the 1944 Act had geared the education system. Now it was dawning that to commit children

---

agree or agreed to disagree. This arose out of the realization, quite empirically arrived at, that in the final analysis punishments and coercion are negative, destructive elements in all circumstances . . . They were found to be ineffective and wasteful.'[7]

to such a ruthlessly competitive system was not the best basis on which education might stand. And there were fairly violent indications that both the 'failures' and the 'successes' of the system were finding it unacceptable.

TALK WITH US
understanding is free
understand us
we are part of one another
no more them against us
each one is indispensable
talking and working together
we create an education
education means
a lifetime growing wiser
is there anything more important?
wisdom equals thought
alive with feeling
what else can answer our questions?
the quiet voice of wisdom working
THAT IS THE REVOLUTION

The students and some staff of the Hornsey College of Art issued this declaration[11] after they had removed from control of their college what they saw to be an effete management interested only in prestige products. In their prolonged occupation of their college they demonstrated their idea of education; its affinity with Neill's is not difficult to discern – 'No more them against us – each one is indispensable – talking and working together – we create an education . . .'

The undercurrent of dissent eroding the foundations of authority began to be expressed in the mid-fifties and was shared in different ways by a surprisingly large proportion of the community. It began, perhaps, with Jimmy Porter's cascade of neurotic, destructive, impotent yet menacingly intelligent fury which seemed to spawn shoals of angry young men. Almost simultaneously the film *Rock Around the Clock* triggered a series of street riots, and rock 'n' roll became the medium of unfocused protest for the less articulate. Towards the end of the same year the Establishment too seemed to join the epidemic of violence with its demoralizing Suez 'adventure'. Violent crime, especially among the young, increased rapidly with an apparently free-floating anger directed against old women, shopkeepers or other gangs of youths who were wearing a different style of clothes. On a larger scale, H-bombs were being 'tested' in different parts of the world and youthful protest focused for a few years in the Aldermaston marches against nuclear warfare. Originally respectful of the law, this movement became more openly subversive with the formation of the Committee of 100 (of which, incidentally, Neill became a member, having himself arrested at a

Polaris base demonstration). It collapsed abruptly and violence generally subsided, giving way to gentler assault by satire and by the progressive discarding of most of the prevalent forms of sexual morality. Again the establishment outdid all subversion in the bizarre episode of the Profumo affair. Authority seemed now to be thoroughly discredited. Life-patterns lost their certainties. It became less easy to assume that the young would meekly step on to the ladders that had been set for them. They were seeking an alternative culture, an anti-culture.

'Our programme is cultural revolution through a total assault on culture which makes use of every tool, every energy and every media we can get our collective hands on . . . our culture, our art, our music, newspapers, posters, our clothing, our homes, the way we walk and talk and fuck and eat and sleep – it's all one message – and the message is freedom.'[12] That was one flamboyant declaration made on the occasion of the notorious 1968 Democratic convention in Chicago. The Paris students pinned a more solemn manifesto to the walls of the Sorbonne during the 'events' there in the same year: 'The revolution that is beginning will call in question not only capitalist society but industrial society. The consumer's society must perish a violent death. The society of alienation must disappear from history. We are inventing a new and original world. Imagination is the seizing power.'[13]

For all its confusing diversity this movement was at least clear in its negations. It expressed a passionate rejection of established moral and aesthetic values, of affluence, of the reification of humanity. It was searching for 'a psychic community, in which one's own identity can be defined, social and personal relationships based on love can be established . . .'[14] Concurrently, another set of changes was being quietly initiated within the schools, changes which, even if not the revolution they were often represented to be, do express a fairly thorough reversal of values by replacing the idea of education as an instrument of the producer-consumer society with the idea of education as a service to children. In the more extreme form (mainly in Infant and Junior schools) the 'needs of the children' became virtually the only criterion for educational choices, but even in the more moderate versions at least these needs were distinguished from the demands of society with a tendency to relegate the social demands to second place. This also involved a radical change in the teacher's exercise of authority for he was no longer defining from without, and imposing within, the classroom ends and means. The children, individually and collectively, were to contribute to classroom decisions. The teachers turned for an appropriate developmental a psychology to such sources as Piaget and Susan Isaacs who had constructed their models in similar open situations. The independent progressive schools had anticipated many of these changes and there is evidence that quite a number of teachers were looking at Neill's example particularly in the development of the new patterns of teacher-pupil relationship which were implied.

Changes in the secondary field are being effected more gradually. They were much more obviously influenced by the disillusionment with the meritocracy and as the inequities and wastage of selection and streaming become apparent the tripartite organization is being gradually superseded by a comprehensive system. But it is not only a question of organization: educational methods are being questioned too. The assumption of academic learning as the primary purpose of a school is no longer automatic, and the inculcation of associated modes of conduct is not necessarily an appropriate aim. Robin Pedley in his book *The Comprehensive School*, the first really influential publication on that subject, expressed the hope that the new schools would be translating 'liberal ideas about equal worth of all men . . . into more democratic social structures . . . If a comprehensive system came into being which merely hotted up the individual struggle for power, the rat-race for social prestige, it might be better that the reform had never been begun.'[15] He wanted pupils to be educated for active participation in a 'free democracy' by having them work and live in a school setting which 'is as democratic as the law of education and the incomplete maturity of the pupils permit'.[16]

The comprehensive schools laid claim to the title of the new progressives. At the Dartington Colloquy (1965) one headmaster, Peter Snape, explained: 'If you are working in a boys' Grammar School . . . your task . . . is to produce a certain type of boy for society. You select on entry those boys who will fulfil this role. If however you throw out that selection method . . . obviously we cannot stand for one type of child: we must stand for as many types of children as we have children on roll. So straightaway you are forced into a position of concentrating on the individual needs of the child.'[17]

Not all the new schools found this philosophy so inescapable, but the problems that many of them had to face provided a discontinuity which discouraged the mere acceptance of the assumptions on which the older schools had been based. Subject teachers began to recast their work in ways that often emphasized the accent on individual development. Teachers of English, for example, shifted their attention from the exclusive study of classical writers and the production of essays in set styles; instead books by contemporary writers were felt to be closer to the pupils' interests and experience, and children were encouraged to develop their own style and form of writing, following their own imagination and concerns with a new freedom. Teachers of mathematics realized that their subject was not solely a matter of learning ready-made techniques for solving peculiarly irrelevant problems, but that children were capable of discovering their own approaches to a mathematical exploration of their own world. Science lessons, likewise, became an active engagement in scientific inquiry rather than just a learning of established theories and an exercise in replicating other people's experiments to verify other people's answers to other people's questions. Some even more adventurously began to move out of the limitations imposed by the traditional subject organization which seemed to embody 'the ambition of the bureaucrat and systems-builder to deal only with foregone conclusions'. Albert Hunt headed a short article on 'The Tyranny of Subjects' with these words of McLuhan. He went on to observe: 'The child becomes a part of a pattern he never fully understands and is powerless to change . . . He is taught by experience that it is normal for other people to organize his life . . . The education system has, in fact, become a reflection of a society which gives the appearance of choice, but in which all major decisions . . . are taken in secret by experts without consultation, a society which deals "only with foregone conclusions".'[18]

With such a shift in values as this Neill was able to re-emerge as one who had developed on the small island of Summerhill a form of education that now looked not so perverse and misguided as it had done for so many years. The fact that his Summerhill *was* such an isolated island with such a select clientele told against him, for the new progressivism was reacting strongly against a 'hierarchical' *élitist*, establishmentarian, static, closed, anti-democratic'[19] society. But many were ready to accept that he had had no alternative but to isolate himself in order to mount his demonstration at all and that even though his pupils had almost all come from middle-class homes his education was not itself hierarchical, *élitist*, anti-democratic, establishmentarian!

As the sixties proceeded, Neill received increasing attention from both the mass media and from educationists. He was awarded honorary degrees by two universities. His observations on various social and educational issues, many of them outside his immediate experience, were welcome copy for the press. He wrote against the use of corporal punishment,[20] he regretted the proposed raising of the school-leaving age;[21] he conversed with Helen Parkhurst about the treatment of delinquents;[22] he supported Michael Duane in the struggle to preserve Risinghill;[23] he argued in favour of the legality of abortion;[24] he criticized contemporary education for ignoring the inner life of the child;[25] he described his use of spontaneous acting at Summerhill;[26] he reflected on old age;[27] he argued in favour of an apprenticeship form of teacher-training;[28] he commented on I.Q. tests[29] and on the permissive society;[30] he argued against all forms of censorship.[31] Additionally, he made several appearances on television, and Summerhill itself was given a national viewing. It was a remarkable reversal of fortune: only a decade earlier he had written: 'My public has been a special one. What might be called the official public knows me not. The BBC would never think of inviting me to broadcast on education; no university, my own Edinburgh included, would think of offering me an honorary degree.'[32]

This vogue was not attained through any modification of his basic tenets. Neill remained as uncompromising as ever. As the editor of the *Spectator* observed: 'While most pioneers tend to grow away from their youthful ideas, moving towards some slightly less unorthodox position, Neill has done the opposite: he has stuck to his early radical views and watched orthodoxy move towards him.'[33] The 'new morality', much discussed in the early sixties, was a case in point. Professor Carstairs had shocked many listeners to his Reith lectures in 1962 when he suggested that charity should be considered a higher virtue than chastity. *Honest to God* came the following year in which the Bishop of Woolwich declared 'Nothing prescribed – except love' – seemingly to return to that essence of Jesus' preaching for which Neill had been pleading for so long. The journal, *Twentieth Century*, devoted its winter issue of 1963 to a debate on contemporary morality: the editorial introduction to this debate started: '"The whole world is sick with morality," says A. S. Neill on a later page: yet what looks to him like a surfeit seems, to others, like chronic malnutrition.' Religious authority had dissolved, the editorial continued, class sanctions were undermined, righteous indignation no longer held power. Even a secular definition of morality, 'a man's conformity to the society he belongs to', did not help, since there was no cohesive society to act as reference. Yet it was not a situation of despair or alarm. 'The area of moral *concern* is enlarging and deepening inside the ideological frontiers although the range of moral *convention* is shrinking.'

This sentence nicely described the position that Neill had held for many years. It was not morality, but moralists that he had inveighed against. 'Any moral system which is imposed on a child,' he wrote, 'is nothing more than a castration of the child in his cradle . . . It is the moralists who are responsible for our present level of sex-crime and for the state of affairs revealed in the Kinsey Report.'[34] It was the familiar message, but expressed more pithily than before, as if he were picking up the Reichian mantle and speaking with Reich's conviction. 'Yet we continue in our anti-life, sex-negative society to mould our children: the child discovers his fingers and toes and the whole family claps with glee, but when he goes on to discover his sexual organs the laughter stops.' Given a sex-positive society, for which Summerhill stood, in which the adolescent is allowed a sex-life ('What else is he supposed to *do* with his sex?') and children are freed from the burden of guilt, the problems would dissolve. It was a long way off, he thought. He had recently proposed the motion in the Oxford Union 'That the Christian ideal of chastity is outdated': the opposition had won with a majority of eighty-seven. 'But in the forty years of Summerhill's existence there has been a steady movement towards freedom. Indeed it is the so-called progressive schools that have stood still, while some state schools, especially the state primary schools, have moved strongly towards freedom.'

The movement towards freedom, such as it is, has not been a steady one. This study has so far suggested that it has happened rather in two lurches, with a partial withdrawal between them and that these were primarily shifts in social orientation with educational repercussions. In the twenties the educational action was largely among the independent progressives, drawing inspiration from people like Edmond Holmes, Homer Lane, Montessori, and from the first wave of New Schools that had been founded at the beginning of the century. In the social and political confusion that preceded the Second World War this movement lost much of its radical conviction and was in no position to prevent the construction of a competitive and academically based education after the war. Almost alone, Neill still insisted that the revolution had been betrayed, and by challenging the consciences of several generations of teachers and by keeping his own alternative alive he may have given the necessary support to those who were ready to use the dramatic changes in social feeling to move educational thought and practice at least partly in his direction during the sixties. How far this was actually the case can only be inferred from what has been said by those involved in these changes.

At the Dartington Colloquy, Harry Rée testified to the influence that Neill had had on his own practice. 'I, personally, remember reading Neill, and as a result of that I introduced a school committee into my school,' said Professor Rée, referring to his days as headmaster of a grammar school. He went on: 'It was a simple thing to do and it made all the difference to the school . . . I wouldn't have done it if it had come just as an idea. Neill himself, sadly enough, doesn't seem to realize what an enormous debt huge numbers of us owe to him – and others like him – because he has put things into practice.'[35] In a similar vein, Mr A. B. Clegg, the Chief Education Officer for West Riding, has spoken of the admiration he had felt for Neill from his days at a London Day Training College at the beginning of the thirties and attributed to Neill some responsibility particularly for the change in opinion as to 'the blunderbuss treatment of bad behaviour by caning' and as to the bigger question of what he called 'forced learning'.[36] Robin Pedley considered the changing relationships between teachers and children as the most significant area in which Neill's influence has been felt. 'Neill, more than anyone else, has swung teachers' opinion in this country from its old reliance on authority and the cane to hesitant recognition that a child's first need is love, and with love, respect for the free growth of his personality . . . The magic of the inspired reformer is there in Neill's books, in his talks to teachers who still (1963) flock to hear him . . . Today's friendliness between pupil and teacher is probably the greatest difference between the classrooms of 1963 and those of 1923. The change owes much to Neill, and to others in independent co-educational schools who have practised similar principles.'[37]

An anonymous reviewer of *Summerhill* commented on 'how strangely unaware he [Neill] is of his deep and effective influence beyond Summerhill . . . Like Pestalozzi, Montessori, Froebel, Neill is primarily important as a teacher of teachers . . . even the Public Schools have felt his reforming power.'[38] Neill has certainly been cautious, even pessimistic, in assessing his own influence. Reflecting on his life's work, he wrote: 'I fear sadly that our progressive schools are not touching the root of the matter. We have little apparent influence . . . We are outwith the great domain of education; millions of school-children never even heard of us and their teachers are so circumscribed by classrooms and curricula and salaries, that even with the best will in the world they can do little to do anything much about education. After all, schools are fashioned by adults, and adults in a mechanized civilization that has so much that is meretricious and banal simply cannot fashion a good education.'[39] He wrote that, it is true, at Summerhill's lowest ebb in 1961, but even in 1967 he seemed no more hopeful: 'I wonder how anyone can be an optimist in this sick world,' he wrote then.[40] The sickness is such that whatever gains have been made over these fifty years are of precarious stability. This is particularly so of the advances in secondary education which is most vulnerable to the repressive forces of society: for it is there that the pressure is most strongly felt to equip the pupils – technically and morally – for their prescribed roles in adult life. Reforms in these schools often have to be carried through, if at all, against strong local opposition, from parents perhaps, or governors, or a local education authority, sometimes even from the pupils themselves when they find themselves caught in the cross-fire of conflicting values. Many such struggles must have been joined which have become causes of no more than local argument. A few have been contested in nationwide publicity, most notably the case of Risinghill School in London the closing of which in 1965 caused such consternation not only to the children and parents immediately involved but to many educationists throughout the country who saw wider implications in the case. The issue seemed to be whether a local authority could be relied upon to show sufficient breadth of vision and generosity as to support an educational experiment that challenged more basic assumptions than those involved by the introduction of teaching machines or new mathematics syllabuses. For the Headmaster, Michael

7. A Saturday-night meeting

8. A. S. Neill in his eighties

Duane, was avowedly trying to extend the essentials of Neill's form of education into the state system; and he tried to do this in a situation that most people would have predicted was an almost impossibly difficult one – in a large school, in one of the most deprived areas of London, with a staff not sharing his ideology and, as it turned out, with an equally unsympathetic local authority and inspectorate.

Although Neill has denied that Duane was a 'disciple' of his – he has always disliked the idea of disciples (by which he seems to mean unquestioning and unoriginal followers) – neither he nor Duane has ever denied a strong mutual admiration. Duane had been a regular visitor to Summerhill since about 1950 when he was headmaster of a school at near-by Lowestoft. Neill for his part quotes Risinghill as evidence that 'one can use love not hate in a state school . . . one answer to those who say that freedom is possible only in a boarding school for middle-class children.'[41]

Another man who, though obviously not a disciple of Neill's in the above sense, has nevertheless been strongly influenced by him, is R. F. Mackenzie. It was as long ago as 1934 that the influence first began to work on him when he was teaching at the Forest School in Fordingbridge. There, 'were teachers and pupils who had previously been at Summerhill and all the books about Summerhill were in the library. Neill brought not peace but a sword into the staff meetings.'[42] For Mackenzie, Neill's 'uncompromising outlook has compelled us to review our own facile compromises.' In the dozen years during which he has been guiding the fortunes of his school, Braehead in Fife, Mackenzie has had to struggle continuously with the local education authorities, councillors and school-governors, to avoid compromises. An account of his work is to be found in his three books about Braehead from which it becomes clear that the child's freedom is most precious to him and he sees examinations as particularly evil for the threat they carry to that freedom, since they are the instrument by which a child's own interests are subjugated. He is obviously keen to involve the children in his own enthusiasm, principally for nature and for history (Neill suspects him of 'a compulsion to teach . . . in spite of his brilliant heresies'[43]) but it is also obvious that he wants them to share his pleasures in their own way and for their own pleasure. His over-riding aim seems to have been that children who are given a large degree of freedom should be able to build confidence in themselves and be able to find their own enthu-siasm: his insistence that this was the aim for all his pupils led him to put into practice the 'comprehensive idea' so that when the local plans for comprehensive reorganization threatened to absorb Braehead into the Grammar School he saw this as a putting back of the clock: he felt that it was part of a process of reversion to the 'comprehensive' pattern that

M

Scotland had in pre-war days, when the Dominie would invest most of his energies to tutoring the 'lads of pairts' in Latin and Greek and set the others sums to do and spellings to learn.

How far this is a justified criticism must be left for those more familiar with the Scottish scene to judge. What seems clear is that Mackenzie has been forging one version of an education that derives much of its feeling from Neill. It is also clear that many other such ventures are being tried in other parts of this country. Even though there may be few schools which have crossed the line into Neill's court in the way that Braehead and Risinghill evidently did, there are many which are moving away from the traditional forms, and roughly in Neill's direction. If he has had any influence outside the independent sector it would be most easily discernible in such schools, and in an effort to make some assessment of the extent and form of that influence I recently approached a number of Heads of schools which independent and informed educationists had described to me as 'progressive'.

The word is notoriously ambiguous, but I was not looking for any ideologically closely-knit group so that it was not important that my selectors (all of whom were involved in teacher-training and as such would be fairly well acquainted with a number of schools in their neighbourhood) should interpret the word all in precisely the same way. I defined the schools that I wanted to contact as being of the kind that would probably not be approved of by most of the Black Paper writers.*

This gave me a list of 102 schools and to the Heads of each I sent a questionnaire. The first most striking thing about their replies was the number and fullness of them – 75 per cent returned completed forms. The fact that such a high proportion took the trouble to respond seems to indicate that they regarded the subject as being of some importance: at least it was one on which they wished to express themselves. This impression was confirmed by the large number who wrote at considerable length in response to the invitation to add any further comments that they felt they would like to make. A digest of these comments appears in Appendix 1.

The questionnaire was designed to inquire into three aspects: (i) what acquaintance did these Heads have with Neill's work? (ii) how much did they feel Neill had influenced developments in various aspects of education? (iii) how much, and in what ways, did they feel they had themselves been influenced by Neill? Details of the questions and responses are given in

---

* Professor C. B. Cox, incidentally, has himself attested to the influence of Neill. In a letter to the *Guardian*[44] he explained that the Black Paper does not oppose 'sensible reforms'. But two things he singled out for special opposition. The first was an exclusive reliance on discovery methods, and secondly 'we oppose the methods of Summerhill and A. S. Neill and argue that extreme progressivism does not prepare children for adult life in modern competitive society.'

Appendix 1: here I shall comment on what seem to be the more significant features of the replies.

Only four (or perhaps I should say as many as four) of the seventy-seven who returned completed forms had no knowledge at all of Neill. Clearly, television has given Neill a lot of publicity – fifty-three (or nearly three-quarters) had seen him on TV, while only thirteen had been to one of his lectures and only four had actually visited Summerhill. These last figures are low compared with those relating to his television appearances, but perhaps the one in six of these Heads who had heard Neill lecture is a quite high proportion. Nor was a television viewing the limit of their acquaintance for most: there were only ten (in addition to the four who had not heard of Neill) who had read none of his books: the average number of his books read was almost exactly three per person. This again strikes me as being fairly high, and would indicate that most of those who had any knowledge of Neill probably had a fairly good knowledge of him. The most widely read of his books were his last two (forty-two had read *Summerhill*, and twenty-seven had read *Talking of Summerhill*) and *That Dreadful School* (which twenty-nine had read). These are the only ones of Neill's books that have been in print over the last half-dozen years so it may be that at least some of this reading was stimulated by his TV appearances. But not all of his earlier books have been neglected: *A Dominie's Log*, *The Problem Child*, and *The Problem Parent* had each been read by at least twenty of my respondents. The book whose title at least was most obviously addressed to the profession – *The Problem Teacher* – was comparatively neglected: only nine of this sample of seventy-odd had read it. But that book had come during one of the troughs in Neill's popularity, while the more widely read books were written nearer the crests.

The second set of questions concerned Neill's influence on educational developments and I asked my respondents to express their assessment of his influence on nine separate aspects of educational practice by using a five-point scale defined as follows: A: no influence; B: some marginal influence; C: quite noticeable influence; D: very considerable influence; E: enormous influence. About 10 per cent of the respondents declined to play this part of the game. This was very understandable for any individual must feel his opinion, expressed in this way, is tentative and rudimentary. However, when a fairly large number of well-informed people do this thoughtfully (and from the way in which other parts of the questionnaire were completed it is obvious that the whole thing was done with care) then I think something emerges from the overall picture. There are two qualifications that must be made: firstly, whatever measurement is being made, it relates to people's *perceptions* of influence, rather than to the 'actual influence'. I do not find this worrying, since it is through these perceptions that influences operate. The second point is that the results can be used most reliably in comparing Neill's influence on the various items. Thus his influence on school curriculum was seen to be minimal compared with his influence on 'pupil participation in school affairs (self-government, etc.)' and on 'Teacher-pupil relations'. The 'curriculum' question I inserted as a kind of sensitivity check and it emerged as one would reasonably expect, I think, as the area of least influence (a mean rating of between A and B), with only three people giving a D rating and one an E. The mean rating for 'teacher-pupil relations' on the other hand was right in the middle of the scale, and seventeen people gave it a D rating, and five gave it an E.

These mean ratings were calculated simply by translating the five letters into figures from −2 to +2 and by taking a simple arithmetic average. The nine items received the following average ratings (they are listed in the order of their averages derived from all respondents, and their averages from primary and secondary Heads are indicated separately):

Item	Overall average	Primary average	Secondary average
What schools teach	−1·06	−0·96	−1·22
Spread of co-education	−0·64	−0·51	−0·75
Moral education	−0·62	−0·64	−0·59
The way teachers teach	−0·58	−0·52	−0·68
Sex education	−0·46	−0·46	−0·46
Use of punishments	−0·30	−0·30	−0·30
School discipline	−0·16	−0·23	−0·08
Pupil participation	−0·02	+0·02	−0·08
Teacher-pupil relations	0·00	0·00	+0·01

If these figures are to be interpreted in any absolute sense they seem to be saying that Neill's influence is seen not to be negligible in many respects, and that in about half the items listed he is being judged to have had 'quite noticeable' influence by a large proportion of these Heads. To take an item half-way down the list, for instance – sex education: exactly half of those who expressed an opinion rated Neill's influence on this matter as 'quite noticeable' (34 per cent) or 'very considerable' (13 per cent) or 'enormous' (3 per cent). As we go down the list these proportions tend (almost uniformly) to increase towards the E end of the scale, until for teacher-pupil relations we find 69 per cent placing their rating in one of these three categories, 25 per cent in the 'very considerable' category and 7 per cent judging his influence in this respect to have been 'enormous'.

In the third area of inquiry the respondents were asked to rate on the same scale their feelings about Neill's influence on their own practice. They were asked to make this a rating of 'overall influence' rather than of any specific aspect, and this may well tend to depress the ratings below those which might have been given in particular areas. Nevertheless nearly one half (45 per cent) of those who expressed an opinion (and only four of those who replied refused the question) rated the influence on themselves as 'quite noticeable' or more. The percentages* in the five categories were as follows:

A	B	C	D	E
19	38	28	11	4

The 15 per cent who placed themselves in the last two categories came mostly from primary schools. No secondary Head rated Neill's influence on himself as 'enormous' though four of them considered it 'very consider-able'. I found these returns surprising, for when it is remembered that Neill is often represented as an unrealistic extremist operating far from the difficult conditions of the average state school, it is easy to suppose that there would be no sizeable number of responsible Heads who would regard his work as at all relevant to their own – especially in a profession which is so often described as 'naturally conservative'. Perhaps that image should change.†

Many of my respondents complained in their comments how difficult it is to assess influence from any particular quarter and I had every sympathy with them for this. It is an almost impossible thing to be sure about, but even though this small inquiry offers no reliable quantitative answers as to the extent of Neill's influence, it does suggest that a fair number of men and women who are now responsible for the way some state schools develop are conscious of the fact that Neill's arguments and example have affected their policies not inconsiderably.

The excerpts in Appendix 1 are mainly from the general remarks that the respondents were invited to make at the end of the questionnaire; but after rating Neill's influence on their own practice they were also invited to indicate in what particular directions they had felt this influence, if at all. The comments made in this section most frequently pointed to the changes in the quality of the relationships in their schools, mainly between teachers and pupils, but also among the staff themselves. 'An attempt to achieve a comradely relationship with students and to break down hier-archical attitudes.' 'Treating pupils with respect.' 'I have looked towards

* These percentages take account of the four who said they had never heard of A. S. Neill.

† It would have been interesting to know how different would be the picture that would emerge from an unselected sample of Heads. I made an attempt to get such a picture by sending the same questionnaire to about forty Heads of comprehensive schools (almost all the secondary Heads in my selected sample were from such schools) taken at random from the Education Committees Directory. A mere 35 per cent responded and it seemed fruitless to pursue the matter since it is probable that I was getting a biased sample still, though this time it was a self-selected one.

freedom in our relationships with the children.' Such remarks were common.

Almost as frequent were comments which drew attention either to the feeling of support which Neill's actions and writing gave to those who were already rebelling against traditional assumptions or to the effect he had in causing the teacher to question the assumptions that were being made. Typical of such expressions were the following: 'Neill's enthusiasm quite a supportive element.' 'One's own approach and methods have been strengthened through his endorsement.' '. . . causes one to have sleepless nights reviewing, clarifying and modifying one's aims and practices.' '. . . significant in demonstrating courage in the face of illiberal pressures. This has been helpful in what is still an authoritarian State system.'

The questioning which Neill provoked was at one level concerned with the fairly wide issues of the teacher's values: 'The only real education is that which has been sought by the child himself.' '. . . to see the school as *for* the children.' 'My belief in original goodness.' '. . . giving less importance to measurable achievement.' But most particularly my respondents considered that Neill had changed their attitudes towards difficult children, causing them to withhold punishments and to attempt rather to understand the child; and also that he was one of a number of educationists who had reinforced ideas of a child-centred education. Harry Rée was by no means alone apparently in being persuaded by Neill's example to introduce some form of self-government.

It was noticeable that very few spontaneously mentioned being influenced at all in their attitudes to moral education as such (though of course changes in relationships and in attitudes to difficult children certainly imply a shift in this respect), and in particular to sexual attitudes. The few who did make specific references were in the main disapproving: 'Admiration for his work, but disapprove of his methods in relation to sex and moral education.' This suggests a non-acceptance of the ideas that lie at the root of Neill's educational philosophy, and this implication is quite consistent with the 'B' or 'C' ratings which were the most common assessments of Neill's influence on the respondents' own professional attitudes and practices. We may infer that Neill has played a significant part in changing educational practice in some respects but that this has not been accompanied by any widely enthusiastic acceptance of his whole philosophy, however much we may compliment (or condemn) ourselves on the permissiveness or child-centredness of modern education. One obvious brake on such a change is the inertia of public opinion, and many of my respondents commented on this difficulty of working against parental opinions and, more commonly, staff attitudes. 'One or two in a large school can destroy the system of "government by consent" and free discipline.'

As one Headmaster summed it up: 'I think a fundamental change of *feeling* is required before any new approaches in punishment (or lack of it), sex education, moral education, relationships, curriculum methods, etc., can make *truly effective changes*. This change of feeling has not occurred in most of the places where the so-called "new ideas" are being tried out. They therefore make no difference. This change of feeling is also a change of philosophy of course. But philosophy of life, and society – not of teaching only.'

Yet it may still be true that, as another of my respondents wrote: 'Neill will prove to have been a very important figure whose influence, directly or indirectly, extends to many teachers even when they (on the conscious level) dismiss his ideas as "hopelessly idealistic".' Certainly there was much truly professional idealism expressed in the replies to this questionnaire. It is therefore not sufficient to brush Neill aside as Brian Jackson tried to do when, in reviewing Neill's last book, he wrote: 'He is part of the private system . . . a family ethos which is just not most people's.'[45] This is to confuse the circumstances in which Neill has been forced to work with what he has been saying and actually doing. As Harry Rée pointed out at about the same time: 'The most important revolution in the schools of tomorrow is not going to come from the introduction of machines or modern methods but from a change which is already observable . . . in the quality of the relationships both within the school and in the community outside . . . We still need Neill,' he concluded.[46]

That this recognition was quite widely shared was demonstrated when action by the Department of Education threatened to close Summerhill. This threat had hovered over the school throughout the sixties when the Department had been moved to undertake a close scrutiny of all the country's private schools, ironically as a result of a case of cruelty in one of them. For Summerhill this threat came to a head in 1968 when a 'final inspection' was to be made. A number of sympathetic articles appeared in the press, and just before the verdict was to be announced *The Times* published a letter from Professors Ben Morris and Robin Pedley which was also signed by another dozen distinguished men – Bertrand Russell among them.[47] The letter was in effect a notice to the Secretary of State that he could not close 'this celebrated school, an acknowledged landmark in educational theory' without facing a public outcry. For, the writers asked, 'although many of Neill's ideas have been absorbed under the skin by modern educationists, can we afford to lose so vital a laboratory of ideas?'

A question in parliament the following week elicited only a cautious and non-committal reply. Neill went off to Exeter to receive his second honorary degree. Then a reprieve was announced by the Department of

Education whose inspectors now found Summerhill in an acceptable condition. But not, however, so acceptable that it could be recognized as efficient: it was to be allowed another five years of life and a final decision would then be made after yet further inspections.

There is a danger in this that Summerhill is being preserved as a mere relic. More hopefully the efforts to keep the school open may be interpreted as a determination to prevent the ideas which it embodies from being symbolically buried. Yet as John Holt has pointed out: 'The worst thing that can happen to any great pioneer of human thought is for his ideas to fall into the hands of disciples and worshippers, who take the living, restless, ever-changing thought of their master and try to carve it into imperishable granite . . . We must take Neill's thought, his writing, his work, and Summerhill itself, not as a final step, but as a first one.'[48]

REFERENCES

1 *News Chronicle*, 30 January 1957.
2 *Daily Mail*, 4 January 1961.
3 *Daily Herald*, 11 January 1961.
4 *New Statesman and Nation*, 30 June 1961.
5 *Queen*, 27 September 1961.
6 *Daily Herald*, 6 April 1962.
7 *Id*, 8, April 1962.
8 H. Hart (ed.), *Summerhill: For and Against*, p. 7.
9 *Look*, 9 November 1963.
10 *Spectator*, 20 April 1962.
11 Students and staff of Hornsey College of Art, *The Hornsey Affair*, p. 2.
12 R. Neville, *Play power*, p. 62.
13 *Times*, 17 May 1968.
14 P. Jacobs and S. Landau, *The New Radicals*, pp. 13–15.
15 R. Pedley, *The Comprehensive School*, p. 167.
16 Ibid. p. 181.
17 M. Ash, *Who Are the Progressives Now?*, p. 16.
18 D. Rubenstein and C. Stoneman (eds.), *Education for Democracy*, p. 41.
19 Ibid. p. 33. (Article by Albert Rowe.)
20 *Where?*, April 1964; *Daily Telegraph*, 11 January 1965; *Times Educational Supplement*, 31 May 1966.
21 *Times Educational Supplement*, 14 February 1964.
22 *Times Educational Supplement*, 8 May 1964.
23 *Guardian*, 2 February 1965.
24 *Observer*, 31 October 1965.
25 *Times Educational Supplement*, 17 June 1966.
26 Ibid. 30 December 1966.
27 Ibid. 2 September 1966.
28 Ibid. 6 January 1967.
29 *News Chronicle*, 30 January 1967.
30 *Evening News*, 9 August 1967.

31 *Times Educational Supplement*, 29 March 1968.
32 *The Free Child*, p. 7.
33 *Spectator*, 3 March 1967.
34 *Twentieth Century*, Winter 1963.
35 M. Ash, *Who Are the Progressives Now?*, p. 53.
36 Reported in *Id*, 9, 1962.
37 R. Pedley, *The Comprehensive School*, p. 174.
38 *Times Educational Supplement*, 13 April 1962.
39 *Id*, 7, 1961.
40 *Talking of Summerhilll*, p. 137.
41 *Talking of Summerhill*, p. 98.
42 *Id*, 16, 1966.
43 Ibid.
44 *Guardian*, 18 April 1969.
45 *Guardian*, 17 November 1967.
46 *New Statesman and Nation*, 17 March 1967.
47 *Times*, 11 June 1968.
48 H. Hart (ed.), *Summerhill: For and Against*, p. 97.

13 The Necessity of Freedom

The most striking expression that emerged, unsolicited, from my inquiry of headteachers (reported in the last chapter) was of a feeling that Neill's example had encouraged and supported those who already felt a dissatisfaction with current assumptions about education; without the knowledge of his tenacity many of these teachers might have subsided into a resigned acceptance of the conventional. Above all things, Summerhill has been a demonstration of an educational alternative at a time when society has been flattening out into what Marcuse has called a one-dimensional form.

In this concluding chapter, I shall attempt to identify what seem to me to be the most significant features of this alternative that Neill has been demonstrating, and I shall suggest some theoretical constructs, relating to both social and individual development, that may provide a helpful framework within which Neill's work can be set. I have already indicated some issues of which Neill's treatment seems to me not to afford a satisfactory resolution, and I shall sketch out some ideas as to how these issues might be faced without abandoning what I take to be the main, and valuable, essence of Neill's practice.

It is clear that freedom is the major part of this essence – freedom, not just as an educational device, but as a necessary condition of education. It is also said to be one of the cornerstones of the western democracies, but in reality the quality of this democratic freedom is, to say the least, uneven. Marcuse argues that as society succeeds in providing more and more of its citizens with 'the concrete substance of all freedom' – freedom from want – the organization against scarcity turns into an organization of domination. The advanced technological apparatus imposes economic and political requirements that demand an ever more complete allegiance to its principles and institutions. It does so by reducing the opposition to the discussion and promotion of alternative policies *within* the *status quo*. It is in this sense that society is becoming one-dimensional. Non-conformity with the system comes to be seen as 'socially useless' when there is a continuously rising standard of living, particularly if that non-conformity threatens the smooth operation of the economic order. There is a totalitarian (though non-terroristic) manipulation of needs that uses the appearance of pluralism in economic semi-monopolies, political parties and mass-media which, while competing against one another, do not compete against the system. It is a policy of domestic containment in which 'competing institutions concur in solidifying the power of the whole over the individual'.[1]

In the earlier stages of the technological society subversive expressions were argued with or even suppressed: the artist was alienated but virile. Now his products are absorbed, commercialized, distributed: he is emasculated by approval, finding it impossible to transcend the daily 'reality' because he is made a part of it. 'The efforts to recapture the Great Refusal ... suffer the fate of being absorbed by what they refute.'[2] One may see a parallel process in education, which may once have been an initiation into an esotericism, or an instrument of revolution, a route by which the proletariat gained access to subversive doctrine, but which has now become a part of the system, universal, compulsory, innocuous, a mere instrument of accepted social purposes. Debate is about methods and organization: protest is about salaries and the size of classes – opposition within the *status quo*. Some part of this educational *status quo* is conveyed, for instance, in the following words, written not in protest but as a matter-of-fact statement from within a sociological orthodoxy that sees no need to disguise the facts: 'The school is a primary agency of socialization. It has come into being, and has progressively lengthened and elaborated its function, in response to the progressively differentiating needs of advanced industrialism ... The school is in fact concerned less with the needs of the individual child than with the ways in which the individual child can respond to the needs of society.'[3]

This takes us to perhaps the most fundamental departure of Neill's form of education from both the traditional and the liberal-progressive forms. He repudiated the assumption that a school had to be an agency of social purposes. He was so far from making such an assumption that he was moved to say, 'Summerhill isn't a school; it is a way of life.'[4] And it was not a school if a school has to fulfil the functions which Maurice Craft spelled out in the quotation above. If he allowed that Summerhill had to offer the possibility of some kind of preparation for adult life, Neill did so reluctantly, and then only from the point of view of his pupils – providing just sufficient facilities as would enable them to get the paper qualifications to give them entry to further training elsewhere. This was a concession to the actuality of the way society organized itself, but it was as far as he would go. He never considered that education should acknowledge any duty to society to ensure that the new generations were trained for its purposes.

Likewise, he did not accept the view that the school had to transmit the social culture to the rising generations. On the contrary, he was at pains to avoid the deliberate process of transmission (he would have used an emotively less neutral word) of either aesthetic or moral values, for he wanted the children to be left free to make their own selection, uninfluenced by years of persuasion and suggestion as to which values were most to be cherished.

To adapt Maurice Craft's words, Summerhill was concerned more with the needs of the individual child than with the ways in which the individual child might respond to the demands of the society outside – but within the school was the 'real', present society to which the children had necessarily to accommodate themselves. In this sense the school became 'a way of life' rather than a preparation for some later state. It was a place of living in its own right, a society catering for its own needs and pursuing its own purposes, not totally uninfluenced by the larger society in which it was set, but yet not determined by the 'needs' of that society.

It is worth pointing out in parenthesis that Summerhill has been less affected by the concerns of its parent society than other schools may be which derive from it in the future. There are two obvious reasons for this: firstly, the fact that Neill was pioneering an idea which was unique and lacking general acceptance caused him to feel beleaguered and so to isolate the school more than he would otherwise have felt to be necessary. The second reason was the fact of Summerhill being a boarding-school. This naturally insulates a school since the children are not daily introducing concerns from outside. A closer relationship with the larger society might be expected in a day-school. This would obviously have its effects, but it would not necessarily remove from the school community its fundamental autonomy any more than in the case of a theatre, say, which fashions its internal arrangements, regulates its relationships and decides on its productions in accordance with its own purposes and function. A creative provincial theatre relates to, and in some sense belongs to, the local community, yet it feels no need to mimic the procedures of other institutions or slavishly to supply what society seems to be demanding.

The actual relationship between a school and the larger society is not one that can be prescribed once for all, and in fact varies enormously from one school to another and from one point in time to another. Primary schools, comprehensive schools and public schools, for instance, each develop different kinds of relationships, and there are obvious variations even within these categories. Neill was not laying down the ideal relationship: he developed one which seemed appropriate to his circumstances. Perhaps its only immutable characteristic was the refusal to be bound by the 'needs of society', an insistence on the priority of the way of life within the school over that outside.

In any case, to talk of the 'needs' of society is to obscure the fact that already some decision has been made as to the kind of society that is to be maintained. It would be more precise to speak of the 'demands' of society. A similar comment may be made about the 'needs of the individual child' most of which are contingent either upon what kind of people we want our children to grow into or upon our understanding of the developmental stages through which children 'naturally' pass. Apart from the child's purely physical growth, there is very little that can be said about these developmental stages which is not tied in some degree to the cultural environment.

Many of the theorists of child-centred education make great play of the 'needs' of children and generally do so with some developmental scheme in mind. This gives the appearance of a scientifically-based pedagogy, but quite unintentionally it removes from the child much of his human individuality. He comes to be seen as a specimen which is considered abnormal if it does not exhibit the expected developmental stages at the appropriate times.

Neill very rarely talked of the needs of children but would speak rather of their 'wants' or 'interests'. He had no elaborately observed map of child development – only a few broad notions as to the 'nature' of children. Perhaps he recognized only two universal psychological needs in children – the need for play and the need for love. These should be unbounded: the child should 'play and play and play'; adults should always be 'on the child's side',[5] supplying all the love and support that were wanted. For the rest, the children themselves should identify their 'needs' and the adults who cared for them should supply them in such measure as was physically practicable, excepting only where the child's wants conflicted with the obvious conditions for his safety. The child would, of course, discover other restrictions stemming from his physical, and immediate social, environment.

Of course, not all of a child's 'needs' or 'wants' are internal products: they change according to his experience of the outside world. As such secondary wants developed, Neill would generally require that they too should be satisfied. When a child has learnt to read he should have access to as many books as he may want, and of the kind he wants – neither proscribed nor prescribed. But Neill refrained so far as he could from the usual educational tactic of constructing the child's environment to produce 'needs' of the particular kinds which an adult may want him to feel. Usually the educator has more honourable motives than the drug-peddler or even the commercial advertiser in his wish to stimulate some pre-determined 'needs' in children. He may consider it his duty to do this in order to provide society with the kind of people (equipped with appropriate knowledge, skills and character structures) that it requires; or, apparently more altruistically, he may see it as the way by which his pupils will be able to develop their full potentialities and thus enjoy a fuller and richer life. Even the former motive may be represented as being in the pupils' own interests since it is supposed to be for the ultimate benefit of its members that society should function efficiently, and in any case each pupil will, it is said, eventually be happier if he is able to play a useful part in society and thus attain a more honoured status. On the other hand the latter motive may not be so disinterestedly directed towards each pupil's happiness – quite apart from the fact that the circumstances in which this purpose is pursued as often have the effect of inhibiting the development of the pupils' interests and potentialities, it is always the case that the potentialities which are to be fostered are only those which are approved of and felt to be worth-while by some other authority or perhaps by general social consensus.

In its starkest representation this view of education was characterized by Freud as society's means of establishing the dominance of the Reality Principle over the Pleasure Principle. However, as Marcuse has convincingly argued, what Freud took to be a necessity of civilization is actually contingent upon the particular forms of social organization which are familiar to us. Freud's Reality Principle was one of a number of possible forms, some of which have been realized in the past, others of which exist now in different cultures, and others still there are which remain possibilities. The form which now obtains in the western technological societies Marcuse has labelled the Performance Principle, 'in order to emphasize that under its rule society is stratified according to the competitive economic performances of its members'.[6] If this is the case the transformation of the raw instinctual demands may be admitted as necessary, but the nature of this adaptation is not permanently settled. The psycho-analysts, whose alliance Neill hoped for in his early days, refused to support him perhaps because their reading of Freud led them to accept his view of the necessity of the repressive actions of society in support of a supposedly inevitable version of the Reality Principle.

Marcuse's wider perspective leads him to examine more critically the nature of these repressive mechanisms. There was a stage in the development of society, he argues, when these repressions were necessary to combat scarcity; in addition to fulfilling this primary function they also enabled man to transform 'the blind necessity of the fulfilment of want into desired gratification'[7] in ways which made available the more elaborate pleasures of civilization. However, as the conquest of scarcity proceeded, specific historical institutions of dominance developed – the dominance of one section of society over another – and this entailed additional controls necessitating what Marcuse calls 'surplus repression' which tends to act against gratification, localizing permissible pleasures rather than extending and elaborating them. 'For a long way, the interests of domination and the interests of the whole coincide: the profitable utilization of the productive apparatus fulfils the needs and faculties of the individuals.' Nevertheless this coincidence cannot be maintained, for although the labour of most people is necessary for the satisfaction of some of their basic needs yet it is 'work for an apparatus which they do not control, which operates as an independent power to which individuals must submit if they want to live. And it becomes the more alien the more specialized the division of labour becomes.' The individual is thus trapped in a system on which he is dependent but which also involves him in alienated labour – he finds himself 'engaged in activities that mostly do not coincide with his own faculties and desires.' The concomitant restrictions on the libido appear the more rational the more they permeate the whole of society. They seem inevitable because the system requires them and the individual comes to feel himself protected and sustained by the system. 'The societal authority is absorbed into the "conscience" and into the unconscious of the individual, and works as his own desire, morality and fulfilment. In the "normal" development the individual lives his repression "freely" as his own life: he desires what he is supposed to desire; his gratifications are profitable to him and to others; he is reasonably happy and often even exuberantly happy.'[8]

Normality, the conformity to norms, is no longer automatically desirable, and can be a painful condition. As R. D. Laing has expressed it: 'What we call "normal" is the product of repression, denial, splitting, projection, introjection and other forms of destructive action on experience. It is radically estranged from the structure of being . . . The condition of alienation . . . of being out of one's mind, is the condition of the normal man.' And he goes on to observe: 'Society highly values its normal man. It educates children to lose themselves and to become absurd, and thus to be normal. Normal men have killed perhaps 100,000,000 of their fellow normal men in the last fifty years.'[9]

It is the 'estrangement from the structure of being' which makes even an exuberant happiness fundamentally destructive of the man himself as well as of 100,000,000 of his fellow men. We are led to enact our own destruction because it is made to appear the only means by which our basic needs can be satisfied and because in having them satisfied we receive the bonus of superfluous gratifications that others have 'chosen' and have persuaded us we want. Knee-deep in the useless products of affluence, who are we to complain? With the all-but complete conquest of scarcity (in at least most parts of the western societies) the conquest of society itself is now well advanced. 'We can be more deliberate, and hence more successful, in our cultural design,' boasts the master-planner in B. F. Skinner's scientifically based utopia. 'We can achieve a sort of control under which the controlled, though they are following a code much more scrupulously than was ever the case under the old system, nevertheless, *feel free*. They are doing what they want to do, not what they are forced to do. That's the source of the tremendous power of positive reinforcement – there's no restraint and no revolt. By a careful cultural design, we control not the final behaviour, but the *inclination* to behave – the motives, the desires, the wishes. The curious thing is that in that case *the question of freedom never arises*.'[10]

Skinner was postulating a small and isolated community in which the planning was total and was 'scientifically' executed. Such self-consistency is not in practice attainable and our technology has not succeeded in perfecting the techniques of 'positive reinforcement' in the way that Skinner hoped might be possible. There *is* restraint and there *is* revolt. Perhaps the human psyche will not succumb so completely however sophisticated the means of manipulation that are used on it; but we do seem to have reached the point where the educational and propagandizing agencies are so powerful and so essentially united in a technological rationality that the individual is losing the certainty of his will. The validity of his own experience is continually in question; his motives, desires and wishes are not clearly his own. Marcuse has attempted to distinguish 'true' needs from 'false' needs – a peculiarly difficult distinction unequivocally to establish. As he says, 'in the last analysis, the question of what are true and false needs must be answered by the individuals themselves, but only in the last analysis: that is, *if and when they are free to give the answer*.'[11] (My italics.) Logical objections to most attempts to differentiate between true and false needs are not difficult to find, yet the feeling that lies behind the distinction is quite widely recognized: but it is a part of the process of subjection that our feelings are made to appear untrustworthy and can only be regarded seriously if they are uncontradicted by logic and if they are verified by empirical evidence. Marcuse defines false needs as 'those which are superimposed upon the individual by particular social interests in his repression: the needs which perpetuate toil, aggressiveness, misery and injustice . . . Most of the prevailing needs to relax, to have fun, to behave and consume in accordance with the advertisements, to love and hate what others love and hate, belong to this category of false needs.'[12]

Jules Henry makes a similar distinction by differentiating between what he calls 'drives' and 'values', both culturally influenced though in different degrees. The former are those urges which impel us towards achievements while the latter are those which guide us in our intimate human relations. He describes our culture as a 'driven culture' – one in which values are swamped by drives, in which a man urged on by drive 'may consume others by compelling them to yield to his driveness'. This subjection of what we consider good to what seems to be necessary is encouraged by a condition of personal uncertainty fostered by 'the assumption of the modern world that one does not really know what one thinks one knows'.[13] Carl Rogers introduces the idea of 'congruence', by which he means a marriage between a person's experience, awareness and action. But for the majority of us he finds individuals with 'values mostly introjected, held as fixed concepts, rarely examined or tested . . . Since these value constructs are often sharply at variance with what is going on in our own experiencing, we have in a very basic way divorced ourselves from ourselves.'[14] Fromm goes further by suggesting that the 'substitution of pseudo acts for original acts of thinking, feeling, and willing, leads eventually to the replacement of the original self by a pseudo self.'[15]

These formulations, among others, may seem to describe our perception of present-day normal man quite accurately, yet it may still not seem justifiable to regard one set of needs as more real than another or one self as psuedo and another lost self as real, since both are recognizable products of individual interaction with a social culture. Perhaps the only ultimate justification is to be found in one's own, and others', experience, and of course, it is this very experience whose social negation is the undermining of our integrity. If a man is moved to acquire some fairly expensive object it is reasonable to assume that he needs or wants that object; but it may be that it is not the object itself that he wants but the enhanced estimation of himself by others that he hopes will result from his possession of the object. Similarly, beliefs may be expressed, values assumed, behaviour adopted not for their own sake, not for the direct satisfaction which they will give, but for the impression that they are felt to make on others. A man may profess a belief in God or in science only because not to do so would bring him into disrepute among people by whom he is anxious to be accepted. His behaviour may not appear to differ from one whose belief is based on genuine conviction, yet he is likely to find that the belief offers him no substantial support for his actions. He is himself able to distinguish between the quality of his experience when he acts according to assumed beliefs and that which results from beliefs and values that are not of a displaced origin – even if his actions deceive others. If this displacement becomes at all habitual, and especially if the dissociation between actions and feelings is unconscious, leaving only a vague feeling of dissatisfaction as the individual finds himself continuously impelled to act in a fashion which he feels is at variance with his deeper interests, it seems legitimate to talk not only of true and false needs but even of true and false selves.

The traditional form of education seems intentionally to aim at this state of affairs – to substitute for the original thoughts and feelings of a child

N

(original in the sense that they originate from his own psychic processes) other thoughts and feelings which are considered to be more socially useful, more civilized or morally more acceptable. It is at this point that Neill differed most fundamentally with the traditional conception. At one level it can be considered that the difference stems from whether it is the dogma of original sin or the dogma of original virtue that is accepted, but perhaps beyond this is a more subtle variation in the views of human growth. In this respect, the traditional mode of education seems to share with Freud the idea of a linear development of an individual in which the primitive is superseded by the sophisticated. The events of childhood were seen by Freud as mere memories, and as being truly functional only in pathological cases where there is some kind of fixation in a stage of development which properly should have been discarded. Such a view tends to devalue the earlier stages because they are regarded as temporary states which each person has to 'grow out of'. An alternative dynamic is the view that each individual in growing is adding experience continually to a permanent core. This is probably the more commonly held view even though the logic of our actions often seems to deny it. Properly held it is a supposition that would tend to place value on present experience rather than to focus attention on the future, mature self. In this view the main problem which an individual faces is to find ways of adapting to society which do not undermine the integrity of his self. If he is persuaded to adopt defensive, rather than adaptive, tactics he is eliminating a part of the meaning of his existence and substituting for it some secondhand meaning which is alien to him.

One way in which this process operates in an 'educational' setting has been sensitively described by John Holt in his book *How Children Fail*. Here he exposes the strategies which children quite commonly adopt in coping with tasks which they find difficult and whose meaning often eludes them. A teacher sets a problem intending and expecting the children to accept it at its face value and bend their efforts towards its solution. If they succeed he will be satisfied, perhaps because he is genuinely concerned with their progress though as often his satisfaction derives from the confirmation of his own skill as a teacher which their success offers. The children understand this, and they see it as their primary task to satisfy their teacher. They know that solving the problem successfully would achieve this goal, but if they find that this is not immediately possible – and after years of experience of similar situations they may well realize that they are unlikely to find such an easy way out – they are acute enough to search for clues in the teacher's behaviour which will enable them to react in ways which will give him at least a secondary satisfaction. This may actually lead them to solving the problem that he gave them, but if so they will have done so by analysing him rather than the problem. In fact, he is their problem. The education has become, not a learning of arithmetic or whatever may have been the teacher's intention, but the learning of how to simulate behaviour which is accorded approval. As a training for 'real-life' situations this may not be a wasted lesson, for these children may well have to find their successes by pleasing other people, particularly those more advanced in the hierarchy of social approval. Children absorb this lesson from their earliest experiences when, for instance, they are taught to suppress the expression of unacceptable feelings, and the teaching is continued through their schooling – in their arithmetic lessons, which Holt mainly describes, but in their art lessons too, and their history lessons, and their science lessons. Inside and outside the classroom the school ethic leads pupils to abandon behaviour which they might otherwise have felt more expressive of their own attitudes, thoughts and feelings. The process is often so complete that teachers are appalled by its success, complaining that their senior pupils lack initiative and imagination and instituting corrective procedures to encourage the qualities that they have so effectively helped to extinguish.

In the context of an education which is conceived of as a process of replacement this may be seen as proper. But there are educationists who have opposite ambitions, who declare their wish to foster initiative, creativity, self-discipline and so on, but who are still bound by contrary attitudes which have the effect of diminishing the possibility of individual autonomy. So-called discovery methods are used, but what is to be 'discovered' is already prescribed, and the children are obliged to infer from various clues that the teacher builds into the situation what it is that he wants them to discover. School councils are instituted; but it quickly becomes clear that these are simply instruments for the implementation of an already formulated policy. In many ways such tactics are more likely to undermine the integrity of children than an openly directive stance, for the more subtly they are applied the more apt they are to obscure from the child the possibility of his own independence, to blur the boundaries between his own decisions and those which are made for him. It is an insinuation of other values into his psyche rather than a clear presentation of an alternative. It is the adaptation to education of the apparatus of domination characteristic of the one-dimensional culture that enslaves by erosion rather than by conquest.

In the frankly authoritarian mode of education, the choices are explicit. The pupil may more or less consciously decide to split his life between the school and the not-school cultures. This is not to advocate such an education, but to point to its saving grace – it may fail, leaving its pupils battered, but more or less intact. But this is small comfort when this mode of education becomes the dominant one, since those who evade its effects are likely to be stranded, isolated individuals, or attached to a deprived sub-culture.

Perhaps, then, these two forms of education – the authoritarian and the progressive-liberal – offer a Hobson's choice between the production of schizoid types and of hysteric types, the one in which a true self continues to live a precarious existence within the individual hating and fearing the false-self system which imprisons it, and the other in which the true self is lost or so atrophied that the pseudo-self is virtually the only operative agent.

Neill's version of this true-false system was always expressed in far less explicit terms though there is no doubt about his conviction and valuation. He spoke in terms of 'naturalness', of sincerity, truthfulness, directness and spontaneity. It is not the case, I think, that he was always so sure of his purposes as he was by the time he wrote *The Free Child* which was, in effect, his final synthesis. But very soon after he had started his work at Gretna he formulated his aim as being 'to make my bairns realise.'[16] He was unsure at that time what it was that he wanted them to 'realise', but said, 'I think I want to make them realise what life means. Yes, I want to give them, or rather help them to find an attitude. I want these boys and girls to acquire the habit of looking honestly at life.' Perhaps he was right to omit the object of the verb in the first place: perhaps it was simply that he wanted his bairns to real-ize.

Under Homer Lane's influence and with the new perspective provided by psycho-analysis, Neill's interest was diverted towards problem children. He followed Lane in thinking that children behaved in difficult ways largely because of the attempts by parents and teachers to impose particular standards of behaviour. A failure to maintain these standards might provoke guilt feelings which were difficult to accommodate; or it might result in the loss of parental love – or at least the fear of such a loss; or the standards might simply be an irrational barrier to legitimate desires, a barrier which might provoke in some children rebellious and anti-social attitudes and in others feelings of inconsolable inferiority. It was these imposed standards, particularly those accompanied by some supposed moral backing (because this aggravated the guilt feelings) which perverted a child's good intentions into problem behaviour. Thus initially Neill's 'removal of the *verbot*' was primarily intended to release the problem child from the unnecessary constraints and guilt-feelings, or at least to remove Neill from the position of sustaining the guilt. Only then could he hope to help the child out of its conflicts.

However, there seems always to have been a more positive motive in his rejections of the value-imposing role that adults usually assume. He did not miss the point of Lane's story of the mother who 'helps' her infant in his struggles to bring his fist to his mouth[17] thus robbing him of the joy of discovery and of the expansion of his power. The guiding hand accentuates possession by devaluing activity; but it also builds the 'other' at the expense of the self. Thus interferences by the well-intentioned adult with the child's exploration of his world so often weaken that child's capability of making his own choices and of pursuing the consequences of his own decisions by which alone he would discover and create himself. Neill's realization of this diminishing effect of a concert of moralizing and guiding adults is apparent in his many scathing remarks about the 'higher lifers' and in particular in his passionate attacks on the Coué system of auto-suggestion.[18] As the years passed this view of freedom as a necessary condition for the personal growth of children took precedence over the view of freedom as a condition for the treatment of problem behaviour.

His attitude to problem children changed as a result of two observations. Firstly, he discovered that children were able to resolve most of their own difficulties when they were given an appropriate environment – that is, a setting in which the children were able to explore the consequences of living unobscured by adult restrictions and compulsions and at the same time were given the knowledge and feeling of adult support and approval. Secondly, he observed that children who came into this non-coercive environment, even if at first they were exhibiting no problem behaviour, would almost invariably find it necessary to live through a period of anti-social expression.

These two observations led to a revision of Neill's ideas, not only about problem children, but about children in general. It now seemed that there was no clear boundary between problem children and normal children – there seemed only to be problems which were more or less intractable, problems which could be suppressed and problems which shouted for attention. Or to look at it from another angle, there was normality which was acceptable and there was normality which was unacceptable; both of them 'the product of repression, denial, splitting, projection, introjection and other forms of destructive action on experience'. The freedom of Summerhill was most importantly a means by which children's experience was acknowledged, rather than denied and destroyed.

One consequence of this revision of his ideas was that Neill began to relinquish his role as a child-therapist. Perhaps it had always seemed as though he was to some extent indulging himself in this activity, but at least it had enabled him to acquire a deeper understanding of children. Now he realized that for most children, 'problem' or 'normal', it was unnecessary – though he kept open the possibility of 'Private Lessons' for those children who seemed to want the more intimate relationship with him. The language of symbols had its own meaning and place – in dreams or fantasy or behaviour – and there was no need to translate them into another medium if through their own actions children were able freely to experience themselves. Neill discarded the techniques of psycho-analysis though he did not altogether reject its theory – that is to say, he continued to accept the main thesis of the significance of unconscious forces, the importance of infantile sexuality, the mechanism of repression, and so on, and he continued to regret the neglect of this knowledge in teacher-training which, it seemed to him, concentrated attention exclusively on learning-theory and animal psychology. In rejecting the relevance of psycho-analytic technique to education he was also following Reich who inferred that the social implications of the theory pointed to the need for prophylaxis rather than for therapy.

In fact Neill has not bothered to follow the development of neo-Freudian psychology beyond Reich, and he has understandably been criticized, notably by David Holbrook,[19] for his own ignorance of more recent theories, an ignorance which seems to nullify his complaints about the teaching profession's apparent lack of interest in what he would regard as the essential psychology. The fact is that he arrived at a practical synthesis which did not seem to him to need the support of the continuously developing formulations of the neo-Freudians. If he had followed these later theories probably he would have found the existentialist psychology most suggestive. The connection has been implied by its foremost practitioner this country, R. D. Laing, when he declared his interest[20] in Reich's work at a time when to do so was apparently to move outside professional boundaries. The perspective which causes the existential psychologist to regard his patients in their social setting rather than in a consulting-room isolation; which leads him to accept neurotic and psychotic expressions as valid commentaries on a person's experience and thus to support, rather than to 'correct', the expression and to accept rather than to deny, and so to destroy, the experience; which requires a more symmetric relationship between 'analyst' and 'patient' than the classical transference relationship presumed; and which impels him to social action, attempting to influence reform in the light of his specialist knowledge and experience – all of these aspects, closely reminiscent of Homer Lane's inspired, though untutored practice, would have attracted Neill's sympathy had he studied them.

But in so far as this school of psychology is based on an existentialist philosophy, there are deeper reasons for such an affiliation of ideas. For the existentialist, freedom is an inescapable condition of human living, the condition of man's process of continuous self-creation, a fact rather than a value – and this in a world whose only values are those which are man-made.

The central peculiarity of man's existence is that he is aware of his existence, and being so aware he is also aware of the possibility that he may not exist. He is, in Sartre's words, 'the being by whom nothingness comes into the world' – nothingness, the obverse of the existence-idea. This is his existential anxiety, that he is ever concerned about his own obliteration – by death, perhaps, but equally about the everyday obliteration by the action of our fellow beings, by their denial of our experience and of the value of our experience which is evidence of the fact and the value of our existence. We are unavoidably in each other's power, for our existence, or rather the idea of our existence which is our creation, requires the corroboration of others recognizing us as independent and unique agents. Without it, we are as good as dead; but more, we should be aware of our own deathness.

'I must keep emphasising,' wrote Neill,[21] 'that when a child cannot get love he will ask for hate and hate in abundance. One lad from an unhappy home gave me months of misery by constantly trying to make me angry. Most of his actions were unconscious . . . he would "accidentally" drop a hammer on my feet, would get in my light, would manage to trip me up when walking with me. Another hefty lad of fifteen hit me playfully but very hard every time he met me during the first month after his arrival. My shoulder was black and blue . . . More than once I have had an adolescent girl who made herself objectionable by staring superciliously at other children and at adults and saying personal things in a sweet voice . . . "I say, Margaret, you really should do something about your thick ankles." This catty variety of girl tries not only to hate but to be hated by the whole community.'

Either love or hate is recognition.* People who are themselves in a state of 'ontological insecurity', as Laing calls it, find it difficult to accept that a child's insistent demand for recognition is a 'legitimate' human demand, and will superciliously refer to the child's 'attention-seeking behaviour' or snubbingly tell him that he is not the only pebble on the beach. The reduction of people to 'pebbles on the beach' having value only as one of a million other such pebbles, perhaps being swept out to sea yet being utterly replaceable, is one of the lessons in the absurd in which children have to be schooled so that they may become normal producer-consumers.

In the process of submerging the individual's personal value in the social ethic the group's welfare takes the place occupied earlier by God's will, and actions come to be judged according to their helpfulness in sustaining the group rather than by the pleasure they give to God. However, the basis of both ethics, social and religious, lie outside man, as did the classical ethic

---

* Though of course love carries a more positive valuing. But as Neill pointed out, 'Love and hate are not opposites. The opposite to love is indifference.'[22]

which erected absolute categories apparently independent of man. Existentialism argues the arbitrariness of these ethics by pointing out that man himself has chosen the basis on which they rest – whether it is society, or God, or a Platonic idealism. The argument is taken to the point that any system of values is dependent on nothing but man's choice, that man himself is the creator of all values.

This baselessness of our value-systems is the origin of our existential freedom. We choose according to our values and our choices reciprocally make our values. We may choose to regard some authority other than ourselves to dictate, or advise upon, our value-system, but even then we have made the choice ourselves through the choosing of our authority. In this sense is our freedom inescapable and necessary for our existence. 'Man is, indeed, a project which possesses a subjective life, instead of being a kind of moss, or a fungus or a cauliflower. Before that projection of the self nothing exists: not even in the heaven of intelligence: man will only attain existence when he is what he purposes to be.'[23]

So far as I know, only one writer has directly connected the existential philosophy with Summerhill. In his short book *Existentialism in Education* Van Cleve Morris suggests that Neill's school alone can be regarded as a paradigm school for an existential education. This, of course, would surprise Neill who has certainly never had any such philosophical pretensions himself and who would very likely ask if the Existentialists were a pop-group – which indeed they may be. Yet it does seem that this system of thought underpins the Summerhill idea in a way which does not leave it as a mere extension of permissiveness.

There are two points in Morris' advocacy, however, which I think are misleading both as regards the actuality of Summerhill and as regards the implications of existentialist philosophy, but which raise interesting issues. He emphasizes the significance of what is called the Existential Moment – the point in a person's life when the awareness first dawns of his existence as a unique, independent and possibly autonomous being. For many people this dawning is sudden and immensely significant, occurring usually in early puberty. It is a boundary in time, on one side of which the individual cannot be held to be 'responsible', for without a degree of self-awareness choices can hardly be felt as choices and freedom cannot have the subjective significance which causes the implications of decisions to be realized as personal consequences. Now because the 'Moment' comes for most people at about the age of twelve, Morris infers that 'the lower grades necessarily deal with the individual before he is existentially awake. Existentialism, as an educational philosophy, can therefore afford to be officially indifferent to and disinterested towards elementary educational theory.'[24] Obviously Neill was far from indifferent to the education of 'the lower grades'; in fact, he would have liked to have started his education 'nine months before the children were born, if not earlier'. He was very much aware that the manner in which a child is reared right from its earliest point of existence has profound and lifelong effects, possibly just because the infant who is not self-aware may be less able to counteract the actions which undermine his eventual autonomy. This does not actually conflict with the existential theory: we may return to Sartre where, discussing the process of a man's self-creation, he observes that 'man will only attain existence when he is what he purposes to be' – that is, after his personal existential moment. But Sartre adds that this does not necessarily mean that he will attain what he may wish to be. 'For what we usually understand by wishing or willing is a conscious decision taken – much more often than not – after we have made ourselves what we are. I may wish to join a party, to write a book or to marry – but in such a case what is usually called my will is probably a manifestation of a prior and more spontaneous decision.'[25] This being the case it is plainly not a matter of indifference to the educator what experiences the child is subjected to before his self-awareness brings the responsibility of his freedom. Quite apart from the fact that the time of this birth into existential being may be quite variable and unpredictable – Morris quotes one person for whom it came as early as four years of age – it has to be recognised that the child's first experiences are crucial in the formation of the base from which he is later to act. We cannot expect that a sudden assumption of freedom will be painlessly accepted by a child hitherto ignorant of its exercise. In Neill's terms, we can never expect a conditioned infant to become more than semi-free: the more the opportunity for the child's regulation of his own life is removed the less secure are the foundations of his being and the stronger are the tendencies to permanent dependence, the 'Peter Pan syndrome', or as Morris calls it 'the pre-existential nostalgia'.

The second point on which I think Morris places a wrong emphasis concerns the relation of the school to the individual. He criticizes the progressive educationists on the grounds that although they set out to engage the personal involvement of their pupils in their own education and although they went a long way towards this engagement, yet they 'finally yielded to the siren song of the social psychologists, who insist that involvement must be understood as a relation between the individual and the *group*'. He regrets the preoccupation with ideas such as group dynamics, human relations, sociograms and peer influence to the exclusion of 'involvement as personal, emotional, or privately *affective* in nature'.[26] He is writing from an American context, of course, possibly with Dewey's influence particularly in mind, but I think that this criticism can be correctly applied to the British progressives though perhaps to a lesser degree. The objection is basically that this tendency can result in the subjection of the individual to the group purposes and in the imposition of a social morality which has all the inhibiting faults in education of any other imposed morality. But it is false to assume that the only alternative is one of unbridled individualism and Morris' testimony for Summerhill as a paradigm of existential education could be understood to be advocating this. It is, he claims, 'a school designed to function on behalf only of the individual learner . . . in which there are no rules, no requirements, no regulations . . .'[27]

In the fuller description which he gives, Morris in fact corrects the impression which this sentence conveys. He makes it clear that it is not the case that at Summerhill there are no rules, requirements or regulations; and although it may be that the school functions primarily on behalf of the individual, it does so only in the realization that the individual is not isolated from, or independent of, his social environment. In fact the interactions with the community are one of the most important sources of learning at Summerhill and there is a definite attempt to articulate the communal will and the various individual wills, and to find a workable balance. This does not contradict the important projections of existential philosophy which is concerned with the Being-in-the-World *and* the Being-for-Itself. An education which turns its back on either of these two aspects of existence is inevitably partial. The Summerhill child is able to experience his aloneness as well as his obvious relatedness to the community, but both are only minimally prescribed. Neill has himself observed: 'In Summerhill there is one perennial problem that can never be solved; it might be called the problem of *the individual vs. the community*.'[28] If it had been solved, this would have implied a denial of the freedom which was intrinsic: in order to preserve this freedom it was necessary not to define it precisely. To attempt such a definition may be an interesting academic exercise, but to use such a definition in order to design a freedom policy for other people to live within is already to deny their freedom. So Neill had indicated only in the broadest terms, and these largely for the guidance of adults, where the boundary between freedom and licence should in his view lie. It has been for succeeding generations of Summerhill children to mark out that boundary for their own use.

Allied problems present themselves from the dichotomy which is so frequently made between freedom and authority. It is true that some forms of authority are in opposition to some forms of freedom and vice versa; but the opposition is not inevitable. In replying to a review by T. C. Worsley of his book *Hearts not Heads in the School*, Neill declared that 'a self-governing school is full of authority, an authority that sincerely tries to balance the rights of the individual and the community.'[29] He claimed, I think justifiably, that his attitude to authority was not negative, as Worsley had asserted, but that it is made to seem so by the current assumptions about authority. Marcuse has pointed out the corresponding difficulty faced by those who find that 'the free society' cannot be adequately defined in traditional terms. 'New modes of realization are needed corresponding to the new capabilities of society . . . Such new modes can be indicated only in negative terms because they would amount to a negation of prevailing modes. Thus economic freedom would mean freedom *from* the economy . . . Political freedom would mean liberation of the individuals *from* politics over which they have no effective control. Similarly intellectual freedom would mean the restoration of individual thought now absorbed by mass communication and indoctrination, abolition of "public opinion" together with its makers.'[30]

I have pointed out earlier[31] that there is no exact parallel between the modes of liberty of the parent society and the freedom that may be considered appropriate in education. Marcuse's point is relevant, not to draw such a parallel but rather to suggest the difficulty that Neill had had in defining new modes with words which still carry the connotations acquired in the context of the forms which he is discarding. Almost inevitably this gives the appearance of a very negative set of ideas. The problem is now to identify those ideas which appear negative for this reason and to understand their positive content, and those ideas which are only negative and are without a positive content.

Authority at Summerhill was vested in the whole community except that, as explained in Chapter 11, Neill did find it necessary to retain a formal personal authority in a few well-defined sectors – to ensure safety, for instance, and to regulate relations of the school with the outside. Apart from this, it was possible for each individual in the community to share in the exercise of this communal authority. As already suggested, there was a very positive rationale for this arrangement – it was in fact of the very essence of the school – and there is abundant evidence[32] to suggest that it resulted in constructive attitudes to other forms of authority being developed in the Summerhill pupils. This policy necessitated the withdrawal of members of staff from most of the traditionally assumed modes of operation. They were given no institutional authority; they were required to exercise their influence only as persons, assuming no special privileges and having no special expectations of conformity to their wishes; they were to discard the traditional postures of dignity of a teacher; they were to refrain from imposing their ideas by persuasion or suggestion – and certainly by intimidation. All of this was definition by negation. It was found by most of the staff – certainly by all of those who stayed for any length of time – as entirely acceptable and proper. But it did lack a positive purpose and caused some to question wryly what they were really there for: half-jokingly the answer seemed to be to stoke the boiler and darn the socks. Neill himself certainly had a positive function in his relations with the children, and in fact the staff too had an essential part to play in their loving and supportive actions. Yet it is probably true to say that beyond this the position of the adults in this child-community was never properly faced.

In fact in so many ways did the children and adults enjoy equality of status that there was always a temptation to pretend that there were no differences. Most importantly, they were given equal voting rights at the decision-making meetings and were subject to the same laws: in more trivial matters, they joined the same dinner-queues, they were called by the same sort of titles (Christian names or nick-names), they used the same bathrooms and lavatories, and so on. In a few other matters there were acknowledged differences: the staff each had their own room, while the children shared theirs with from two to four others; there was a staff-room which generally the children did not use (though its boundaries were not so sacrosanct as in most schools). The number of such overt differences was really quite small; but in fact the staff were there for a different set of purposes, and although it would be an exaggeration to say that this was ignored, I think it is not unfair to suggest that its implications were not fully recognized.

It is of course often argued that another set of significant differences between adults and children derive from their varying expertise and range of experience. In the Summerhill context, this takes us into greater uncertainties: we have to ask how relevant such accumulated experience is to the main purposes of the school. If the method of learning (I mean not just learning in the academic sense) is intended to be personal and experiential, then other people's experience may be only marginally relevant and in fact may even be obstructive. On the other hand, accepting the thesis that learning is to be based on individual decisions by the children and is to be pursued by them through their own living, one is still faced with the question as to what is the nature of the special part that the teacher may play in the process. Does he have a special part to play at all? Is he there in a purely advisory capacity? Or as a kind of interpreter? Or as a resource librarian?

The question does not seem to me to have been satisfactorily answered at Summerhill. For reasons discussed in Chapter 11, Neill has been almost paralysingly chary of allowing his teachers to function in any but a very self-effacing way. Partly because of his relegation of their activity to a necessary, but largely unwanted, function, and partly because of his own limited vision on this front, with a few rare exceptions teaching has remained close to the traditional stereotype. His response to the Inspectors' criticism on this score was symptomatic: classroom activities related only to examination-passing. This now seems unnecessarily limited: in many state primary schools, especially in those unrestricted by eleven-plus requirements, the new approaches to teaching and learning have been making sufficient progress to suggest that, though uncertainties remain, there is available a mode of learning that would fit well with the more basic principles on which Summerhill rests. Secondary schools are now at the stage that junior schools reached some ten years ago, and unless a reaction hopelessly inhibits progress there is a good chance of similar advances in that area. The pioneers of these new methods have been experienced practitioners working more or less intuitively with only a fairly rough and ready rationale. It was the same with the progressives at the beginning of this century who worked on the basis of their feelings that certain changes were proper, acting on a set of passionately held, rather than rationally argued, values. This is the way of pioneers; but in persuading others to follow a firmer argument becomes necessary.

The most hopeful foundations for such a rationale that I have come across are suggested in a short article by Professor David Hawkins.[33] He introduces as a 'central theoretical assertion . . . the rich and indissoluble connection between two human attributes. One is the human "aptness for culture", the necessary transmission of culture from one generation to another; the other is the human causality of self-direction and choice.' To assert the first by itself would leave us where we were educationally, but this connection between the aptness for culture and the characteristic human causality which Professor Hawkins identifies leads to the important recognition that 'culture is not simply "transmitted" but is assimilated selectively in accordance with the dictates of a constructive process in which, as sentient and self-organizing creatures, children cannot help being engaged.' So Professor Hawkins asserts the necessity for 'the provision of wide and significant choice for children's learning' – and it is precisely this that was lacking at Summerhill once the children entered their lesson-huts. The choice to enter or to remain outside was certainly open to them and a similar choice remained open, for there was no compulsion, real or disguised, to stay. But so long as they stayed, they put themselves in the hands of their teachers, their opportunity for significant choices being suspended.*

However, the provision of choice in the learning situation does not mean that the teacher adopts a *laissez-faire* policy. He may have the definite intention, in Professor Hawkins' words, 'to lead [the children] to a wider

---

* There are some lessons which had been taped reproduced in Snitzer, *Living at Summerhill*, pp. 80–8. In addition my comments are based on more direct knowledge. They do not apply to Art or Drama – but then these were not called lessons!

experience, and to a richer information-match with the resources of our culture'. How this match is to be achieved is the critical question. The answer is not to be found, however, in making a polar opposition between 'authoritarian' and 'permissive' teaching, and then looking for the ideal as 'somewhere in-between'. This, Professor Hawkins argues, is a 'theoretical misconstruction'. The authoritarian stereotype portrays a teacher who arrogates all the significant choices to himself, whilst the permissive teacher is supposed to leave all choices to the children. In-between we might expect to find the teacher who is 'giving some choices to children but keeping others for himself, like a dealer in poker.'

To confine our thinking to this single dimension is to obscure the inter-actions between teacher-choices and child-choices – and, I would add, group-choices. The value and range of the children's choices are affected by their teacher's choices, and these can, and should, be affected by his know-ledge of the children's choices through which their predilections and personalities become manifest. But this can happen only if the situation is such as to allow a diversity of actions and reactions.

Thus the teacher has to relate to the children in the context of his own expertise and resources, but it is a reciprocal relation and the children's various resources and their expertises are as significant an ingredient in the interaction as the teacher's. Similarly there has to be a continuing interplay between the purposes of the children and those of the teacher – not simply a mixture, as suggested by the idea of lessons in the mornings and 'free activity' in the afternoons – or more often, just on Friday afternoons! But the relation is crucially affected by the nature of the institution in which it functions and by the purposes and assumptions that are built into that institution.

When Neill declared that 'Summerhill isn't a school – it is a way of life' he was anticipating the realization of the current deschooling movement that the kind of institutions which, typically, schools are commits teachers to actions which are all too often anti-educational and forces children into a way of life which is unprofitable for most of them. Neill in fact estab-lished a small deschooled society in which facilities for learning were available but their use optional. The facilities may have been inadequate, and for historical reasons his small 'island' community may have been too much insulated from a larger society, but the essential structure for an open education was there.

The failure of compulsory schooling is unavoidably apparent when children reject it dramatically – by violence or by truancy – and the author-ities are then apparently not averse to alternatives (such as the Free School in Liverpool) being offered to these children. There is, however, a danger that such 'safety-valves' will assist the fiction that the more docile children are being satisfactorily educated, just as the freedom of Summerhill was partially accepted as being a useful way of catering for 'problem' children but irrelevant to the needs of 'normal' children. It is necessary that the acquiescent, if apathetic, majority should not be fed with an ersatz education just because they appear to accept it. The fact, for instance, that more pupils are now voluntarily extending their schooling into our sixth forms does not necessarily indicate their educational needs are being met since most of them are staying at school just to acquire more O- and A-level passes. Examinations are not merely measures of educational attainments: they are what education has come to mean. And since the knowledge which is needed to obtain these passes is quickly forgotten, being educated is a temporary condition and therefore an unimportant one.

Neill too saw school-learning in this way and he tried to minimize the time that children wasted on it. So long as it remains a passport to well-paid occupations, it remains necessary to provide facilities for children to make the temporary acquisitions of skills and knowledge. But there are better things for them to be spending their time on – interests to be explored, understandings to acquire, skills to be mastered, modes of expression to be developed, which like the learning of infancy are durable because they are personally assimilated. This quality of learning is needed if, in Friere's words, education is to be a process of 'becoming critically aware of one's reality in a manner which leads to effective action upon it.'

This takes us back to Neill's starting-point, his resolve to make his bairns 'realise'. Though this is certainly not something that adults can ever do for children, it seems probable that in the present condition of society it is not something which can just be left to happen. The present de-schooling alternatives, such as Illich's proposals for 'learning networks', do not seem fully adequate, although they are sensible ideas for the area they appear to concentrate on – that of skill-acquisition. But it seems more sensible to think of de-schooling schools rather than society: that is to say, children should still be offered the use of some kind of institution to which they can *belong*, but it needs to be non-coercive – at the 'convivial' end of Illich's institutional spectrum.[34] Schools today are mostly at the opposite pole, of the type that Illich calls 'manipulative', with a coerced membership, complex and costly institutions, having effects quite contrary to their avowed aims, their 'hidden curriculum' which demands a learning of obedience, conformity, the acceptance of other-choices, the suppression of the implications of experience, of one's reality, and the substitution for it of secondhand interpretations of thirdhand experience – all of this being anti-educational, a cultural action for submission, rather than for liberation.

The deschooled 'convivial' institutions would include an adult presence to meet the children's 'aptness for culture' whilst respecting and welcoming the creativeness of their selective assimilation of that culture. It seems necessary that such an institution should be small so that the nature of the relationships within it and the individual purposes which it would be intended to facilitate would not become obscured by institutional require-ments. These small schools may need to be supplemented by the kind of 'learning networks' which Illich describes, but neither the schools nor the networks could claim any monopoly for learning nor impose any obligation to use them without contradicting their own purposes. They would be service institutions. If childhood is playhood, then playrooms and adven-ture playgrounds must be there: if it is love and support that a child wants, then a loving and supportive setting should be available; if it is hate, or curiosity, or the need for quiet withdrawal that a child feels, then these feelings have to be accepted and their personal and social exploration facilitated.

It was a demonstration of such an anti-school that was Summerhill.

REFERENCES

1 Marcuse, *One-Dimensional Man*, p. 50.
2 Ibid. p. 70.
3 M. Craft, in *Colston Papers*, No. 20, p. 49.
4 *Id*, No. 11, 1963.
5 *The Problem Teacher*, p. 57.
6 Marcuse, *Eros and Civilization*, p. 50.
7 Ibid. p. 46.
8 Ibid. p. 51.
9 R. D. Laing, *The Politics of Experience*, p. 24.
10 B. F. Skinner, *Walden Two*, p. 262.
11 Marcuse, *One-Dimensional Man*, p. 6.
12 Ibid. p. 5.
13 Jules Henry, *Culture Against Man*, p. 15.
14 C. Rogers, *Freedom to Learn*, p. 247.
15 E. Fromm, *Fear of Freedom*, p. 177.
16 See p. 12.
17 See p. 68.
18 See Chapter 4.
19 *Times Educational Supplement*, 9 May 1969.
20 *New Society*, 28 March 1968.
21 *The Problem Parent*, p. 210.
22 *The Problem Child*, p. 62.
23 J-P Sartre, *Existentialism and Humanism*, p. 28.
24 Van Cleve Morris, *Existentialism in Education*, p. 116.
25 J-P Sartre, op. cit. p. 28.
26 Van Cleve Morris, op. cit. p. 118.

27 Ibid. p. 147.
28 *Summerhill*, p. 53.
29 *New Statesman and Nation*, 19 January 1946.
30 H. Marcuse, *One-Dimensional Man*, p. 4.
31 See p. 39.
32 See Chapter 11.
33 *Forum*, vol. 12, No. 1, Autumn 1969, pp. 4–9.
34 Ivan D. Illich, *Deschooling Society*, Chapter 4.

o

Appendix 1
Questionnaire to Head-teachers

The details of the responses to the questionnaire (see Chapter 12) which was circulated to 102 selected head-teachers are set out below. The first question asked was: Do you know of A. S. Neill? The replies show the number of Heads in the various categories of schools who responded to the questionnaire:

	Infant	Junior	Primary	Secondary	Total
Yes	11	11	22	30	74
No	2	0	2	0	4

The respondents were then asked which, if any, of Neill's books they had read. The totals for each book were:

A Dominie's Log	20	Is Scotland Educated?	0
A Dominie Dismissed	9	That Dreadful School	29
The Booming of Bunkie	0	Last Man Alive	1
A Dominie in Doubt	7	The Problem Teacher	9
Carroty Broon	0	Hearts Not Heads in the School	13
A Dominie Abroad	5	The Problem Family	6
A Dominie's Five	6	The Free Child	6
The Problem Child	25	Summerhill: A Radical Approach	
The Problem Parent	22	to Education	42
		Talking of Summerhill	27

The average number of these books that each person had read was 3·0 (Primary Heads: 2·85; Secondary Heads: 3·2).

The next question was also directed towards gaining some impression as to how familiar the respondents were with Neill's work:

Number of Heads who had	Primary	Secondary	Total
(a) heard Neill lecture	11(23%)	3(10%)	14(18%)
(b) visited Summerhill	3 (8%)	1 (3%)	4 (5%)
(c) heard Neill on TV/radio	33(69%)	20(69%)	53(68%)

(Percentages are of the total responding to the questionnaire.)

The next question was phrased as follows: 'In this question, I am asking you to rate Neill's influence on the way things have developed over the last few decades in the various aspects of education listed below. No one can do this precisely, of course, but a collective opinion about it may have some significance. Please ring whichever of the ratings seems nearest to your assessment of his influence on each item. The following coding is used: A—no influence at all; B—some marginal influence; C—quite noticeable influence; D—very considerable influence; E—enormous influence.'

In the table below, the figures under each of the ratings (A—E) indicate the *percentage* of those responding in each category who made the respective rating. The figures in brackets are the *mean ratings* which were calculated by translating the five letters into figures from −2 (for A) to +2 (for E) and by taking a simple arithmetic average. (See p. 166.)

Item	Primary Heads' ratings					Secondary Heads' ratings					Overall ratings				
	A	B	C	D	E	A	B	C	D	E	A	B	C	D	E
School use of punishments	5	35	45	15	0(−0·30)	0	52	26	22	0(−0·30)	3	42	37	18	0(−0·30)
Spread of co-education	17	35	33	12	3(−0·51)	26	37	26	11	0(−0·75)	21	36	30	12	1(−0·64)
Sex education	13	36	38	10	3(−0·46)	17	35	28	17	3(−0·46)	15	35	34	13	3(−0·46)
Moral education	17	40	33	10	0(−0·64)	21	34	28	17	0(−0·59)	19	37	31	13	0(−0·62)
Teacher-pupil relations	12	18	35	38	7(−0·00)	3	28	41	21	7(+0·01)	9	21	37	25	7(−0·00)
What schools teach	36	33	23	5	3(−0·96)	45	35	17	3	0(−1·22)	40	34	21	4	2(−1·06)
The way teachers teach	23	26	36	10	5(−0·52)	14	54	18	14	0(−0·68)	19	38	28	12	3(−0·58)
School discipline	8	30	45	13	5(−0·23)	4	34	28	34	0(−0·08)	6	32	37	22	3(−0·16)
Pupil participation in school affairs (Self-government, etc.)	8	18	38	36	0(+0·02)	4	34	28	34	0(−0·08)	6	25	34	35	0(−0·02)

In the same way the Heads were asked to rate Neill's influence on their own professional attitudes and practices. Their responses are summarized below:

Primary Heads						Secondary Heads						Overall					
A	B	C	D	E		A	B	C	D	E		A	B	C	D	E	
17	39	27	10	7	(−0·49)	22	36	29	13	0	(−0·67)	19	38	28	11	4	(−0·57)

After these questions the respondents were asked (*a*) to particularize on the directions in which they may have felt to have been influenced by Neill, and (*b*) to add any further comments that they might wish to make. Many wrote at length, and excerpts from their comments are reproduced below. There is an excerpt from every one of those replies which included comments in this section and in each case this excerpt has been chosen to convey the spirit and main content of the comment.

From Head-teachers of Infant schools:

I only wish I had met Neill, or could do so. And it would be worth a lower salary to work with A. S. Neill, to share his knowledge, understanding and beliefs. For in the State system of education the hardest thing is to stick to what one believes in, in spite of parental opposition. It is still parents who need most help to know their children.

I think A. S. Neill's work has confirmed many of the observational practices of Nursery and Infants teachers – but the influence was much more Susan Isaacs, D. E. May, Schiller – than Neill.

I feel I have been more influenced by the work of Piaget.
[Influenced particularly in respect of] (*a*) I give less importance to measurable achievement; (*b*) my staff have more liberty and responsibility; (*c*) need to know children as individuals.

I expect that A. S. Neill's influence is felt very widely and deeply because the people who taught me and with whom I have been associated in my profession must have been influenced by him.

A questioning of former traditionally accepted practices. The accent on 'wholeness' of learning. A move away from subject matter – qualitative aspect rather than quantitative. A growing interest in psychology of child development and individual learning.

First interested in education through reading *Dominie's Log* at about 12 years of age – opened my eyes to an approach to children in school different from the methods I had experienced as a child. Also Neill's enthusiasm quite a supportive element.

I feel that Neill is one of several educationists who have caused us to look critically at traditionally accepted ideas about children, education and society.

My own whole teaching has been influenced in a general way in that the knowledge of the way he runs his school made me re-think my attitude towards children in school. Probably the most important aspects were:
    (1) that problems which I saw in children's behaviour could be my fault.
    (2) that certain aspects of child care (physical health, for example) were my responsibility and a child couldn't be allowed freedom in areas which might adversely affect this.
    (3) Punishment – personal relationships.

As an assistant in my first teaching post I was encouraged by those in authority to punish severely all those disturbed children who were stealing, swearing, etc. I rebelled and found many answers to my questions in Neill's books – often causing arguments in the staffroom and being accused of too much leniency. There are two boys in this school at present who are thrashed frequently at home by vicious step-fathers or 'lodgers' and who are desperate for affection and understanding from their teacher. In my dealings with them I often recall how Neill has dealt with similar incidents.

From Head-teachers of Junior Schools:
A. S. Neill's greatest influence has been on teacher-pupil relationships. The old type of formal education and discipline was obviously wrong to the post-war teachers who began to move towards informality, and most of them never heard of Neill.*

It is difficult to state directions since the influence has been largely negative. Neill is one of those infuriating people with whom one finds it difficult to agree but who, nevertheless, cause one to have sleepless nights reviewing, clarifying and modifying one's aims and practices.

I doubt whether Summerhill can be regarded as a 'model' since it is too exotic and although it represents a cross-section of difficult students it does not contain enough children who are well orientated to the world and to school life. We shall always be grateful to Neill for stating the 'problems' clearly, but too many people are inclined to find his 'solutions' too 'instant'. This is the price that any innovator extraordinary must pay.

I am not conscious of Neill's influence at all. No doubt his books made me

* This latter suggestion is not borne out by the responses to this questionnaire which suggest that less than 5 per cent of those actively engaged in this kind of change had 'never heard of Neill'.

think; e.g. I do not believe in 'rules'. Most of these seem to be developed to protect the teacher and are negative.

[Influenced particularly as regards] Role and authority of teacher; attitude to children. . . . I know that Neill considers learning in the academic sense quite peripheral to education – even so I think this is why his influence on 'the way teachers teach' is negative.

I find it difficult to take a lot of Neill's work very seriously (in relation to large, 'non-selected' classes in State schools) . . . He is not very consistent in his outlook or theories.

I do not think Neill's ideas have in any way influenced my own professional attitudes or practices.

From Head-teachers of Primary Schools:
It is difficult to differentiate between the sources of influence on my practice – some ideas are directly from A. S. Neill (e.g. very definitely the withholding of punishment and the attempt to understand underlying causes of behaviour problems); some probably indirectly from others of like thinking (e.g. un-streaming – though in an indirect way from Neill's writings).

Obviously, Neill is one influence but significant in demonstrating courage in the face of illiberal pressures. This has been helpful in what is still an authoritarian state system. Neill not so important as people like Robin Tanner, in practice and standards.

I read his books early in my career and they made me take a long look at educational methods, children's approaches to work, etc. school discipline – I think they had a far deeper influence on my own thinking than I have given Neill credit for. I probably took what I felt to be the best in his approach and adapted the ideas and practices to my own work.

The first school I taught in had been greatly influenced by Neill through the Headmaster, Vicars Bell. I came to Neill's ideas second-hand through Mr Bell. What I have tried to do in this school which could be directly related to Neill's work (ideas) is to have free discussion by the children of behaviour and punishments. Last year at a Symposium on Education run by the Cambridge Union there was a question on Summerhill followed by discussion. The people influenced by Neill far outweighed the others, which was interesting to see in Cambridge.

I discovered Neill in 1948 when I was browsing in a second-hand bookshop. I was an unqualified teacher in a special school for delicate children and 'That Dreadful School' made a great impact on me. At College the following year I was warned not to mention Neill as this could prejudice my chances of qualifying. Since then I have met few teachers who are interested but this has not deterred me from introducing his books to young teachers . . . Maintained schools cannot be run just like Summerhill but much of Neill's philosophy can be tried out.

The noticeable diminution in authoritarian and coercive methods in educational organization and teaching is to a considerable extent due to his initiative and example. On the other hand I feel that his methods and ideas have remained rather static . . .

I pricked up my ears at Neill's doings – as being a chap after my own heart – but have felt lately that some of his ideas have been somewhat far-fetched . . . Neill's work and ideas form one little bit of the bombarding mass of ideas from which we pluck our help and inspiration.

Neill possibly reinforced ideas already there but I was more influenced I think by Lowenfeld, Hartley, Boyce, Catty, Isaacs and others when I began to teach.

I feel that Neill's belief in total child involvement has had great influence on patterns of school work, particularly in Primary Education.

(Influenced particularly as regards) (*a*) very definitely the withholding of punishment and the attempt to understand underlying causes of behaviour problems (E); (*b*) unstreaming (though in an indirect way from Neill's writings) (D); (*c*) somewhat insignificant (or is it?) the calling of staff, amongst ourselves, by christian names (E).

Most of my knowledge of A. S. Neill has come from a Mr Christian Schiller when I was on a course at the London Institute. We were 12 in the group . . . and I suppose we continued many things that A. S. Neill has started but not to the extreme he goes.

The ideals on which I run my own school have some approximation to Neill's but they were developed during my Froebel training.

Feel that Neill's experiment brought to the attention of many that there were other sides of Education, other than 'subjects'. Has reverse action too – e.g. makes teachers feel that if A. S. Neill's pupils are allowed freedom of comment and action then staff should be allowed exactly the same. Could cause chaos. . . . Children all vary in the amounts of freedom, etc., they can manage.

He was a voice which helped to establish the climate of opinion which so obviously influenced the humanising of education since the 39–45 war. Individual differences, the true nature of the child, emotional growth must all be considered in the light of his work.

Neill visited the college where I was training and gave a lengthy talk, answered questions, etc., which I remembered mainly as being about the most interesting of the whole course. His anecdotal treatment of moral education (honesty, theft, etc.) influenced my own attitude, but what sticks most perhaps is the inspiration of his *humanity*, his concern for children as *people*, with individuality. It was this I felt, rather than his Freudian slanted psychology, which led to his emphasis on opportunities for the working out of interests, urges and inhibitions when and while they occurred . . .

Typical of all innovators – one must overstress to impress. Neill's overstressing particularly adult/child relationships created an initial negative reaction in me – but which quite definitely affected my ultimate decisions in running a school.

I feel that Neill is really a forerunner or pioneer of what has come to be a general climate of opinion but that his actual direct influence on the general teaching world or on myself has been marginal at best. In fact he may have to some extent had an adverse influence owing to his extreme policies – common to pioneers in any field.

From Head-teachers of Secondary Schools:
Neill's emphasis on freedom places too great a strain on many children especially those who need the support of a regular system until they can stand alone. He over-emphasises certain aspects of punishment and forgets that children have bodies as well as minds.

I cannot attribute any influence directly from Neill on me. I am very conscious of a number of other clearly identifiable influences. These may in turn have received the impetus to the development of their ideas from A. S. Neill.

My own views have been clarified but not strongly influenced. Most powerfully present in my own school administration and philosophy are a school council and my whole approach to (a) pupil/staff relationship and (b) staff/Head relationships.

I think Neill's influence is much less than commonly supposed because the environment in which he developed his ideas had little in common with the environment in which 90 per cent of pupils and teachers are engaged.

Neill, working under the conditions he does, has developed ideas which are basically sound but only modifications of certain of them are generally applicable.

We have tried in our community to implement some of Neill's ideas . . . progress made in follow-up procedures have given us much satisfaction.

I have no doubt that Neill will prove to have been a very important figure whose influence, directly or indirectly, extend to many teachers even when they, on the conscious level, dismiss his ideas as 'hopelessly idealistic'.

Although I knew of and discussed Neill long before I qualified, many of his ideas were already part of my own philosophy of education and of my family (with a long interest in education) . . . I have little doubt that many of Neill's principles are a vital part of the development of this comprehensive school – not consciously but fundamentally, because his ideas are largely right for my school. . . . I cannot honestly feel that Neill has shaped our thinking directly, except in so far as his practice and thinking have affected educational thought generally over the years. Of this, I am more certain.

I think that so much of what Neill started as a revolutionary has become accepted that schools are very different today, but few people realise where the ideas came from. The greatest difficulty I find as a Head is to introduce a school council/democracy in a real form. [He goes on to point the need for staff unanimity of belief, and skill in handling, this 'real school democracy'. Both he finds lacking.] I wish I had been able to visit the school [Summerhill] in the early days. My memories of the two books I read are very vague, but I have always had a great respect for what Neill did.

I am still far from convinced that Neill's methods are suitable for all children even in his own 'complete' environment. In the state system I believe the system to be quite unworkable, with day schooling and unsympathetic parental attitude the method is completely undermined. I still believe discipline in study and behaviour is a positive and good aspect of education. [This man however acknowledges to Neill 'considerable influence' on his own attitudes and practice in the matter of 'pupil participation in school government'.]

Admiration of his work but disapprove of his methods in relation to sex and moral education.

We should all, I am sure, like to introduce more of his ideas and methods. But (*a*) numbers are our greatest enemy, and (*b*) I don't think we can go too far ahead of society's attitudes. I have found his approach most rewarding with deprived children needing remedial teaching.

My own movement towards a more 'liberal' outlook, especially in pupil/teacher relations, and in pupil/staff involvement in school organisation stems largely I think from my own experiences in a variety of schools. However, I feel that Neill's influence has had some bearing on this 'move' – even if it is difficult to be precise as to how and when. And certainly, many younger colleagues seem to be imbued with his ideas nowadays.

I'm more inclined to look at things from kids' point of view, to see the school as *for* children, to accept certain sorts of noise and disorder as proper to childhood; also the idea of equality between persons (i.e. teacher and children), but the habits formed in 30 years before I read Neill have not vanished entirely!

As a man who first taught as a pupil-teacher in 1928 I was, originally, a firm disciplinarian who thought of 'the class' rather than the pupils. I was still a bit of a Duke of York when I took my first headship of a boys' school. Neill – and the off-spinnings of his influence – changed my approach completely so that I would like to think that my approach is now child-centred and that I have a real concern for the underprivileged child, who in general responds to me. Since I have tried to adopt some of his ideas I have found a marked increase in the amount of minor vandalism and damage to school property but I think he has taught me that damage to property is less important than damage to human personality. I do not think the problems of freedom and responsibility have yet been solved here and I do note a tendency for younger teachers to complain that I do not 'back them up' by beating those who irritate them. Will the pendulum swing back?

I believe more in Zeitgeist than I do in Neill. One constantly meets people who endorse the principles of freedom (within reason), compassion, child-centred education, objections to corporal punishment, etc., which may perhaps be associated with him but I suspect that they may be no more influenced by him than I have been – which is absolutely not at all.

I was always interested in Neill's methods but it has only been in the last twenty-five years of my career that I have really appreciated what he was after. As an assistant I had a fairly conventional outlook. As a head I have consistently looked towards freedom in our relationship with the children. This to me is a key concept and much of this I feel came from Neill.

The difficulty of applying his ideas is the innate conservatism and authoritarianism of assistant teachers, their insistence on punishment. One or two of these in a large school can destroy the system of 'government by consent' and free discipline.

P

There is almost no influence on my own work (since I have learned the little that I know of Neill only during the last two years). Nevertheless my own practice and beliefs coincide with his in a number of areas. I may have been influenced by him through others (i.e. at second-hand) without realising it.

Neill's work – school, lectures, books – serve to crystallise what many teachers have thought and practised for a long time. In this respect, one's own approach and methods have been strengthened through his endorsement.

I am not conscious of Neill's influence. Nor am I conscious of the influence of other revolutionaries. Undoubtedly they have had their effect.

I can't be sure, after reading the first Summerhill book, how much of it, so to speak, entered my bloodstream . . . I do not believe that a great deal of what Neill has stood for, particularly over the last two or three decades, is either valid or relevant in the State system. . . . To put it in a nutshell, I should want to separate the few true and essential things that Neill has said and stood for from the peripheral chaff that over the years, because of the general neglect he's undeservedly suffered from, he's been forced to say and write.

I think that a fundamental change of *feeling* is required before any new approaches in punishment (or the lack of it) sex education, moral education, relationships, curriculum methods, etc., can make *truly effective changes*. This change of feeling has not occurred in most of the places where the so-called 'new ideas' are being tried out. They therefore make no difference. This change of feeling is also a change of philosophy of course. But philosophy of life and society – not of teaching only.

The comprehensive school I run is as near as one can get to Neill's in the state system (so I have been told by an H.M.I. !). I don't think this is correct but the school wouldn't be the same if I'd not met Neill's ideas.

Humanising influences cannot be tied up with one man.

I read the Dominie books in the home of my aunt. She was a village schoolmistress in Cambridgeshire and A. S. Neill's books were my first experience of any educational theory. I grew up accepting his thesis as reasonable and understandable . . . I regard him as the source of inspiration to whom I owe a great deal. I'm not brave enough to do all he has done but I'm sure I derive a lot of strength in such liberal practices as obtain here from the regard in which I have always held him.

Appendix 2
The Press and A. S. Neill

Ever since *The Weekly Dispatch* discovered the titillating parts of Neill's first book in 1915, the national press has kept an ear alert to him. Both the frivolous and serious sections of the press have appreciated his news-value, and Neill himself, though no doubt sometimes finding this attention embarrassing and at times irritating, seems on the whole to have welcomed any publicity as at least a first step towards his intention to get people to question their educational assumptions. The list below of reports, articles, letters-to-editors, etc., does not pretend to be complete, but it will give some indication of the kind of press coverage that Neill has received over the years. I have not included reviews of his books, and the more substantial articles by Neill are also excluded from this list since they are noted in the bibliography.

1915 *The Weekly Dispatch*, 14 Nov. Headed 'A New Type of Schoolmaster', the article gave substantial quotes from *A Dominie's Log*.

    The New Age, 2 Dec. A sarcastic quote from *A Dominie's Log* in the 'Current Cant' (a feature similar to the *New Statesman*'s 'This England').

    The New Age, 16 Dec. Letter from Neill *re* the above quote.

1916 *Forfar Dispatch*, 10 Feb. A note on *A Dominie's Log*.

    The New Age, 20 Apr. Letter from Neill *re* review of *A Dominie's Log*.

1921 *Forfar Dispatch*, 20 Jan. Notice of a meeting at which Neill was to speak.

    Forfar Dispatch, 27 Jan. Report of the above meeting.

1932 *Daily Mail*, 10 Aug. Report on Neill's talk to the Independent Labour Party Summer School. Headline: 'Kicks for Teacher: Scholars encouraged to break windows.'

    News Chronicle, 10 Aug. ditto. Headlines: 'School without rules / Pupils may smoke and swear / Edgar Wallace for reading.'

    Daily Sketch, 11 Oct. 'Do-as-you-like School': a report on Summerhill (with picture).

1933 *Daily Express*, 10 Jan. 'Do-as-you-please schools'. Report on progressive schools in Europe, including Summerhill.

1937 *News Chronicle*, 12–16 Apr. Five lengthy extracts from *That Dreadful School*.

    News Chronicle, 20 Apr. Letters relating to above extracts.

    New Statesman and Nation, 15 May. Letter from Neill *re* Prof. Joad's review of *That Dreadful School*.

1944 *Daily Express*, 13 Apr. Report by William Hickey on an exhibition of paintings by Summerhill children. Headline: 'No "Sir", He.'

    Evening Standard, 13 Apr. Report on exhibition of paintings.

    Evening Standard, 3 May. Report: Mrs A. S. Neill dies in nursing-home in Wales.

Daily Sketch, 6 Dec. Report on Kingsmuir, 'branch' of Summerhill.

1945 *Sunday Pictorial*, 21 Oct. Report on Summerhill, with pictures. Headline: 'Here's the most amazing school in the world.'

1946 *New Statesman and Nation*, 19 Jan. Letter from Neill *re* review of *Hearts Not Heads in the School*.

John Bull, 12 Jan. Feature article headed: 'Mr Neill's cock-eyed college.'

1947 *Evening Standard*, 1 Sept. Report (through *Time Magazine*) of Neill's lecture-tour in U.S.

1948 *Daily Graphic*, 5 March. Report of a visit to Summerhill by Kenneth Mason.

Evening Standard, 16 Nov. Report: 'Dominie returns from U.S.'

1949 *News Chronicle*, 17 Feb. Report by Louise Morgan, headed 'No-one said "Don't" to Zoe.'

Daily Herald, 16 May. Report by Marjorie Proops, headed 'Experiment with Zoe'.

Daily Herald, 23 May. Correspondence on above report.

Picture Post, 11 June. Report by Susan Hicklin, headed 'The child who never gets slapped'.

1951 *Daily Express*, 28 July. Report on the refusal by U.S. of a visa for Neill.

1953 *Guardian*, 4 Feb. Letter from Neill *re* refusal of visa by U.S.

Daily Sketch, 7 Oct. Report on the financial crisis at Summerhill, headed: 'Britain's craziest school, Summerhill, is facing the end of its long, long term.'

Guardian, 26 Oct. Feature article: 'A. S. Neill at 70.'

1955 *News Chronicle*, 17 Feb. Report of Neill's address at the London Institute of Education Foundation week. Headline: 'Do-as-you-like school head says teachers must shed dignity.'

1956 *Guardian*, 17 Dec. Article by A. V. Wood on 'Self-government' with special reference to Summerhill.

Guardian, 22 Dec. Letter on the above from C. Butler.

Guardian, 29 Dec. Reply to above from A. V. Wood.

1957 *News Chronicle*, 30 Jan. Report: Neill comments on the 11 + exam.

News Chronicle, 11 Feb. Report on Neill's attempt to stop smoking at Summerhill. Headline: 'Laying down the law.'

Sunday Graphic, 17 Feb. Report on the above, with description of the school.

Sunday Mirror, 24 March. Feature article on Summerhill. Headline: 'Everything is topsy-turvy at the most amazing school in Britain.'

Daily Mail, 10 Aug. Report on inspection of Summerhill and on formation of the Summerhill Society. Headline: 'Smoke-and-swear school not up to standard, say men from Ministry.'

Sunday Dispatch, 18 Aug. Report of one teacher's (M. Hardiment) discomfiture at Summerhill. Headline: 'Kiss-and-smoke school is a nightmare.'

Sunday Dispatch, 25 Aug. Letter from a former pupil *re* above report.

Daily Mirror, 7 Sept. Opinions from four notable personalities (including Neill) under heading: 'Don't talk to strange men' (apropos a scare following assaults on children).

News Chronicle, 18 Sept. Report on financial difficulties at Summerhill. Headline: 'Who will help the Do-as-you-please School?'

1958 *Times Educational Supplement*, 27 June. Letter from Neill about Homer Lane.
1959 *Reveille*, 2 July. Feature article: 'The school where they kiss and cuddle.'
1960 *Daily Mail*, 21 Dec. Report: 'Summerhill's 40th birthday next month.'
1961 *Daily Mail*, 4 Jan. Report: 'Unhappy birthday for that dreadful school.'
   Daily Herald, 11 Jan. Report: 'Neill is coming' (to London for 40th anniversary).
   Daily Mail, Report on 40th anniversary, with comments from ex-pupils. Headline: 'The wild ones are so tame now.'
   Today, 11 March. Feature article on Summerhill. Headline: 'Should Bobby have a knife?' Also editorial comment.
   Guardian, 22 March. Report on conference on new trends in education including a comparison, with 'surprising similarities', between a Borstal institution and Summerhill.
   New Statesman and Nation, 30 June. Report of a week-end visit to Summerhill, with the suggestion 'Why can't Nuffield help?'
   Guardian, 25 Sept. Letter from Neill *re* Committee of 100.
   Queen, 27 Sept. Feature article on Summerhill, headed 'The happiest days of their lives'.
1962 *Guardian*, 17 March. Letter from Neill *re* smoking.
   Daily Herald, 6 April. Article by Henry Fielding: 'The market in happiness: modest boom for "Freedom" schools.'
   Spectator, 27 April. Editorial comment on *Summerhill*.
   Daily Herald, 25 June. Account of week-end visit to Summerhill by Henry Fielding. Headline: 'The school they said was dreadful.'
   Reveille, 12 July. Feature article on Summerhill: 'School where (almost) anything goes.'
   Daily Express, 18 Oct. Report: 'Birthday of A. S. Neill.'
1963 *Sunday Pictorial*, 27 Jan. Report on Neill's attitude to adolescent sex. Headline: 'Sex – and a Headmaster.'
   News of the World, 27 Jan. Report on Neill's contribution to symposium in *Twentieth Century* on contemporary morality. Headline: 'Too much morality, says Head.'
   Times Educational Supplement, 16 Aug. Article by Donald Maclean. 'A. S. Neill looks back.'
   Times Educational Supplement, 23 Aug. Letter on Maclean's article.
   Times Educational Supplement, 18 Oct. Article: 'Neill at 80.'
   Daily Express, 18 Oct. Report: 'Neill gets a car for 80th birthday from pupils.'
   Daily Mail, 1 Nov. Report on Neill's 80th birthday.
   Look, 19 Nov. Feature article on Summerhill: 'School run by children.'
   Daily Telegraph, 29 Nov. Letter from Neill about American developments.
   Guardian, 12 Dec. Letter from Neill about contemporary drama.
1964 *Where?* No. 16. Neill replies to Scottish headmaster who advocated the use of the strap.
   Woman's Mirror, 11 July. Article on A. S. Neill.
1965 *Daily Telegraph*, 11 Jan. Letter from Neill about corporal punishment.
   Guardian, 2 Feb. Letter from Neill about Risinghill.
   Sunday Mirror, 22 Oct. Article: 'Birthday greetings to one of the most significant rebels of our time.'

Observer, 31 Oct. Letter from Neill about abortion.

1966 *The Times*, 10 May. Report on honorary degree awarded to Neill at Newcastle. Headline: 'Honour for a rebel.'

Times Educational Supplement, 13 May. Report on Newcastle honorary degree. Headline: 'Dynamic headmastership.'

Times Educational Supplement, 19 Aug. Letter from M. Duane on Neill's influence.

Times Educational Supplement, 26 Aug. Letters about M. Duane and Neill.

1967 *News Chronicle*, 30 Jan. Neill's comments on I.Q. tests. Headline: 'They beat the Head.'

Times Educational Supplement, 11 Aug. Comment on inspection of independent schools with reference to Summerhill.

Daily Telegraph, 23 Nov. Letter from Neill about the training of teachers.

Times Educational Supplement, 1 Dec. Report on the Inspectors' report on Summerhill in 1959 and on present expectations. Headline: 'Unrepentant freedom.'

1968 *Guardian*, 5 June. Article by Leila Berg on the inspection of Summerhill.

Guardian, 11 June. Letter from Neill *re* above article.

The Times, 11 June. Report: 'Summerhill ready for inspection.'

The Times, 11 June. Letter about a possible closure of Summerhill from Professor Ben Morris, *et al.*

Evening Standard, 12 June. Report: 'Improving Summerhill.'

Sunday Telegraph, 16 June. Report by Nicholas Bagnall headed 'Saviours for Summerhill'.

Daily Telegraph, 28 June. Report on Neill's award of an honorary degree at Exeter: 'The maker of Summerhill.'

The Times, 3 July. Report on inspection: 'Good marks for Summerhill.'

Times Educational Supplement, 5 July. Report on inspection: 'Good news for Summerhill.'

Times Educational Supplement, 5 July. Report on Neill's honorary degree award at Exeter.

Evening News, 17 Oct. Report: 'Neill being proved right at 85.'

Daily Express, 18 Oct. Interview with Neill on occasion of his 85th birthday.

Bibliography

A. Books by A. S. Neill
A Dominie's Log, Herbert Jenkins, 1915.
A Dominie Dismissed, Herbert Jenkins, 1916.
Booming of Bunkie, Herbert Jenkins, 1919.
A Dominie in Doubt, Herbert Jenkins, 1920.
Carroty Broon, Herbert Jenkins, 1920.
A Dominie Abroad, Herbert Jenkins, 1922.
A Dominie's Five, Herbert Jenkins, 1924.
The Problem Child, Herbert Jenkins, 1926.
The Problem Parent, Herbert Jenkins, 1932.
Is Scotland Educated?, Routledge, 1936.
That Dreadful School, Herbert Jenkins, 1937.
Last Man Alive, Herbert Jenkins, 1938.
The Problem Teacher, Herbert Jenkins, 1940.
Hearts Not Heads in the School, Herbert Jenkins, 1945.
The Problem Family, Herbert Jenkins, 1949.
The Free Child, Herbert Jenkins, 1953.
Summerhill: A Radical Approach to Education, Gollancz, 1962.
Talking of Summerhill, Gollancz, 1967.
Freedom – not License!, Hart Pub. Co., New York, 1966.
Wilhelm Reich, Ritter Press, 1958. (Joint authors: P. Ritter and A. S. Neill.)

B. Articles by A. S. Neill
Below is a list of the more important published articles of Neill's, especially those to which reference is made in the text.
Editorials in *The Student* (undergraduate journal of Edinburgh Univ.), 1911/12
    'The Lunatic' (a short story); *The New Age*, 4 February 1915.
'Psycho-analysis in Industry'; *The New Age*, 4 December 1919.
Editorials in *The New Era*, 1920–23.
'The psychology of the flogger'; *The New Era*, vol. 1, No. 4, October 1920.
'Right and wrong'; *The New Era*, vol. 2, No. 7, July 1921.
'Education in Germany'; *The New Era*, vol. 3, No. 10, April 1922.
'Summerhill'; *The New Era*, vol. 9, No. 34, April 1928.
'Summerhill'; *The New Era*, vol. 10, No. 39, July 1929.
'Inspection of schools'; *The New Era*, vol. 13, No. 9, October 1932.
'Summerhill'; in *The Modern Schools Handbook*, (ed. T. Blewitt), 1934.
'Authority and freedom in schools'; *The New Era*, vol. 16, No. 1, January 1935.
Contribution to *G.B.S.90*. (ed. S. Winsten); Hutchinson, 1946.
'Dominie looks at the Secondary School'; *Secondary Education*, September 1947.

'Love-discipline yes, hate-discipline no'; *New York Times Magazine*, 7 November 1948.

'Freedom and licence'; *Times Educational Supplement*, 26 July 1957.

'Why have exams? Culture and futility'; *Times Educational Supplement*, 8 May 1959.

'Realities of life'; *Times Educational Supplement*, 6 May 1960.

'My scholastic life'; *Id*, Nos. 2–7, September 1960–August 1961.

'Summerhill mistakes'; *Id*, No. 10.

'A dirty word'; *Id*, No. 11 (undated).

Contribution to a symposium on contemporary morality; *Twentieth Century*, Winter 1963.

'Tony and the gang' (conversation with Helen Parkhurst); *Times Educational Supplement*, 8 May 1964.

'Using the extra year'; *Times Educational Supplement*, 14 February 1964.

'Radical Private Schools' (conversation with Mario Montessori); *This magazine is about schools*, vol. 1, No. 1, April 1966.

'Corporal punishment' (Conversation between A. S. Neill, M. Duane and I. Cook), *Times Educational Supplement*, 31 May 1966.

'Learning or living'; *Times Educational Supplement*, 17 June 1966.

'A dominie grows old'; *Times Educational Supplement*, 2 September 1966.

'Drama in Summerhill'; *Times Educational Supplement*, 30 December 1966.

'What shortage?' (on teacher-training); *Times Educational Supplement*, 6 January 1967.

'You've got to be free to be happy'; *Evening News*, 9 August 1967.

'Can I come to Summerhill? I hate my school'; *Psychology Today*, May 1968.

'All of us are a part of this sick censorship'; *Times Educational Supplement*, 29 March 1968.

'Life without father'; *Times Educational Supplement*, 11 April 1968.

C. Books consulted in the preparation of this volume (other than those by A. S. Neill):

Adams, Sir John. *Modern Development in Educational Practice*, U.L.P. 1928 (2nd edn.).

Ash, M. *Who Are the Progressives Now?*, Routledge & Kegan Paul, 1969.

Auden, W. H. *Poems 1928*, Private edition 1928.

— *Poems 1930*, Faber & Faber, 1933 (2nd edn.).

— *The Orators*, Faber & Faber, 1932.

— *Look, Stranger!*, Faber & Faber, 1936.

— *Letters from Iceland*, Faber & Faber, 1937.

Auden, W. H. and Worsley, T. C. *Education – Today and Tomorrow*, Hogarth Press, 1939.

Barrie, J. M. *A Window in Thrums*, Hodder and Stoughton, 1892.

— *Sentimental Tommy*, Cassell, 1896.

Bazeley, E. T. *Homer Lane and the Little Commonwealth*, Allen & Unwin, 1928.

Boyd, W. *Towards a New Education*, A. A. Knopf, 1930.

Boyd, W. and Rawson W. *The Story of the New Education*, Heinemann, 1965.

Caldwell Cook, H. *The Play Way*, Heinemann, 1917.

Clarke, F. *Freedom in the Educative Society*, U.L.P., 1948.

Cole, G. D. H. *Essays in Social Theory*, Macmillan, 1950.

Douglas, G. *The House with Green Shutters*, Classics Book Club, 1952.

Eyles, L. *For My Enemy Daughter*, Gollancz, 1941.

Fromm, E. *The Fear of Freedom*, Routledge & Kegan Paul, 1942.

Gardner, D. E. M. *Susan Isaacs*, Methuen, 1969.

Garnett, D. *The Familiar Faces*, Chatto & Windus, 1962.

Grainger, A. J. *The Bullring*, Pergamon Press, 1969.

Hart, H. *Summerhill: For and Against*, Hart Pub. Co., New York, 1970.

Henry, Jules. *Culture Against Man*, Random House, 1963.

Hindus, M. *Humanity Uprooted*, Cape, 1931.

Holmes, E. *What Is and What Might Be*, Constable, 1911.

— *In Defence of What Might Be*, Constable, 1914.

Holt, J. *How Children Fail*, Pitman, 1964.

— *The Underachieving School*, Pitman, 1970.

Illich, Ivan D., *Deschooling Society*, Calder and Boyars, 1971.

Isaacs, S. *Intellectual Growth in Young Children*, Routledge, 1930.

— *Social Development in Young Children*, Routledge, 1933.

Isherwood, C. *Lions and Shadows*, Methuen, 1953.

Jacobs, P. and Landau, S., *The New Radicals*, Penguin, 1967.

Judges, A. V. (ed.) *Education and the Philosophic Mind*, Harrap, 1957.

King, B. *Changing Man*, Gollancz, 1936.

Klein, M. *Contributions to Psychoanalysis, 1921–1945*, Hogarth Press, 1948.

Lehmann, J. *The Whispering Gallery*, vol. I, Longmans, Green, 1955.

MacIntyre, A. *Marcuse*, Fontana/Collins, 1970.

MacKenzie, R. F. *Escape from the Classroom*, Collins, 1965.

— *A Question of Living*, Collins, 1963.

— *The Sins of the Children*, Collins, 1967.

MacMunn, N. *A Child's Path to Freedom*, Bell, 1914.

— *A Path to Freedom in the School*, Bell, 1921.

Mannin, E. *Commonsense and the Child*, Jarrolds (revised edn.), 1947.

— *Commonsense and the Adolescent*, Jarrolds, 1937.

— *Confessions and Impressions*, Jarrolds, 1930.

— *Privileged Spectator*, Jarrolds, 1939.

Marcuse, H. *Eros and Civilization*, Sphere Books, 1969.

— *One-Dimensional Man*, Routledge & Kegan Paul, 1964.

— *An Essay in Liberation*, Allen Lane (The Penguin Press), 1969.

Martin, K. *Father Figures*, Hutchinson, 1966.

Morris, Van Cleve. *Existentialism in Education*, Harper & Row, N. Y., 1966.

Muir, E. *The Story and the Fable*, Harrap, 1940.

Muir, W. *Belonging*, Hogarth Press, 1968.

Nearing, Scott. *Education in Soviet Russia*, The Plebs League, 1926.

Newson, J. and E. *Patterns of Infant Care*, Penguin, 1965.

Park, J. *Bertrand Russell on Education*, Allen & Unwin, 1964.

Pedley, R. *The Comprehensive School*, Penguin, 1963.

Pekin, L. B. *Progressive Schools*, Hogarth Press, 1934.

Perry, L. R. (ed.) *Four Progressive Educators*, Collier–Macmillan, 1967.

Pfister, O. *Some Applications of Psychoanalysis*, Allen & Unwin, 1923.

Pinkevich, A. *Science and Education in the U.S.S.R.*, Gollancz, 1935.

Revel, D. *Cheiron's Cave*, Heinemann, 1928.

Rawson, W. *The Freedom We Seek*, New Education Foundation, 1937.

Reich, W. *Character Analysis*, Vision Press, Peter Nevill, 1940.

— *The Sexual Revolution*, Orgone Institute Press, N. Y., 1945.

— *The Function of the Orgasm*, Panther Books, 1968.

Ritter, P. and J. *The Free Family*, Gollancz, 1959.

Robinson, P. A. *The Freudian Left*, Harper & Row, N. Y., 1969.

Rogers, C. *On Becoming a Person*, Constable, 1961.

— *Freedom to Learn*, Merrill Pub. Co., 1969.

Rousseau, J-J. *Confessions*, Glaisher, 1925.

Rubenstein, D. and Stoneman, C. (eds) *Education for Democracy*, Penguin, 1970.

Russell, B. *Principles of Social Reconstruction*, Allen & Unwin, 1916.

— *On Education*, Allen & Unwin, 1926.

— *Education and the Social Order*, Allen & Unwin, 1968.

— *Autobiography*, vol. II, Allen & Unwin, 1968.

Rycroft, C. (ed.) *Psychoanalysis Observed*, Constable, 1966.

Schar, E. (ed.) *The Family and the Sexual Revolution*, Indiana Press, 1964.

Segefjord, B. *Summerhill Diary*, Gollancz, 1970.

Selleck, R. J. W. *The New Education, 1870–1914*, Pitman, 1968.

Simpson, J. H. *Schoolmaster's Harvest*, Faber, 1954.

Skidelsky, R. *English Progressive Schools*, Penguin, 1969.

Snitzer, H. *Living at Summerhill*, Collier Books, 1968.

Spears, M. K. *The Poetry of W. H. Auden*, Oxford, 1963.

Spender, S. *World Within World*, Hamish Hamilton, 1951.

Spock, B. H. *Baby and Child Care*, Bodley Head, 1955.

Stewart, W. A. C. *The Educational Innovators*, vol. II, Macmillan, 1968.

Students and staff, Hornsey College of Art, *The Hornsey Affair*, Penguin, 1969.

Taylor, W. (ed.) *Towards a Policy for the Education of Teachers* (Colston Papers No. 2), Butterworth, 1969.

Walmsley, J. *Neill and Summerhill*, Penguin, 1969.

Wells, H. G. *The Open Conspiracy and Other Essays*, printed by Waterlow & Sons, London, 1933.

Wills, D. W. *Homer Lane*, Allen & Unwin, 1964.

Worsley, T. C. *Barbarians and Philistines*, Hale, 1940.

Index